CASSELL'S DICTIONARY OF FRENCH SYNONYMS

ARRANGED IN GROUPS FOR THE CONVENIENCE OF ENGLISH STUDENTS

BY

P. O. CROWHURST

Diplomé de l'Université de Lille

DODD, MEAD & COMPANY
NEW YORK—1931

Copyright, 1931
By Dodd, Mead & Company, Inc.

Ref.

PRINTED IN THE UNITED STATES OF AMERICA

INTRODUCTION

FRENCH is without doubt the foreign language most frequently studied in English-speaking countries today, a fact which may be accounted for in several ways. First, the history of France has in past centuries been closely interwoven with that of England, revealing, here, the spirit of unity linking the two nations, there, the misunderstanding or hostility which divided them. As a result the French tongue found its way into England from the Norman invasion onward, remained in use at the Court until the fourteenth century, shared with Latin the distinction of being the literary language of Europe and became the diplomatic and social speech of the world. Secondly, the geographical situation of France as regards England and the close relationships with the French since the Revolution in America, have facilitated the study of the language, but a third and more potent reason for its present-day popularity was the advent of the Great War in 1914, that gigantic upheaval which threw the nations into physical touch with each other and permitted us to study, at close range, the character and language of our French allies during that unprecedented struggle.

It may be said, therefore, that the French language has come to stay, but we must remember that it is infinitely rich in *nuances* and *finesse* or, as we should say, shades of meaning, so much so that the possibilities of expressing oneself exactly, or making mistakes, are alike unbounded. As an example, the words *pendant* and *durant* are generally given as French equivalents for "during", while *affreux, effrayant, effroyable* and *épouvantable* may all be taken as meaning "fearful". Yet few there are, perhaps, who understand the difference in meaning between *pendant* and *durant*, while how many realize the various degrees or kinds of human apprehensiveness represented by the words *affreux, effrayant, effroyable* and *épouvantable*. And so on throughout the whole language. Nearly every word has a separate and distinct meaning, which makes it so easy to express oneself exactly in French. This is one of the reasons why the French language became the diplomatic tongue of the world.

We find, therefore, that a superficial knowledge of French is insufficient, not to say dangerous, and the author's object in presenting this work is to help those who use it to select the right word which they need for correctly rendering in French what they wish to say or translate.

The title of this book may perhaps seem paradoxical. It has been said that the French language has no synonyms, and when we come to study the subject we are forced to admit that words really synonymous or

INTRODUCTION

having exactly the same meaning are few in number. Yet when a student consults the average English-French dictionary for the exact translation of any given term he is met with a haphazard array of words, some of which might give him the required equivalent, many of which certainly would not. He therefore needs some sort of guide which, it is hoped, the present work will supply. It must be borne in mind, however, that this book is intended for use in conjunction with, rather than in preference to, a French dictionary. A dictionary, as such, is necessarily more complete since it contains a multitude of dissimilar expressions, etc., with which we have no concern. It is only with the more commonplace or everyday terms that we have to deal here—the simplest words are the hardest to translate correctly.

Arrangements have been made for the inclusion of all words which, though not French synonyms, claim the special attention of the English-speaking student as such. For instance, the words *anse, manivelle, poignée, manche, queue* and *brimbale* bear no relationship whatever to each other in French, which explains why a Frenchman instinctively and unhesitatingly employs the correct term. The American, however, can only render them in his own language by the one word "handle" and, as a result, his choice of a French equivalent might not always be a happy one.

The Index at the end of the book contains a complete list of all those French terms, etc., which are in everyday use. All words having no interest from a synonym point of view have, however, been deliberately excluded as their inclusion would not only have been contrary to the purpose of the book as implied by its title, but would also have burdened the index itself with a host of words serving no other purpose than to render reference thereto a more lengthy and complicated procedure. The number placed against each word refers to the group in which will be found the exact meaning, carefully explained, of all its synonyms.

A special supplement containing information of a general nature is also included.

The Author desires to express his deep gratitude to Mr. de V. Payen-Payne for the valuable aid and most helpful suggestions received from him in connection with the present work.

P. O. C.

LIST OF ABBREVIATIONS

adj.	Adjective.
adv.	Adverb.
adv. exp.	Adverbial expression.
colloq.	Colloquial.
conj.	Conjunction.
e.g.	For example.
Ex.	Example.
i.e.	That is.
interj.	Interjection.
inv.	Invariable.
n.f.	Noun feminine.
n.m.	Noun masculine.
prep.	Preposition.
prep. exp.	Prepositional expression.
pron.	Pronoun.
pa. p.	Past participle.
pr. p.	Present participle.
q.v.	Which see.
v.i.	Verb intransitive.
v. imp.	Verb impersonal.
v.r.	Verb reflexive.
v.t.	Verb transitive.

CASSELL'S DICTIONARY OF FRENCH SYNONYMS

SYNONYM GROUPS

WORDS having more than one meaning are repeated in each group to which all such meanings respectively belong.

1.

Abandon, *n.m.* The state of that which is abandoned. Ex.: *L'enfant est dans l'abandon.*
Abandonnement, *n.m.* The act of abandoning. Ex.: *L'abandonnement d'une propriété.*
Renoncement, *n.m.* Renunciation, spiritually or morally speaking. Ex.: *Le renoncement aux honneurs.*
Renonciation, *n.f.* Renunciation, legally or practically speaking. Ex.: *La renonciation à ses droits.*
Désistement, *n.m.* Exclusive legal term signifying renunciation or abandoning of any claim, action, etc. Ex.: *Le désistement d'une action civile.*

2.

Annuler, *v.t.* To annul or cancel, generally speaking.
Abroger, *v.t.* To abolish (a law). To abrogate.
Casser, *v.t.* To do away with, by one authority, what exists by virtue of another. Ex.: *Casser un officier.*
Révoquer, *v.t.* To revoke. To return to what was originally established. Ex.: *Révoquer un ordre.*
Infirmer, *v.t.* To reverse, by appeal, a previous law-court decision. Ex.: *Infirmer un jugement.*
Abolir, *v.t.* To abolish, generally speaking.

3.

Opprimer, *v.t.* To oppress tyrannically. To inflict hardship. Ex.: *Opprimer un peuple.*
Accabler, *v.t.* To crush, figuratively speaking. Ex.: *Accabler d'impôts.*
Oppresser, *v.t.* To oppress, i.e. to cause a physical feeling of pressure or heaviness. Ex.: *Mon angoisse m'oppresse.*

4.

Abstrait, *adj.* Lack of attention to what is being said or taking place. Ex.: *Une personne abstraite.*
Distrait, *adj.* Distracted. Attention diverted from anything to something else. Ex.: *Répondre d'une façon distraite.*

[1]   B

5.

Abjurer, *v.t.* To abjure. To renounce solemnly or publicly.
Renier, *v.t.* To deny, for some special reason, what one really respects. Ex.: *Renier ses parents.* To disown. Ex.: *Renier un ami.*

6.

Finir, *v.t.* To finish. Refers to the work or occupation itself. Ex.: *Finir un livre.*
Terminer, *v.t.* To terminate. To bring to an end. Refers to the duration of any work, etc. Ex.: *Terminer un discours.*
Achever, *v.t.* To complete. To finish off. Implies the accomplishment of the various stages of any work, undertaking, etc. Ex.: *Achever une maison.*
Parachever, *v.t.* To perfect by completion. Ex.: *Parachever une œuvre.*
Compléter, *v.t.* To complete in a general sense. To make entire. Denotes the addition of what is missing. Ex.: *Compléter une collection de timbres-poste.*

7.

Accumulation, *n.f.* Accumulation. The result of continued heaping up or gathering together. Ex.: *Une accumulation d'objets.*
Amas, *n.m.* An irregular heap or mass. Ex.: *Un amas d'objets.*
Tas, *n.m.* A collection of articles, etc., piled up closely together. Ex.: *Un tas de pierres.*
Monceau, *n.m.* A heap or collection of articles, etc., larger and more irregular than a *tas.* Ex.: *Un monceau de ruines.*
Amoncellement, *n.m.* The action or result of heaping up. Ex.: *L'amoncellement de la neige.*
Pile, *n.f.* Pile. A collection of similar objects, generally round in shape, carefully placed one on top of the other. Ex.: *Une pile de louis d'or.*

8.

Très, *adv.* Very, generally speaking. Ex.: *Un homme très instruit.*
Beaucoup, *adv.* Much or extremely, with reference to quantity. Ex.: *Il m'a beaucoup ennuyé.*
Bien, *adv.* Well. Very. Implies the addition of admiration, approval, etc. Ex.: *Cet acteur a bien joué.*
Fort, *adv.* To an extreme degree. Denotes energy or intensity. Ex.: *Être fort indigné.*
Fortement, *adv.* Very much. Ex.: *Avoir le moral fortement ébranlé.*
Largement, *adv.* Liberally. Ex.: *Donner largement aux œuvres de charité.*

9.

Payer, *v.t.* To pay. To settle, by payment, what one owes. Ex.: *Payer une dette.*
Verser, *v.t.* To pay. Refers to the act itself. Ex.: *Verser cinq cents francs.*

Régler, *v.t.* To settle a bill, debt, etc. Ex. : *Régler une facture.*
S'acquitter de, *v.r.* To clear oneself entirely of any obligation, financial or otherwise. Ex. : *S'acquitter d'un devoir.*

10.

Abaisser, *v.t.* To lower, generally speaking. Ex. : *Abaisser la voix.*
Rabaisser, *v.t.* To lower what is considered too high or exalted. Ex. : *Rabaisser un orgueilleux.*
Abattre, *v.t.* To lower in the sense of reducing or diminishing. Ex. : *Échec qui abat le moral.*
Rabattre, *v.t.* To bring or pull down. Ex. : *Rabattre le prix d'un article.*
Humilier, *v.t.* To lower in the sense of confuse. To humiliate. Ex. : *La pénitence humilie.*
Avilir, *v.t.* To lower in quality or estimation. To degrade. Ex. : *Le crime avilit l'homme.*
Ravaler, *v.t.* To lower, denoting a contrast between the position held and that to which reduced. Ex. : *L'ivrognerie ravale aux yeux du monde.*

11.

Actionner, *v.t.* To cause movement in any machine, apparatus, etc.
Commander, *v.t.* To drive (a machine). Ex. : *Scie commandée électriquement.*
Mouvoir, *v.t.* To propel or drive.
Faire tourner, *v.t.* To make revolve.
These four verbs have practically the same meaning when used in the above technical sense.

12.

Auparavant, *adv.* Before, in the sense of "beforehand". Ex.: *Achetez, si vous voulez, mais refléchissez auparavant.*
Avant, *adv.* Before. Requires *de* or *que* followed by a verb. Ex. : *Étant enrhumée, elle s'est excusée avant de chanter.*
Préalablement. Au préalable, *adv.* First or previously. Ex. : *Il avait demandé préalablement l'autorisation du ministre.*

13.

Actif, *adj.* Active. Applied more to the character or disposition of a person. Ex. : *Une femme active.*
Agissant, *adj.* Active. Refers to the actual movement or activity itself. Ex. : *Des préparatifs agissants.*

14.

Acrobatisme, *n.m.* Acrobatism. The profession of an acrobat. Ex. : *L'acrobatisme est un métier dangereux.*
Acrobatie, *n.f.* Acrobatics. Refers to the performance itself. Ex. : *Un tour d'acrobatie.*

15.

Aborder, *v.t.* To approach and speak to a person at any meeting, gathering, etc.
Joindre, *v.t.* To meet, by going towards a person.
Accoster, *v.t.* To stop a person in the street. To accost.
Rejoindre, *v.t.* To rejoin or catch up with a person.

16.

Enfanter, *v.t.* To give birth to. Refers only to the actual birth itself.
Accoucher, *v.i.* To give birth to. Denotes the whole process of confinement.
Engendrer, *v.t.* To procreate or beget. Ex.: *Isaac engendra Jacob.*

17.

Affubler, *v.t.* To dress badly or slovenly. Ex.: *Affublé d'une vieille redingote.*
Accoutrer, *v.t.* To dress in a grotesque manner. Ex.: *Enfant accoutré d'une manière ridicule.*
Fagoter, *v.t.* To dress badly or outrageously. Generally used in an absolute sense. Ex.: *Vous voilà fagoté !*

18.

Coutume, *n.f.* Custom, generally speaking. Ex.: *Une fois n'est pas coutume.*
Accoutumance, *n.f.* The act of getting accustomed to anything. Ex.: *L'accoutumance avec le climat.*
Habitude, *n.f.* Habit, or natural impulse. Ex.: *Avoir de bonnes habitudes.*
Us, *n.m.* Use. Only used with *coutumes* in the expression *us et coutumes.*
Usage, *n.m.* Use. The word has a more restricted meaning than *coutumes.* Ex.: *Les usages des gens.*

19.

Abréger, *v.t.* To abbreviate or condense. Ex.: *Abréger un exposé.*
Accourcir, *v.t.* To shorten the length of. Ex.: *Accourcir un manteau.*
Raccourcir, *v.t.* To shorten again or further. *Raccourcir* is, however, more often employed in preference to *accourcir* as meaning "to shorten" generally.
Écourter, *v.t.* To cut short. Denotes insufficient length or development. Ex.: *Écourter un exposé.*

20.

Abrutir, *v.t.* To besot, or make a beast of. Ex.: *L'excès d'alcool finit par abrutir.*
Hébéter, *v.t.* To dull the mind or intelligence. Ex.: *Avoir un air hébété.*

21.

Effronté, *adj.* Impudent in the sense of being without modesty. Ex.: *Gamin effronté.*
Hardi, *adj.* Impudent in the sense of being fearless. Ex.: *Une réponse hardie.*

22.

S'adonner, *v.r.* To be addicted to, or fond of. Ex.: *S'adonner à la boisson.*
Se donner, *v.r.* To give oneself up entirely to. Ex.: *Se donner à la science.*
Se livrer, *v.r.* To give oneself up to with confidence. Ex.: *Se livrer à une occupation.*
S'abandonner, *v.r.* To abandon oneself. To give oneself up to without reserve or restraint. Ex.: *S'abandonner à la providence.*
Se laisser aller, *v.r.* To forget oneself. To go so far as to. Ex.: *Se laisser aller jusqu'à manquer de respect.*

23.

Stupéfier, *v.t.* To stupefy, figuratively speaking.
Abasourdir, *v.t.* To amaze, causing confusion or consternation. Ex.: *La pauvre femme resta abasourdie devant la nouvelle.*
Ébahir, *v.t.* To cause to be wonderstruck. Implies open-mouthed astonishment. Ex.: *Les paysans ébahis.*
Ébaubir, *v.t.* To cause to be wonderstruck. Implies open-eyed astonishment. Ex.: *La foule ébaubie.*

24.

Abattement, *n.m.* Moral dejection or low-spiritedness. Ex.: *Abattement d'esprit.*
Accablement, *n.m.* Extreme moral or physical dejection. Ex.: *La maladie entraîne souvent l'accablement du corps.*
Anéantissement, *n.m.* The state of mind of a person having succumbed completely to moral or physical suffering. Ex.: *L'anéantissement devant la douleur.*
Prostration, *n.f.* Prostration. Moral and physical collapse as a result of illness, etc.

25.

Affairé, *adj.* Busy, i.e. occupied with business matters. Ex.: *Un quartier très affairé.*
Occupé, *adj.* Busy or occupied in a general sense. Ex.: *Il était occupé à ranger ses papiers.*

26.

Abstraire, *v.t.* To abstract, with the intention of attending to what is abstracted.
Faire abstraction, *v.i.* To abstract, with the intention of putting aside, without considering, what is abstracted.

27.

Abstractivement, *adv.* Abstractly; by abstraction. Implies action.
Abstraitement, *adv.* Abstractedly; with absence of mind. Implies a condition.

28.

Administration, *n.f.* The organization for carrying out the laws, etc., of a government. Ex.: *Règlement d'administration publique.*
Gouvernement, *n.m.* The government itself, politically speaking. Ex.: *Gouvernement socialiste.*
Régime, *n.m.* The form of government. Ex.: *L'ancien régime.*

29.

Attraper, *v.t.* To catch what one is pursuing or waiting for. Ex.: *La police a attrapé l'assassin.*
Gripper, *v.t.* To catch skilfully. Ex.: *Un chat grippe tout ce qu'il peut attraper.*
Happer, *v.t.* To catch suddenly or unexpectedly. Ex.: *Le pauvre vieillard fut happé par la locomotive.*

30.

Actuellement, *adv.* At the actual moment when speaking or writing. Ex.: *Mon frère est actuellement en France.*
À présent, *adv. exp.* At present. Now. Used more in connection with a state or condition having originated previously. Ex.: *Il n'a rien dit jusqu'à présent.*
Présentement, *adv.* At present. *Présentement* is less precise than *actuellement.* Ex.: *Maison à louer présentement.*
Maintenant, *adv.* Now. Implies a continuation. Ex.: *La mode est changée maintenant.*
Aujourd'hui, *adv.* Nowadays, as contrasted with some other period. Ex.: *Aujourd'hui la mode est moins compliquée.*

31

Avéré, *adj.* Proved to be true. Ex.: *Ce fait est avéré par l'histoire.*
Véritable, *adj.* True, i.e. conforming to or abiding by what is true. Ex.: *Un récit véritable.*
  Real or genuine as opposed to false or an imitation. Ex.: *Un diamant véritable. C'est pour moi un véritable ami.* (*Vrai* is also used in this sense.)
Véridique, *adj.* Capable of being believed. Truthful. Ex.: *Un homme véridique.*
Vrai, *adj.* True, i.e. agreeing with fact. Ex.: *Une histoire vraie.*

32.

Acte, *n.m.* Act. Refers more to the will or power of the mind. Ex.: *Acte irréfléchi.*
Action, *n.f.* Action. The manifestation or result of an act. Ex.: *Une bonne action.*

33.

Humiliation, *n.f.* Humiliation or confusion. Ex. : *L'humiliation d'un prétentieux.*
Abaissement, *n.m.* Reduction in height or position, figuratively or materially speaking. Ex. : *La concurrence amène l'abaissement des prix.*
Avilissement, *n.m.* Disgrace or degradation. Ex. : *La débauche est un avilissement.* A cheapening or reduction in value. Ex. : *L'abondance de l'or occasionne son avilissement relatif.*
Bassesse, *n.f.* Lack of moral elevation or dignity. Ex. : *L'avarice est une preuve de bassesse d'esprit.*
Abjection, *n.f.* The lowest degree of degradation or moral corruption. Ex. : *L'abjection n'attire que le mépris.*

34.

Acide, *adj.* Acid. Implies the opposite to sweet. Ex. : *Un goût acide.*
Âcre, *adj.* Acrid. Implies a natural condition. Ex. : *Des vapeurs âcres.*
Acerbe, *adj.* Sharp. Refers to something not yet sweet. Ex. : *Une pomme acerbe.*
Aigre, *adj.* Sour. Refers to something which has lost its sweetness. Ex. : *Du vin aigre.*

35.

Accusateur, *n.m.* Accuser. Person who charges openly, and generally with proof of his accusation.
Dénonciateur, *n.m.* Denouncer. Person who informs against another.
Délateur, *n.m.* Person who informs against another in secret, often without proof.

36.

Achat, *n.m.* Purchase. Refers more to the act than to the article purchased.
Emplette, *n.f.* Purchase. Refers to what is purchased and denotes small objects of everyday use. Ex. : *Faire des emplettes.*
Acquisition, *n.f.* Purchase. Legal term used in connection with real estate. Ex. : *L'acquisition d'un terrain.*

37.

Reçu, *n.m.* General term for a receipt for money or an article. Receipt, i.e. the act of receiving. The word is confined, in this sense, to the expression "On receipt of". Ex. : *Au reçu de votre lettre.*
Quittance, *n.f.* Receipt for total payment. Ex. : *Timbre de quittance.*
Acquit, *n.m.* Receipt. Denotes complete settlement of any financial obligation. The expression *pour acquit* on a receipted invoice corresponds to "Received" in English when the bill is fully paid.
Récépissé, *n.m.* Receipt, i.e. a written acknowledgment of receipt, generally of goods. Ex. : *Récépissé de chemin de fer.*

Réception, *n.f.* Receipt, i.e. the act of receiving. **Ex.** : *Accuser réception d'une lettre.*
Recette, *n.f.* Receipts or takings. **Ex.** : *La recette et la dépense. La recette d'hier est satisfaisante.*
Receipt or recipe, i.e. a formula for any preparation.

38.

Aigreur, *n.f.* Sourness of temper, character, etc. **Ex.** : *Être d'une aigreur insupportable.*
Acrimonie, *n.f.* Acrimony. **Ex.** : *Paroles pleines d'acrimonie.*
Âcreté, *n.f.* Bitterness in speech, etc. Implies the addition of hatred. **Ex.** : *L'âcreté d'une dispute.*

39.

Accéder, *v.i.* To comply accessorily with what has already been agreed to by others. To accede.
Consentir, *v.i.* To consent, generally speaking.
Acquiescer, *v.i.* To acquiesce. To agree to what is proposed by others.
Adhérer, *v.i.* To adhere to. To be in agreement with. **Ex.** : *Adhérer à un projet.*
Souscrire, *v.i.* To approve of. *Souscrire* is more formal than *adhérer*. **Ex.** : *Souscrire à un arrangement.*
Tomber d'accord, *v.i.* To come to terms after disagreement.
Céder, *v.i.* To consent in the sense of yielding or giving way. **Ex.** : *Il céda au désir de son ami.*

40.

Sentiment, *n.m.* Feeling regarding anything under discussion. **Ex.** : *Il nous a fait part de ses sentiments sur l'affaire.*
Avis, *n.m.* Opinion. Denotes the conclusion drawn from one's feelings prior to any expression of same. **Ex.** : *A mon avis je laisserais la chose telle quelle.*
Opinion, *n.f.* The definite opinion expressed. **Ex.** : *Donner son opinion.*

41.

Amasser, *v.t.* To amass. Implies the collection or gathering together of things of the same kind. **Ex.** : *Amasser une fortune.*
Accumuler, *v.t.* To accumulate. To continue to amass. **Ex.** : *L'avare ne songe qu'à accumuler.*
Entasser, *v.t.* To heap or pile up. To place closely together. **Ex.** : *Entasser des meubles dans une pièce.*
Amonceler, *v.t.* To heap confusedly in large quantities. **Ex.** : *Amonceler la neige.*

42.

Mollir, *v.t.* To soften. Denotes a depreciating effect. **Ex.** : *Fruit qui mollit.*
Amollir, *v.t.* To soften that which is hard or firm. **Ex.** : *La chaleur amollit la cire.* Also used figuratively. **Ex.** : *La pitié amollit le cœur.*
Ramollir, *v.t.* To soften that which has become very or too hard. **Ex.** : *Ce beurre est trop dur ; il faut le ramollir.*

43.

Cabaret, *n.m.* Drink shop where, originally, wine only was sold. The word is now applied to certain modern night restaurants in Paris.
Guinguette, *n.f.* Public-house in the country frequented especially by merrymakers during holiday time. Tea garden.
Café, *n.m.* That which corresponds, in France, to the English public-house.
Estaminet, *n.m.* A country *café*.
Buvette, *n.f.* Small general shop licensed to sell alcoholic liquor for consumption on the premises.

44.

Accélérer, *v.t.* To accelerate. To increase a movement already commenced.
Hâter, *v.t.* To hasten. Refers generally to things. Ex.: *Hâter la fin d'une séance.*
Presser, *v.t.* To hasten, referring more to persons. Ex.: *Presser une personne de sortir.*

45.

Abondamment, *adv.* Abundantly, implying more than necessary for any specific purpose. Ex.: *Livre abondamment enrichi d'illustrations.*
En abondance, *adv. exp.* In abundance. Refers more to the superfluous. Ex.: *Des vivres en abondance.*
Copieusement, *adv.* Copiously. Plentifully.
Amplement, *adv.* Amply. Refers more to the use or application of things and implies that a portion remains over.
À foison, *adv. exp.* Denotes a profusion of similar objects or things. Ex.: *Des fruits à foison.*

46.

Aisance, *n.f.* Easy circumstances.
Richesses, *n.f.* Wealth. Denotes more than *aisance*.
Opulence, *n.f.* Extreme wealth. Opulence.

47.

D'abord, Tout d'abord, *adv. exp.* Firstly. *Tout d'abord* is more emphatic.
De prime abord, *adv. exp.* In the first instance.
Au premier abord, *adv. exp.* At first sight.
Dès l'abord, *adv. exp.* From the commencement.
Premièrement, *adv.* Firstly. In the first place. Generally followed by a sentence commencing with *Deuxièmement, en second lieu,* etc.

48.

Agrandir, *v.t.* To enlarge or increase in extent, size. Ex.: *Agrandir une photographie.*
Accroître, *v.t.* To increase, figuratively or materially speaking. Ex.: *La vieillesse fait parfois accroître la méfiance.*
Augmenter, *v.t.* To augment. To increase in quantity or number.
Ajouter, *v.t.* To add, generally speaking. Ex.: *Ajouter à une somme.*
Croître, *v.i.* To increase gradually. To grow. Ex.: *Les jours croissent.*

49.

Accommodement, *n.m.* Agreement between persons in dispute. Ex. : *Accommodement par transaction.*
Raccommodement, *n.m.* Personal reconciliation between friends, relations, etc. Ex. : *Raccommodement de deux brouillés.*

50.

Accorder, *v.t.* To reconcile, by discussion, etc. Ex. : *Accorder deux adversaires.*
Concilier, *v.t.* To conciliate or pacify, generally speaking.
Raccommoder, *v.t.* To patch up (a quarrel). Ex. : *Raccommoder une dispute.*
Réconcilier, *v.t.* To reconcile, or restore friendship. Ex. : *Réconcilier deux amis.*

51.

Abêtir, *v.t.* To make stupid through lack of care. Ex. : *Abêtir un enfant faute de soins.*
Rabêtir, *v.t.* To make stupid through interference with natural development. Ex. : *Les mauvais traitements rabêtissent l'enfant.*

52.

Abandonner, *v.t.* To abandon or give up, in a general sense, either as regards things or persons. Ex. : *Abandonner un projet.* When referring to persons *abandonner* carries with it the idea of neglect or suffering. Ex. : *Abandonner son enfant.*
Délaisser, *v.t.* To abandon in the sense of leaving quite alone, without support of any kind. Ex. : *Dieu ne nous délaissera point.*
Quitter, Laisser, *v.t.* Both mean to leave, purely and simply. *Quitter* is generally used in connection with persons or places, *laisser* with things. Ex. : *Il quittera Paris ce soir. J'ai laissé votre livre sur la table.*
Renoncer, *v.i.* To give up or renounce, either in the sense of abandoning a claim, or having an interest in anything. Ex. : *Renoncer à une succession. Renoncer aux plaisirs du monde. Renoncer* is also employed transitively in the sense of having nothing to do with, or refusing to recognize. Ex. : *Renoncer quelqu'un pour son ami.*
Se désister, *v.r.* To give up or renounce, legally speaking. Ex. : *Se désister d'un appel.*

53.

Accepter, *v.t.* To accept. To take what is offered.
Recevoir, *v.t.* To receive. To take what is sent or given.
Agréer, *v.t.* To receive that with which one is in agreement. Ex. : *Agréer des marchandises.*

54.

Abattre, *v.t.* To bring down forcibly. Ex. : *Abattre un arbre.*
Démolir, *v.t.* To demolish what is built.
Renverser, *v.t.* To knock over what is standing. Ex. : *Renverser une statue.*

Jeter à bas, *v.t.* To knock down forcibly. Ex.: *Jeter à bas une idole.*
Mettre à bas, *v.t.* To bring down without physical effort. To overthrow. Ex.: *Mettre à bas le gouvernement.*
Raser, *v.t.* To demolish, leaving no trace of previous existence. Ex.: *Raser un village.*
Ruiner, *v.t.* To ruin. To cause to fall to pieces.
Détruire, *v.t.* To destroy. To deprive anything of its quality, condition, etc.
Exterminer, *v.t.* To exterminate. To wipe out of existence.

55.

Auprès de, *prep. exp.* Attached to (persons). Ex.: *Ambassadeur auprès du Roi d'Angleterre.*
Près, *prep.* Attached to (things). Ex.: *Ambassadeur près le Vatican. Médecin près les tribunaux.*

56.

Contrat, *n.m.* A contract. An agreement having a legal aspect. Ex.: *Un contrat de mariage.*
Marché, *n.m.* A contract or agreement by which a sale, purchase or exchange is effected. Ex.: *Conclure un marché.*
Accord, *n.m.* An agreement between rivals, enemies, etc. Ex.: *Établir l'accord entre adversaires.*
Convention, *n.f.* A convention. An agreement, generally speaking. Ex.: *La Convention de Genève.*
Pacte, *n.m.* A pact. A convention made to remain in force for a certain length of time. Ex.: *Le Pacte de Londres.*
Traité, *n.m.* A treaty. A convention made as the result of negotiation. Ex.: *Le Traité de Versailles.*

57.

Acclimatation, *n.f.* The act of acclimatizing or being acclimatized.
Acclimatement, *n.m.* The state or result of being acclimatized.

58.

Naturaliser, *v.t.* To naturalize. Refers to species only.
Acclimater, *v.t.* To acclimatize. Refers to individuals as well as species.

59.

Attirant, *adj.* Attractive. Used figuratively in connection with persons. Ex.: *Manières attirantes.*
Attractif, *adj.* Attractive. Denotes power of attraction in the literal sense of the word. Ex.: *La force attractive d'un aimant.*
Attrayant, *adj.* Attractive as applied figuratively to anything. Ex.: *L'étude de la musique est très attrayante pour beaucoup.*
Attracteur, *adj.* Attractive. Refers to power or a force which acts by attraction. Ex.: *C'est la force attractrice de l'électro-aimant qui fait marcher une sonnerie électrique.*

60.

Adoucir, *v.t.* To sweeten or soften. Ex.: *Adoucir l'acidité d'un fruit.*
Radoucir, *v.t.* To restore sweetness or softness to. Ex.: *Radoucir un regard.*

61.

Gérer, *v.t.* To manage. Refers to a business or similar concern. Ex.: *Gérer un établissement.*
Diriger, *v.t.* To direct or manage. Implies a certain authority given for the maintenance of order. Ex.: *Diriger une usine.*
Conduire, *v.t.* To direct or be at the head of. Implies the addition of experience or knowledge. Ex.: *Conduire des travaux.*
Administrer, *v.t.* To administer. Refers to important matters such as the finance, commerce, etc., of a country. Ex.: *Administrer les finances d'un pays.*
Régir, *v.t.* To manage, with reference to property. Ex.: *Régir une propriété.*

62.

Abrégé, *n.m.* An abridgment. Ex.: *Un abrégé de grammaire.*
Extrait, *n.m.* A part or collection of parts taken from a work. An extract.
Précis, *n.m.* A concise extract, containing essentials only. A "précis"
Résumé, *n.m.* A recapitulation placed at the end of any chapter, book, in the form of a conclusion.
Sommaire, *n.m.* A preliminary notice, list, etc., indicating the principal contents of any work. A summary.

63.

Caler, *v.t.* To hold in position by wedging. Ex.: *Caler un chargement.*
Soutenir, *v.t.* To hold or prop up. To sustain. Ex.: *Piliers qui soutiennent un pont.*
Accoter, *v.t.* To sustain or hold in position from one side. Ex.: *Accoter un mur.*

64.

Attenant, *adj.* Adjoining. Implies an accessory or part. Ex.: *Basse-cour attenante à une ferme.*
Contigu, *adj.* Contiguous. Denotes contact with. Ex.: *Deux maisons contiguës.*
Adjacent, *adj.* Adjacent. Used generally in connection with geometry or geography. Ex.: *Angles adjacents.*
Voisin, *adj.* Neighbouring. Near, but not touching. Ex.: *Deux maisons voisines.*

65.

Louer, *v.t.* To praise with no ulterior motive. Ex.: *Je n'ai qu'à me louer de ses services.*
Flatter, *v.t.* To flatter. To praise in order to please.
Flagorner, *v.t.* To fawn upon. Implies insincerity or hypocrisy. Ex.: *Flagorner un supérieur.*

Aduler, *v.t.* To adulate. To flatter with servility. Ex.: *On adule souvent par intérêt.*
Louanger, *v.t.* To praise, generally in the form of a speech or on some similar occasion. To laud.
Préconiser, *v.t.* To praise or vaunt. To say much, either rightly or wrongly, in praise of. Ex.: *Préconiser un remède.*
Prôner, *v.t.* To praise to a great or ludicrous extent. To extol. Ex.: *Prôner un exploit.*

66.

Décevoir, *v.t.* To deceive, by falling short of what is hoped or expected. To disappoint. Ex.: *Espoir déçu.*
Tromper, *v.t.* To deceive by false representation. Ex.: *L'horloge nous a trompés.*
Duper, *v.t.* To dupe. To deceive a person at his expense. Ex.: *Duper un commerçant.*
Abuser, *v.t.* To deceive by taking advantage of another's credulity, etc. Ex.: *Abuser la confiance de quelqu'un.*
Leurrer, *v.t.* To deceive with the intention of entrapping. To lure.
Donner le change, *colloq.* To deceive by making accept what is believed to be something else. To put on a wrong scent. Ex.: *Donner le change à la meute.*
En imposer, *v.i.* To impose on.
Attraper, *v.t.* To deceive, generally for fun. To take in.
Enjôler, *v.t.* To deceive by soft words. To cajole.

67.

Inculpé, *n.m.* Term applied to an accused person before his trial.
Accusé, *n.m.* Term applied to an accused person as soon as his case is taken to the assizes.
Prévenu, *n.m.* The accused in an ordinary police-court case.
Prisonnier, *n.m.* General term for a civil or military prisoner. Ex.: *Prisonnier d'état, de guerre, sur parole.*
Détenu, *n.m.* Person actually imprisoned or sentenced to imprisonment.

68.

Tact, *n.m.* Tact. Ex.: *Avoir du tact.*
Savoir-faire, *n.m.* The art of doing the right thing at the right moment. Ex.: *Le savoir-faire est mieux que le savoir.*
Savoir-vivre, *n.m.* Good breeding.

69.

Adresse, *n.f.* Adroitness. Applies to the manner in which anything is accomplished. Ex.: *S'échapper avec adresse.*
Dextérité, *n.f.* Dexterity. Refers to cleverness displayed by the hands themselves. Ex.: *La dextérité d'un prestidigitateur.*
Habileté, *n.f.* Cleverness. Denotes the ease or skill with which anything is done or accomplished. Ex.: *Traiter une affaire avec habileté.*

70.

D'avance, *adv. exp.* In advance (of things). Ex. : *Payer d'avance.*
En avance, *adv. exp.* In advance. Before the appointed time. Ex. : *J'arrive en avance.*
Par avance, *adv. exp.* In advance. Beforehand. Implies some special reason or intention. Ex. : *Il a réglé par avance afin d'obtenir un escompte.*

71.

Affinité, *n.f.* Natural connection in the sense of relationship. Ex. : *L'affinité entre deux langues.*
Alliance, *n.f.* Union or agreement between things which are in opposition to each other. Ex. : *L'alliance de la lumière et de l'ombre donne à la nature son relief.*
Connexion, *n.f.* Direct relationship or connection. Ex. : *La connexion des idées.*
Connexité, *n.f.* Relationship, more or less remote. Ex. : *La connexité entre deux crimes.*
Liaison, *n.f.* Connection. Refers to the actual union itself. Ex. : *Officier de liaison.*
Union, *n.f.* Union. Denotes close or intimate relationship. Ex. : *L'union fait la force.*
Rapport, *n.m.* Connection or relation, in the sense of having anything to do with. Ex. : *Réponse sans rapport à la question posée.*

72.

Affecter, *v.t.* To affect. Implies pretence. Ex. : *Affecter du chagrin.*
Afficher, *v.t.* To show any quality, fault, etc. Ex. : *Afficher la bonté.*
Se piquer, *v.i.* To hold a certain opinion about oneself. Ex. : *Se piquer de son autorité.*

73.

Attentat, *n.m.* Attempt in the sense of attack or assault. Ex. : *Attentat contre la vie de quelqu'un.*
Tentative, *n.m.* Attempt or endeavour to do anything. Ex. : *Sa tentative d'évasion échoua.*

74.

Affermer, *v.t.* To let. Refers to rural property, and implies generally for a lengthy period. To farm out. Ex. : *Affermer ses terres à un cultivateur.*
Louer, *v.t.* To let. General term applied to house property, rooms or anything else. Ex. : *Louer un chalet.*

75.

Affres, *n.f.* Pangs, in the sense of dread or terror. Ex. : *Les affres de la mort.*
Angoisses, *n.f.* Anguish, mentally or physically speaking. Ex. : *Les angoisses d'une mère.*
Transes, *n.f.* Fright, in the presence of danger, harm, etc. Ex. : *Être dans de grandes transes.*

76.

Affaibli, *adj.* Weakened. Denotes the effect of exertion, suffering, etc. Ex.: *Être affaibli par la maladie.*
Faible, *adj.* Weak. Refers to the general condition of the mind or body. Ex.: *Faible d'esprit.*

77.

Affermir, *v.t.* To make firm. To strengthen. Ex.: *Affermir une monarchie.*
Confirmer, *v.t.* To strengthen what is already strong. To confirm. Ex.: *Confirmer un jugement.*
Raffermir, *v.t.* To strengthen what is weak or liable to fail. Ex.: *Raffermir le courage de quelqu'un.*

78.

Habiller, *v.t.* To dress. To put on one's clothes. Ex.: *S'habiller avec soin.*
Vêtir, *v.t.* To clothe. Ex.: *Vêtu d'un complet gris.*
Revêtir, *v.t.* To clothe for ceremonial purposes. To invest. Ex.: *Revêtir un dignitaire de ses insignes.* To supply with clothes. Ex.: *Revêtir les pauvres.*

79.

Afflouage, *n.m.* The act of refloating a stranded vessel.
Afflouement, *n.m.* The result of refloating a stranded vessel.
Renflouage, *n.m.* The act of refloating a sunken vessel.
Renflouement, *n.m.* The result of refloating a sunken vessel.

80.

Peines, *n.f.* Troubles. Denotes the trials with which human life is afflicted generally. Ex.: *Confier ses peines à quelqu'un.*
Afflictions, *n.f.* Afflictions. Mental suffering as the result of serious misfortune, etc.
Croix, *n.f.* Troubles. A pious way of referring to the trials which God sends Christians. Ex.: *Porter sa croix.*
Tribulations, *n.f.* Trials resulting from adversity, persecutions, etc. Tribulation. Ex.: *Les tribulations de ce monde.*
Peine, *n.f.* Trouble in the sense of inconvenience. Ex.: *Se donner de la peine.*

81.

Douleur, *n.f.* Acute pain or suffering, physically or mentally speaking. Ex.: *Éprouver une douleur.*
Mal, *n.m.* Pain. Refers generally to the body. Ex.: *Avoir mal à la tête.*
Souffrance, *n.f.* Suffering, physically or mentally speaking. Implies a less acute and more sustained pain. Ex.: *Une vie de souffrance.*
Peine, *n.f.* Mental suffering. Ex.: *Faire de la peine à quelqu'un.*
Tourment, *n.m.* Extreme mental or physical suffering. Torment. Ex.: *Souffrir des tourments.*
Agitation, *n.f.* Agitation. Denotes a less acute mental suffering than that indicated by *tourment.*

82.

Affreux, *adj.* Frightful. Implies repugnance to the extent of being unbearable. Ex.: *Caractère affreux.*
Effrayant, *adj.* Fearful. That which causes fear, often without grounds. Ex.: *Aspect effrayant.*
Effroyable, *adj.* Fearful. Applies to anything really to be feared. Ex.: *Subir une mort effroyable.*
Épouvantable, *adj.* Fearful. Denotes astonishment mingled with terror. Ex.: *Accident épouvantable.*

83.

Affluence, *n.f.* A crowd of people who arrive continuously and in succession at the same place. Ex.: *Aux heures d'affluence l'accès de la gare est difficile.*
Concours, *n.m.* A crowd of people who arrive together at the same place. Ex.: *Un concours de gens.*
Foule, *n.f.* Crowd. Implies a lack of order. Ex.: *La foule se rua vers la sortie.*
Multitude, *n.f.* A large number of people gathered together. A multitude.
Presse, *n.f.* An unruly crowd. Ex.: *La presse devint menaçante.*
Cohue, *n.f.* A tumultuous crowd or throng. A mob.
Rassemblement, *n.m.* A crowd or gathering. Refers more to the assembling of those forming the crowd. Ex.: *L'accident occasionna un rassemblement.*

84.

Affranchir, *v.t.* To free of one's own authority or power. Ex.: *Affranchir une esclave.*
Délivrer, *v.t.* To free by an effort. To liberate. Ex.: *Délivrer un pays de ses ennemis.*
Libérer, *v.t.* To discharge or set free. Ex.: *Libérer d'une dette.*
Élargir, *v.t.* To release or set free with reference to prisoners, captives, etc. Ex.: *Élargir un prisonnier.*

85.

Affecté, *adj.* Affected in the sense of being unnatural. Ex.: *Langage affecté.*
Affété, *adj.* Affected in the sense of being finical. Ex.: *Des manières affétées.*

86.

Aération, *n.f.* Aeration. The circulation of fresh air in buildings, etc. Ex.: *L'aération d'un batiment.*
Ventilation, *n.f.* Ventilation. The expulsion of vitiated or bad air from rooms, etc. Ex.: *Ventilation d'un atelier.*
Aérage, *n.m.* Aeration. Refers more to the apparatus or means employed. Ex.: *Tuyau d'aérage.*

87.

Amorce, *n.f.* Bait. Term restricted to fishing.
Appât, *n.m.* Bait, with reference to animals, game or fish.
Leurre, *n.m.* Bait used for hawking.

88.

Affectueusement, *adv.* Affectionately. Implies a deeper sentiment than that expressed by *avec affection*. Ex.: *Obéir affectueusement à son père.*
Avec affection, *adv. exp.* With affection (see above). Ex.: *Soigner quelqu'un avec affection.*
Affectionnément, *adv.* With affection, in the sense of devotion. Ex.: *Servir affectionnément un supérieur.*

89.

Adversité, *n.f.* Adversity. The state of having fate or fortune against one. Ex.: *L'adversité est quelque fois un bienfait.*
Infortune, *n.f.* Misfortune. Implies a series of adverse circumstances. Ex.: *Tomber dans l'infortune.*
Malheur, *n.m.* Misfortune. Refers more to a single event. Ex.: *Il lui est arrivé un grand malheur.*
Misère, *n.f.* Destitution, poverty. Denotes a condition. Ex.: *Être dans la misère.*
Détresse, *n.f.* Distress. Extreme destitution which may, however, only be temporary. Ex.: *La détresse éloigne beaucoup de soi-disant amis.*

90.

Honnête, *adj.* Polite. Implies a keeping within the bounds of decorum. Ex.: *Un honnête homme.*
Poli, *adj.* Polite. Denotes a somewhat more ceremonious behaviour than *honnête*. Ex.: *Des manières polies.*

91.

S'agenouiller, *v.r.* To kneel. Applies more to kneeling for the purpose of worship, prayer, etc.
Se mettre à genoux, *v.r.* To kneel, generally speaking.

92.

Agiter, *v.t.* To perturb or agitate. Implies uncertainty or extreme anxiety of mind.
Emouvoir, *v.t.* To affect or move. Denotes the influence of pity, joy, etc., on the soul. Ex.: *Rien ne l'émeut.*
Troubler, *v.t.* To perplex or confuse the mind, conscience, etc. Implies disorder or disturbance. Ex.: *Être troublé par la présence de quelqu'un.*

93.

Agreger, *v.t.* To receive as a member of any public body or association.
Associer, *v.t.* To appoint as member or partner of any private company, business, etc.

94.

Agrès, *n.m.* Rigging in the sense of rope, tackle, sails, etc.
Gréement, *n.m.* Boat equipment such as anchor, oars, helm, etc.

95.

Agriculteur, *n.m.* Farmer having his own land and his own workmen.
Agronome, *n.m.* Agricultural expert or scientist.
Cultivateur, *n.m.* Farmer who grows a certain kind of crops.
Laboureur, *n.m.* Farmer who actually tills the land. Ploughman.

96.

Agreste, *adj.* Rural or belonging to the country, in the sense of being wild or uncultivated. Ex.: *Paysage agreste.*
Champêtre, *adj.* Rural, as opposed to urban. Ex.: *Garde champêtre.*

97.

Agression, *n.f.* An unexpected and unprovoked attack. Ex.: *Agression dans la rue.*
Attaque, *n.f.* An attack. Implies open hostility on the part of the person or persons attacking.

98.

Auprès de, Près de, *prep. exp.* These two words both mean "near". *Auprès de* implies, however, a more precise or definite proximity. Ex.: *Restez auprès de moi un moment. Elle demeure près de l'église.*

99.

Attrister, *v.t.* To make sad or sorrowful. Ex.: *Déception qui attriste.*
Contrister, *v.t.* To grieve or afflict. Implies a deeper sorrow than that expressed by *attrister*. Ex.: *Être contristé de la mort de quelqu'un.*

100.

Affûter, *v.t.* To sharpen by means of a flat stone, file, etc.
Aiguiser, *v.t.* To sharpen on a grindstone.

101.

Affront, *n.m.* Open contempt or scorn to a person's face. An affront. Ex.: *Essuyer un affront.*
Outrage, *n.m.* Excessive or violent abuse. An outrage. Ex.: *Supporter des outrages.*
Insulte, *n.f.* Insolent abuse. An insult.
Avanie, *n.f.* A humiliating affront.

102.

Agacer, *v.t.* To annoy in the sense of irritate. Ex.: *Personne dont la vanité agace.*
Harceler, *v.t.* To annoy in the sense of worry or torment. Ex.: *Harceler quelqu'un en l'importunant.*
Provoquer, *v.t.* To rouse to action as the result of annoyance, irritation, etc. To provoke. Ex.: *Affront qui provoque.*

103.

Âgé de, *adj.* Aged. Merely denotes the age of any thing or person. Ex. : *Homme âgé de quarante ans.*
A l'âge de, *colloq.* At the age of. Implies some specific circumstance in addition to the actual age. Ex. : *Elle s'est mariée à l'âge de vingt ans.*
Avoir . . . ans, *colloq.* To be . . . years old. Has the same meaning as *âgé de.* Ex. : *Cet homme a quarante ans.*

104.

Agréable, *adj.* Pleasant or agreeable. Refers to a person's mind or character.
Gracieux, *adj.* Pleasant or agreeable, with reference to appearance or behaviour.

105.

Aimer, *v.t.* To love, generally speaking. Refers either to things or persons.
Chérir, *v.t.* To love, with reference to persons only. *Chérir* is more expressive than *aimer.*
Affectionner, *v.t.* To like (persons). Implies a more moderate sentiment than that expressed by *chérir.*

106.

Aide, *n.f.* Help. Denotes active or physical help. Ex. : *Venir en aide.*
Appui, *n.m.* Support to moral or physical weakness. Implies strength or authority. Ex. : *J'ai réussi grâce à son appui.*
Assistance, *n.f.* Assistance. Used generally in a pecuniary sense. Ex. : *L'assistance publique.*
Secours, *n.m.* Help given promptly when required. Ex. : *Porter des secours à un blessé.*
Soutien, *n.m.* Mainstay or chief support. Ex. : *Être le soutien de sa famille.*
Main-forte, *n.f.* Physical help or assistance. The word accentuates the physical element. Ex. : *Prêter main-forte à la loi.*

107.

Aiguillonner, *v.t.* To incite by playing on a particular weakness or desire. To goad. Ex. : *Être aiguillonné par la faim.*
Animer, *v.t.* To infuse activity, enthusiasm, etc. To animate. Ex. : *Animer une nation en faisant appel à son patriotisme.*
Encourager, *v.t.* To encourage. Applies to those who are timid, afraid, etc. Ex. : *Encourager quelqu'un par l'exemple.*
Exciter, *v.t.* To urge on the irresolute. Implies that the desire already exists. To excite. Ex. : *Exciter des ouvriers mécontents à la grève.*
Inciter, *v.t.* To urge on the uninclined. Ex. : *Inciter des ouvriers à la grève.*
Porter à, *v.i.* To tend or incline. Ex. : *Le manque d'exercice porte à l'embonpoint.*
Pousser a, *v.t.* To spur or urge on the unwilling or half-hearted. To impel. Ex. : *Pousser quelqu'un au vol.*

108.

D'ailleurs, *adv. exp.* Besides. Implies a new reason but of a different kind. Ex.: *D'ailleurs la loi ne le permet pas.*
En outre, Outre cela, *adv. exp.* Moreover. A reason added to strengthen what is already sufficient. Ex.: *Traitement avec, en outre, une pension en perspective.*
De plus, *adv. exp.* Furthermore. A reason added to those already given. Ex.: *De plus l'homme était armé d'un long couteau.*

109.

Pères, Aïeux, Ancêtres, *n.m.* These three words may be taken as generally meaning "forefathers" or "ancestors". *Pères* refers, however, to our immediate forefathers; *aïeux* implies more distant periods, while *ancêtres* denotes those who lived in the very earliest times.

110.

Ainsi, *conj.* So. Denotes resemblance or connection, and not necessarily the reason. Ex.: *Comme la vague meurt et renaît sans cesse, ainsi en est-il de l'existence ici bas.*
C'est pourquoi, *adv. exp.* Wherefore. Denotes reason or logical conclusion. Ex.: *La terre tourne sur son axe ; c'est pourquoi nous avons le jour et la nuit.*
Aussi, *conj.* So. Therefore. Indicates equality or complete relationship between two sentences. Ex.: *Son innocence a été établie, aussi a-t-il été acquitté.*

111.

Aisé, *adj.* Easy. Refers to the nature or character of the thing itself. Ex.: *Il est aisé de traverser une route unie.*
Facile, *adj.* Easy. Denotes the possibility of doing anything without effort, trouble, etc. Ex.: *Il est facile de traverser une route lorsqu'il n'y a pas de circulation.*

112.

Absolution, *n.f.* The absolution pronounced after general or auricular confession.
Absoute, *n.f.* The absolution given at a funeral service.

113.

Allégeance, *n.f.* The action of lightening as regards weight.
Allégement, *n.m.* The result of lightening or lessening a load, weight, etc.

114.

Anse, *n.f.* The handle of a basket or jug.
Poignée, *n.f.* The handle of a door or bag.
Manche, *n.m.* The handle of a broom, shovel, etc.
Manivelle, *n.f.* A cranked handle for turning.
Brimbale, *n.f.* Handle (of a pump).
Queue, *n.f.* Metal handle (of a saucepan, frying pan, etc.).

115.

Aliment, *n.m.* Food. Denotes a particular aliment. Ex.: *Le poulet est un aliment propre au convalescents.*
Nourriture, *n.f.* Food, generally speaking. Ex.: *La Sainte Communion est une nourriture spirituelle.*

116.

De même que, *conj. exp.* Just as. Denotes a comparison as regards ways of acting, thinking, etc. Ex.: *De même que lui, j'ai dû y renoncer.*
Ainsi que, *conj. exp.* Just as. Denotes a comparison between the actions or thoughts themselves. Ex.: *Ainsi que son père, il est devenu avocat.*
Comme, *conj.* As. Denotes a comparison with regard to the quality, etc., of things or persons. Ex.: *Jurer comme un templier.*

117.

Aisance, *n.f.* Easy circumstances. Well off. Ex.: *Être dans l'aisance.*
Aise, *n.f.* Ease, physically speaking. Denotes a temporary condition only. Ex.: *Être à l'aise dans un fauteuil.*

118.

Commodités, *n.f.* Conveniences (of life).
Aises, *n.f.* The comforts or enjoyments of life. Refers more to the luxury provided by wealth.

119.

Ajustement, *n.m.* Dress or clothing. Refers to a person's attire as a whole. Ex.: *Porter un ajustement sobre.*
Parure, *n.f.* Dress or attire. Refers more to superfluous finery or ornament. Ex.: *Se passionner pour la parure.*

120.

Alarme, *n.f.* Alarm. Denotes the actual warning given. Ex.: *Sonner l'alarme.*
Alerte, *n.f.* Alarm. Refers to the state or condition as a result of warning. Ex.: *Une fausse alerte.*

121.

Alentours, *n.m.* Surroundings. Denotes what is included within a certain radius. Ex.: *Les alentours d'une maison.*
Environs, *n.m.* Environs. Refers more to certain places surrounding any town, etc. Ex.: *Les environs de Paris sont très agréables.*

122.

Algue, *n.f.* Seaweed. The name applied to certain classes of seaweed. The *algæ*.
Varech, *n.m.* Seaweed. Popular term for marine vegetation generally.

123.

Ajourner, *v.t.*   To adjourn.   Used generally in connection with meetings, law courts, etc.   Ex. : *Ajourner une séance.*
Remettre, *v.t.*   To put off, generally speaking.   Ex. : *Remettre une affaire de jour en jour.*
Renvoyer, *v.t.*   To adjourn, pending a decision.   Ex. : *Renvoyer une affaire à huitaine.*
Reculer, *v.t.*   To delay or postpone.   Ex. : *Reculer la date de son départ.*
Différer, *v.t.*   To defer or put off.   Ex. : *Différer un paiement.*
  Of the above *ajourner* and *renvoyer* imply that the question, etc., is dealt with to a certain extent before being adjourned.   *Remettre, reculer* and *différer* denote a postponement or putting off without anything being done.
Surseoir à, *v.i.*   To put off or to defer.   Largely used in connection with legal matters.   Ex. : *Surseoir aux poursuites.*

124.

Alinéa, *n.m.*   Paragraph.   Refers more to the beginning of a fresh line, as implied by the word itself.
Paragraphe, *n.m.*   Paragraph, generally speaking.

125.

S'aliter, *v.r.*   To take to one's bed through illness.
Se mettre au lit, *v.r.*   To go to bed for rest or sleep.
Se coucher, *v.r.*   To go to bed or lie down.   Marks the recumbent position.

126.

Alléger, *v.t.*   To alleviate or lessen.   Refers to the actual pain or suffering alleviated.   Ex. : *Alléger sa déception par la résignation.*
Soulager, *v.t.*   To relieve or comfort.   Implies a more general effect on the person, etc., relieved.   Ex. : *Soulager quelqu'un dans son chagrin.*

127.

Attirer, *v.t.*   To attract.   Implies the absence of any special desire on the part of the person attracted.   Ex. : *Son charme nous attira tous.*
Allécher, *v.t.*   To entice or attract.   Presupposes a keen desire on the part of the person attracted.   Ex. : *Être alléché par les salles de jeu.*

128.

Être allé, *v.i.*   To have been.   Implies that the person is still in the place referred to.   Ex. : *Il est allé vivre à Paris il y a quatre ans.*
Avoir été, *v.i.*   To have been.   Denotes having been to a place and returned.   Ex. : *Son père a été à Londres plusieurs fois.*

129.

Alouette, *n.f.*   The sky or singing lark.
Mauviette, *n.f.*   The field lark relished, in France, as a savoury dish.

130.

Altier, *adj.* Haughty. Implies the will to intimidate. Ex.: *Regard altier.*
Haut, *adj.* Haughty. Denotes pride or loftiness. Ex.: *Avoir la parole haute.*
Hautain, *adj.* Haughty in the sense of being arrogant or disdainful. Ex.: *Manières hautaines.*

131.

Amoureux, *n.m.* Lover. One whose sentiments are genuine, whether reciprocated or not.
Amant, Galant, *n.m.* These two words both mean "lover" and imply the existence of improper relations. *Amant* is, however, more modern than *galant*.

132.

Ambiguité, *n.f.* The defect of having a meaning liable to more than one interpretation, thus causing doubt or uncertainty. Ex.: *Parler sans ambiguité.*
Amphibologie, *n.f.* A sentence, the grammatical construction of which allows of two different meanings. Amphibology. Ex.: "*Une lettre mal écrite*" *est un exemple d'amphibologie.*
Double sens, *n.m.* A double meaning, the one generally understood, the other remaining more or less in the nature of an allusion. Ex.: *Phrase à double sens.*
Équivoque, *n.f.* A double meaning, the one natural and intended for the hearer, the other distorted as understood by the speaker. Ex.: *Réponse sans équivoque.*

133.

Amaigrissement, *n.m.* The action of growing thin. Ex.: *La maladie entraîne presque toujours l'amaigrissement.*
Maigreur, *n.f.* The state of being thin. Ex.: *Être d'une maigreur inquiétante.*

134.

Alphabétaire, *adj.* Concerning the alphabet. Ex.: *Discussion alphabétaire.*
Alphabétique, *adj.* In the order of the letters of the alphabet. Alphabetical. Ex.: *Liste alphabétique.*

135.

Aller à la rencontre, *colloq.* To go to meet. Implies the desire to meet a person sooner. Ex.: *Aller à la rencontre de son ami.*
Aller au devant, *colloq.* To go to meet. Denotes respect or honour due to the person being met. Ex.: *La Municipalité alla au devant du Président.*

136.

Amiablement, *adv.* In a friendly manner as between friends. Amiably.
Ex. : *Traiter une affaire amiablement.*
À l'amiable, *adv. exp.* In a friendly manner. *À l'amiable* is more formal than *amiablement* and denotes the settlement of transactions, differences, etc., privately without legal or official intervention. Ex. : *Vente à l'amiable.*

137.

Amendement, *n.f.* The improvement of something which is bad. Ex. : *L'amendement d'un caractère vicieux.*
Correction, *n.f.* The act of correcting or rectifying what is defective. Ex. : *La correction d'une épreuve.*
Réforme, *n.f.* The state of that which is re-established as it should be or given a new form. Ex. : *La réforme du calendrier.*
Réformation, *n.f.* The act of altering or re-establishing the form of anything. Reformation. Ex. : *La réformation d'un règlement.*
Amélioration, *n.f.* Improvement or change for the better. Ex. : *Son état indique une amélioration.*

138.

Emmener, *v.t.* To take away. Refers to persons. Ex. : *Emmenez-moi à la campagne.*
Emporter, *v.t.* To take away, with reference to things. Ex. : *Emporter un livre pour le lire.*
Enlever, *v.t.* To remove or carry away. Refers to persons or things. Ex. : *Se faire enlever. Le vent a enlevé le toit de cette maison.*

139.

Remener, *v.t.* To take again to the same place, with reference to persons. Ex. : *Remenez-moi au théâtre.*
Remmener, *v.t.* To take back again to where a person originally was. Ex. : *Remmener un prisonnier à sa cellule.*
Reconduire, *v.t.* To go back or return with a person. Ex. : *Reconduire quelqu'un chez lui.*

140.

Allure, *n.f.* Natural or habitual manner. Ex. : *Reconnaître quelqu'un à son allure.*
Démarche, *n.f.* Manner or behaviour adapted to circumstances. Ex. : *Démarches qui se font remarquer.*

141.

Amener, *v.t.* To bring. Refers to persons only (from *mener* = to lead). Ex. : *Amenez-moi votre père demain.*
Apporter, *v.t.* To bring things. Ex. : *Apportez-moi un journal illustré.*

142.

Baisser, *v.t.* To lower with a view to bringing to a certain point or position. Ex. : *Baisser un pont-levis.*

Abaisser, *v.t.* To lower from a certain height or position, whence the idea of comparison. Ex. : *Abaisser le niveau d'une route.*

Rabaisser, *v.t.* To lower what is considered too high. Ex. : *Rabaisser un tableau placé trop haut.*

143.

En attendant, *adv. exp.* Until then. Pending a certain event, circumstance, etc. Ex. : *En attendant son arrivée aucune décision ne sera prise.*

Entretemps, *adv.* In the meantime. Meanwhile. Indicates the intervening period between two events. Ex. : *L'affaire a été plaidée jeudi dernier mais le jugement n'est pas encore rendu. Entretemps il ne désespère pas.*

Sur ces entrefaites, *adv. exp.* Meanwhile. Denotes the occasion on which something is done pending a later event. Ex. : *Sur ces entrefaites la commande fut annulée.*

144.

An, *n.m.* Year. Used only in connection with dates or periods of time and, as a rule, is never qualified by an adjective except numbers. Ex. : *L'an 1879. La Guerre de Trente Ans.*

Année, *n.f.* Year. Indicates a period of time and may refer to what takes place during such period by being qualified adjectivally. Ex. : *Une mauvaise année pour la récolte. Bonne année.*

145.

Amuser, *v.t.* To occupy the mind idly in order to beguile time. To amuse. Ex. : *La contemplation de la foule l'amusa beaucoup.*

Divertir, *v.t.* To give pleasure to. To make agreeable. Ex. : *Divertir ses invités.*

Distraire, *v.t.* To turn the attention to something else with a view to amusing, making forget, etc. Ex. : *Le travail le distrait de son chagrin.*

146.

Anciennement, *adv.* Of old. Refers to what happened in bygone ages.

Autrefois, *adv.* Formerly. Serves to denote the change or contrast between past and present. Ex. : *Autrefois les moyens de transport étaient moins rapides.*

Jadis, *adv.* Formerly. Term used to mark a separation between past and present. Ex. : *Jadis la France était une monarchie.*

Naguère, *adv.* Lately. Not long ago. Ex. : *Les danses modernes ont moins de grâce que celles que nous dansions naguère.*

147.

Âne, *n.m.* Jackass. Donkey.

Baudet, *n.m.* Male donkey. *Baudet,* although commonly employed in everyday conversation, strictly applies to the animal used for breeding purposes.

148.

Ânesse, *n.f.* She-ass.

Bourrique, *n.f.* She-ass, considered as a beast of burden.

[25]

149.

Inimitié, *n.f.* Ill-will. Implies that the feeling is open.
Rancune, *n.f.* Rancour. Dissimulated ill-will following an injury, affront, etc.

150.

Annoncer, *v.t.* To announce. Ex. : *Les journaux ont annoncé la guerre.*
Dénoncer, *v.t.* To announce officially or solemnly. Ex. : *On dénonce la guerre par voie diplomatique.*

151.

Anoblir, *v.t.* To ennoble socially. To confer the rank of nobility.
Ennoblir, *v.t.* To ennoble morally. To dignify.

152.

Ampoulé, *adj.* Bombastic. Denotes the use of big words in connection with unimportant things. Ex. : *Style ampoulé.*
Emphatique, *adj.* Pompous. Implies unnecessary exaggeration.
Boursouflé, *adj.* Inflated. Denotes the treatment of a simple subject in a grandiloquent manner.

153.

Apercevoir, *v.t.* To perceive or catch sight of. Implies that the ocular impression received is imperfect owing to distance, obstacles, etc. Ex. : *Nous l'avons aperçu de loin.*
Découvrir, *v.t.* To perceive. Denotes that the impression received is complete. Ex. : *De cette hauteur on découvre toute la campagne environnante.*
Percevoir, *v.t.* To perceive in the sense of receiving the impression of objects, etc. Ex. : *Percevoir la vérité.*

154.

Anneau, *n.m.* A metallic ring for the finger, curtains, etc. Ex. : *Anneau épiscopal. Anneaux gymnastiques.*
Bague, *n.f.* Term reserved for rings worn on the finger. Ex. : *Bague de fiançailles. Bague d'améthyste.*
Alliance, *n.f.* Wedding ring. Ex. : *Alliance en or.*
Rond, *n.m.* Ring (generally other than metallic) for various uses. Ex. : *Un rond de serviette. Faire des ronds dans l'eau.*

155.

Ramener, *v.t.* To bring back again, with reference to persons (from *mener* = to lead). Ex. : *Ramener un accusé au banc.*
Rapporter, *v.t.* To bring back anything. Ex. : *Rapporter-moi le livre que je vous ai prêté.*

156.

Aube, *n.f.* Dawn. Denotes the first glimmer of daybreak.
Aurore, *n.f.* Dawn at the moment when the sky is tinged with a reddish glow. Ex. : *Les lueurs de l'aube annoncent l'aurore.*

157.

Apparaître, *v.i.* To appear. Refers to things, etc., out of the ordinary. Ex. : *Dieu apparut à Abram.*
Paraître, *v.i.* To appear generally. Ex. : *Paraître en public.* Also employed in a figurative sense. Ex. : *A ce qu'il paraît.*
Comparaître, *v.i.* To appear (before a Court of Justice). Ex. : *Comparaître en justice.*

158.

Appareil, *n.m.* The preparation or display connected with any ceremony, etc. Ex. : *L'appareil d'une revue.*
Apparat, *n.m.* Ostentation or exaggerated display. Ex. : *Un festin d'apparat.*

159.

Appas, *n.m.* Charm in the sense of allurement. Refers more to form or appearance. The term is often used in connection with things without merit, but against the attraction of which resistance is difficult. Ex. : *Les appas de la fortune.*
Attrait, *n.m.* Attraction. Denotes that a thing is agreeable on its own merit. Ex. : *Se sentir de l'attrait pour la littérature.*
Charme, *n.m.* Charm. Denotes a mysterious or irresistible attraction. Spell. Ex. : *Être sous le charme de.*

160.

Apprêts, *n.m.* Preparations immediately before anything is done. Ex. : *Les apprêts d'un voyage* (packing bags, etc.).
Préparatifs, *n.m.* Preparation for an event which is more or less distant. Ex. : *Les préparatifs d'un voyage* (decide route, clothing required, etc.).

161.

Apetisser, Rapetisser. These two words both mean " to make smaller ", *rapetisser* implying a slower procedure. The latter term is, however, now generally used in preference to the former. Ex. : *L'éloignement rapetisse les objets.*

162.

Apprivoisé, *adj.* Tame. Refers to animals which have been caught wild and tamed.
Privé, *adj.* Tame. Said of animals born amongst, and reared by, human beings.

163.

Approbateur, *adj.* Approving. Implies the approval of persons. Ex. : *Battre des mains pour applaudir est un geste approbateur.*
Approbatif, *adj.* Approving. Denotes the approval of things. Ex. : *Lever la main en geste approbatif.*

164.

Apprendre, *v.i.* To learn from others voluntarily or involuntarily. Ex. : *Apprendre la musique. Apprendre à mentir.*
S'instruire, *v.r.* To acquire knowledge by one's own effort. Implies the will to learn. Ex. : *S'instruire dans la jurisprudence.*

165.
Creuser, *v.t.* To go into or study a subject, etc.
Approfondir, *v.t.* To go into fully. *Approfondir* denotes a more thorough operation than that expressed by *creuser.*

166.
Apprécier, *v.t.* To value or estimate. Implies that the quality, condition, etc., of the object valued is taken into consideration. Ex.: *Apprécier le contenu d'une bibliothèque.*
Estimer, *v.t.* To estimate. To fix an approximate value based on one's own opinion. Ex.: *Estimer une propriété.*
Évaluer, *v.t.* To fix a value for any specific purpose. Ex.: *Evaluer une propriété aux fins d'hypothèques.*
Priser, *v.t.* To value. The term is restricted to goods, etc., intended for sale by auction or otherwise.

167.
Apprêter, *v.t.* To prepare in the sense of getting ready for immediate use or action. Ex.: *Apprêter à manger.*
Disposer, *v.t.* To prepare in the sense of arranging or putting in order. Ex.: *Disposer une salle pour une conférence.*
Préparer, *v.t.* To prepare. Refers to more or less lengthy preparation carried out some time beforehand. Ex.: *Il est avocat et il prépare son fils à suivre la même carrière.*

168.
Apprendre, *v.t.* To teach. Implies the inculcation of knowledge. Ex.: *Apprendre à lire à un enfant.*
Enseigner, *v.t.* To give lessons. Ex.: *Enseigner une langue étrangère.*
Instruire, *v.t.* To teach in the sense of educating or bringing up. Ex.: *Instruire ses enfants est le premier devoir d'un père.*

169.
S'approprier, *v.r.* To take possession of what is not one's property. Ex.: *S'approprier un terrain.*
S'attribuer, *v.r.* To claim on one's own authority. Ex.: *S'attribuer un mérite.*
S'arroger, *v.r.* To claim as a right. Ex.: *S'arroger un privilège.*

170.
Appointements, *n.m.* Wages. Salary. Applies to those employed in departments, offices, etc.
Gages, *n.m.* Wages, with reference to servants.
Salaire, *n.m.* Wages paid to professional workmen.
Traitement, *n.m.* Salary. Applies only to managers, directors, high officials, etc.

171.
Appréhender, *v.t.* To fear that which may possibly happen, whence the idea of taking precautions. Ex.; *Elle se couvre bien car elle appréhende le froid.*

Craindre, *v.t.* To fear that which may probably or will certainly happen. Ex. : *Craindre la mort.*
Avoir peur, *v.i.* To be afraid of (any present or imminent danger). Ex. : *Cet enfant a peur de l'orage.*
Redouter, *v.t.* To fear (that against which resistance is difficult or impossible). Implies a kind of respect for the thing feared. Ex. : *Criminel qui redoute la justice.*

172.

Appliquer, *v.t.* To apply by spreading or laying over. Ex. : *Appliquer une couche de peinture.* Is also used figuratively. Ex. : *Appliquer la loi.*
Apposer, *v.t.* To apply in the sense of fixing or fastening. Ex. : *Apposer les scellés.*

173.

Appui, *n.m.* Support given to that which is likely to fall. Ex. : *Se servir d'une canne comme appui.*
Soutien, *n.m.* Support given to that which bears a load. Ex. : *Colonne de soutien.*
Support, *n.m.* Support given to keep anything in position. Ex. : *Les supports d'une grille.*

174.

Armes, *n.f.* Heraldic arms. Refers to the shield only.
Armoiries, *n.f.* Armorial bearing as a whole.

175.

Après, *adv.* Afterwards. Denotes posteriority with the idea of a break or interval between the two events. Ex. : *Il est mort dix ans après.*
Puis, *adv.* Then. Afterwards. Implies a certain order. Ex. : *Il m'a parlé de sa mère, puis de son père.*
Ensuite, *adv.* Then. Implies that the two events or circumstances follow each other without any intervening lapse of time. Ex. : *La nouvelle de sa démission a été reçue et ensuite communiquée à la presse.*

176.

S'améliorer, *v.r.* To improve. Implies that a certain quality already exists (*améliorer = rendre meilleur*). Ex. : *Sa santé s'améliore de jour en jour.*
Se bonifier, *v.r.* To improve. Literally to make good (*bonifier = rendre bon*). Ex. : *Le vin se bonifie en bouteille.*

177.

Arrêt, *n.m.* Judgment given by a high court such as the appeal court, assizes, etc.
Jugement, *n.m.* Judgment given by a *tribunal civil*, court martial, etc.
Sentence, *n.f.* Sentence as pronounced by a justice of the peace.

178.

Arrosement, *n.m.* The act of watering. Ex.: *L'arrosement d'un jardin.*
Arrosage, *n.m.* Watering. Does not necessarily refer to the act itself. Ex.: *Service d'arrosage.*

179.

Asile, *n.m.* Refuge. Formerly used with reference to a retreat respected as inviolable; the word is now reserved to indicate a workhouse, infirmary or other similar refuge. Ex.: *Les églises furent longtemps regardées comme des asiles inviolables. Asile de nuit.*
Refuge, *n.m.* Refuge in the sense of retreat from danger, pursuit. Ex.: *Dieu est un refuge pour l'opprimé.*

180.

Arranger, *v.t.* To arrange. To put in order in the sense of assigning a place for anything. Ex.: *Arranger des livres sur un rayon.*
Ranger, *v.t.* To put away a thing in its proper place. Ex.: *Rangez ces livres dans la bibliothèque.*

181.

Assemblage, *n.m.* Collection of things having little or no connection with each other. Ex.: *Assemblage de qualités et de défauts.*
Assortiment, *n.m.* Collection or assortment of things of the same kind. Ex.: *Un bel assortiment de soieries.*

182.

Arracher, *v.t.* To wrest. Denotes violence with resistance or opposition. Ex.: *Arracher des pommes de terre.*
Ravir, *v.t.* To take away either by violence or stealth. Ex.: *Ravir l'honneur à quelqu'un.*

183.

Assiette, *n.f.* Permanent or topographical situation. Site. Ex.: *L'assiette d'une ville.*
Position, *n.f.* Position. Denotes more the manner in which placed. Ex.: *Position prise par l'armée pour l'attaque.*
Situation, *n.f.* Situation, with regard to the surroundings of anything. Ex.: *La situation de cette ville est très agréable.*

184.

Assemblée, *n.f.* Meeting of a more or less formal nature. Applies to creditors, shareholders, government, etc. Ex.: *Assemblée Constituante.*
Réunion, *n.f.* Meeting, public or private. Implies that those present are, to a certain extent, in agreement with one another. Ex.: *Réunion de famille.*
Séance, *n.f.* Meeting. Refers more to the duration of same. Ex.: *Ouvrir la séance. La séance fut interminable.*

185.

Assister, *v.i.* To attend or be present intentionally. Ex.: *Assister à la messe.*
Etre présent, *v.i.* To be present unintentionally or by chance. Ex.: *Il était présent au départ du bateau.*
Suivre, *v.t.* To attend several times in succession such as a course of lectures, etc. Ex.: *Les cours de musique furent très suivis.*

186.

Étancher, Désaltérer, *v.t.* These two words both mean " to quench " or " to slake ". *Désaltérer*, however, is sufficient by itself when translating " to quench one's thirst ", whereas *étancher* requires the addition of the word *soif*. Ex.: *Étancher sa soif. La citronnade est une boisson qui désaltère.*

187.

Assembler, Rassembler, *v.t.* These two words are employed indifferently in the sense of " to collect " or " assemble ". *Rassembler* implies, however, the collection of things more or less scattered. Ex.: *Assembler des troupes. Rassembler ses idées.*

188.

Asservissement, *n.m.* Servitude. Implies tyranny or oppression. Ex.: *Tenir une nation dans l'asservissement.*
Assujettissement, *n.m.* State of subjection. Denotes dependence on the part of the subject. Ex.: *Assujettissement à la mode.*
Sujétion, *n.f.* Subjection. Refers to the obligation itself to which one is subjected. Ex.: *La mort est la porte par laquelle nous nous échappons enfin des sujétions de ce monde.*

189.

Assurer, *v.t.* To make fast. Literally to make sure. Ex.: *Assurer la passerelle d'un bateau.*
Affermir, *v.t.* To make firm by consolidating. Ex.: *Affermir un échaffaudage contre le vent.*

190.

Attaquer, *v.t.* To attack. Implies that the aggression is sudden and of short duration. Ex.: *Attaquer quelqu'un dans la rue.*
S'attaquer à, *v.r.* To attack. Denotes a prepared attack which may last some time. Ex.: *S'attaquer à la réputation de quelqu'un.*

191.

Attache, *n.f.* Attachment or liking for things of a worldly nature. Ex.: *L'attache au pouvoir.*
Attachement, *n.m.* Attachment in the sense of real affection for a person. Ex.: *Ce chien a un grand attachement pour son maître.*

192.

Atteindre, *v.t.* To reach. Implies the accomplishment of the act normally or without effort. Ex.: *Les inondations ont atteint le chemin de fer.*

Atteindre à, *v.i.* To reach. Denotes attainment by perseverance with a view to overcoming difficulty. Ex.: *Atteindre au plus haut point de son ambition.*

193.

Attiédissement, *n.m.* The act of cooling down or becoming lukewarm.
Tiédeur, *n.f.* The state of that which is lukewarm.

194.

Attouchement, *n.m.* The act of touching with the hand. Ex.: *Jésus Christ guérit souvent par le simple attouchement.*
Tact, *n.m.* The sense of touch. Ex.: *Chez les aveugles le tact remplace souvent la vue.*
Toucher, *n.m.* Touch. Ex.: *Le tact est le sens du toucher.*

195.

Attendre, *v.t.* To expect that which may happen. Ex.: *Je l'attends pour demain.*
S'attendre à, *v.r.* To expect that which one is certain will happen. Ex.: *Je m'attends à ce qu'il vienne demain.*
Vouloir, *v.i.* To expect, i.e. to imagine. Expresses impossibility or extreme difficulty. Ex.: *Comment voulez-vous que j'écrive avec une plume aussi mauvaise?*

196.

Considération, *n.f.* Consideration. Respect for what is due to a person. Ex.: *Jouir d'une haute considération.*
Égard, *n.m.* Consideration in the sense of deference to propriety. Ex.: *Manquer d'égards envers quelqu'un.*

197.

Atterrage, *n.m.* The approach to land.
Atterrissage, *n.m.* The actual landing itself.

198.

Autres, *pron.,* **Autrui,** *n.m.* These two words both mean "others". *Autrui* is, however, confined to proverbs, poetical expressions, etc. Ex.: *Il est de retour avant les autres. Ne convoitez pas le bien d'autrui.*

199.

Avare, *adj.* Miserly. Denotes possession for the sake of possession only. Ex.: *L'homme avare se prive de tout.*
Avaricieux, *adj.* Said of persons who take all they can get and give as little as possible. Avaricious.

200.

Avènement, *n.m.* Coming, with reference to special or important events. Ex.: *L'avènement du Messie.*
Venue, *n.f.* Coming, generally speaking. Ex.: *Allées et venues.*

201.

Avenir, *n.m.* Future. Refers more to the flight of time or succession of events. Ex.: *À l'avenir vous me préviendrez avant de partir.*
Futur, *n.m.* Future, with reference to human existence. Ex.: *Nous ne savons pas ce que le futur nous réserve.*

202.

Avarier, *v.t.* To damage or spoil. Used generally in connection with perishable foodstuffs, crops, etc. Ex.: *Ces marchandises ont été avariées pendant le transport par chemin de fer.*
Endommager, *v.t.* To damage property, belongings, etc. Ex.: *La foudre a endommagé cette église.*
Abîmer, *v.t.* To damage or spoil any article by crushing, dirtying, illuse, etc. Ex.: *La pluie a abîmé mon chapeau.*
Gâcher, *v.t.* To spoil through bad workmanship, incompetence, interference, etc. Ex.: *Le mauvais temps a gâché notre excursion.*
Gâter, *v.t.* To spoil or render unfit with reference to food. Ex.: *L'humidité gâte les fruits.*
To spoil (children). Ex.: *Enfant gâté.*

203.

Avérer, *v.t.* To prove that a thing is true or real.
Vérifier, *v.t.* To examine in order to see whether a fact is true or otherwise. To verify.
Constater, *v.t.* To ascertain the truth of anything.

204.

Il y a, Il est, *colloq.* Both these expressions mean "there is" or "there are". *Il y a* refers, however, to a definite instance or instances whereas *il est* denotes vagueness and is only used in the abstract. Ex.: *Il y a quarante membres de l'Académie Française appelés Immortels. Il est des crimes qui ne sont jamais découverts.*

205.

Avertir, *v.t.* To inform beforehand. To warn. Ex.: *Un coup de sifflet nous avertit de l'approche du train.*
Aviser, *v.t.* To inform beforehand or advise, commercially speaking. Ex.: *Je l'ai avisé de l'expédition des marchandises.*
Conseiller, *v.t.* To advise in the sense of giving advice. Ex.: *Je vous conseille de renoncer à ce projet.*
Prévenir, *v.t.* To warn. Implies that the person warned will or should act on the information received. Ex.: *Nous l'avons prévenu du danger qui le guettait.*

206.

À l'aveugle, *adv. exp.* Blindly. Denotes lack of intelligence or understanding. Ex. : *Juger à l'aveugle.*
Aveuglément., *adv.* Blindly, that is, without study or reflection. Ex. : *Acquiescer aveuglément à une demande.*

207.

Aveuglement, *n.m.* **Cécité,** *n.f.* Both these words mean "blindness". *Aveuglement* is, however, generally used in the figurative sense, *cécité* never.

208.

Avisé, *adj.* Cautious in the sense of taking everything into consideration.
Circonspect, *adj.* Cautious in the sense of leaving nothing to chance. Circumspect.
Prudent, *adj.* Acting only after mature reflection. Prudent.

209.

Empire, *n.m.* Power or dominion acquired over, and as a result of, human weakness. Ex. : *Exercer un empire absolu.*
Pouvoir, *n.m.* Power delegated or communicated to any person or authority. Ex. : *Il n'est pas en mon pouvoir de vous accorder cela.*
Puissance, *n.f.* The effective power or authority of any person whether acquired by delegation, right or might. Ex. : *Les hommes n'ont pas toujours mis leur puissance au service de la justice.*

210.

Autour, *prep.* Round about. Denotes immediate proximity. Ex. : *Tourner autour de la question. Les ministres sont autour du roi.*
Alentour, *adv.* Round about, in the sense of being in the neighbourhood. Ex. : *La campagne d'alentour.*

211.

Babiller, *v.i.* To say an abundance of things the substance of which amounts to nothing.
Caqueter, *v.i.* To talk loudly, to the inconvenience of others. To chatter.
Jaser, *v.i.* To talk for any length of time simply for the pleasure of talking.
Jacasser, *v.i.* To talk volubly.
Bavarder, *v.i.* To gossip. Implies an inclination to tell tales.
Jaboter, *v.i.* To talk softly, as of people conferring together.

212.

Bâche, *n.f.* **Prélart,** *n.m.* These two words both mean "tarpaulin". *Prélart,* however, strictly applies to tarpaulins used on boats or ships.

213.

Babiole, *n.f.* Trifle or knick-knack, intended to amuse children.
Bagatelle, *n.f.* Trifle. Denotes something of little value. Ex. : *Acheter des bagatelles.*
Brimborion, *n.m.* Familiar term for any small object of little or no value.
Colifichet, *n.m.* Small trinket or trifle usually for personal attire.

214.

Bachot, *n.m.* Punt or small flat-bottomed boat for crossing rivers, etc.
Canot, *n.m.* Boat (rowing, life-saving, motor, etc.).
Barque, *n.f.* Boat, larger than a *canot* and usually with sails.
Bateau, *n.m.* General term for a boat.
Chaloupe, *n.f.* A boat or launch. Ex. : *Chaloupe canonnière. Chaloupe de pêche.*

215.

Badaud, *n.m.* Simpleton who gapes with astonishment at everything he hears or sees.
Benêt, *n.m.* Simpleton whose extreme good nature or simplicity is imposed on by others.
Niais, *n.m.* Simpleton in the sense of being innocent or unsophisticated.
Nigaud, *n.m.* Simpleton. Implies childish innocence coupled with a lack of refinement.

216.

Bagatelle, *n.f.* That which is of little importance. Ex. : *Cette histoire n'est qu'une bagatelle.*
Rien, *n.m.* That which is of no importance or value whatever. Ex. : *Il s'emporte pour un rien.*
Vétille, *n.f.* Trifle or insignificant obstacle unworthy of attention. Ex. : *Il ne s'arrête pas à des vétilles.*

217.

Badiner, *v.i.* To trifle or play with. Ex. : *On ne badine pas avec l'amour.*
Folâtrer, *v.i.* To be playful or frolicsome. Ex. : *Folâtrer comme un enfant.*

218.

Bafouer, *v.t.* To scoff at.
Conspuer, *v.t.* To revile or treat with scorn. Implies an unreserved expression of one's feelings.
Honnir, *v.t.* To scorn for the purpose of making one blush with shame.
Vilipender, *v.t.* To revile or abuse. Denotes the desire to degrade or lower in estimation.

219.

Balbutier, *v.i.* To stammer. Denotes indistinct articulation. Ex. : *Les ivrognes balbutient.*
Bégayer, *v.i.* To stammer in the sense of hesitating or stuttering. Ex. : *Nos sentiments nous font quelquefois bégayer.*
Bredouiller, *v.i.* To stammer or splutter as a result of talking too quickly. Ex. : *Son empressement le fait bredouiller d'une façon lamentable.*

220.

Balancer, *v.i.* To hesitate between two alternatives.
Hésiter, *v.i.* To hesitate, generally speaking.

221.

Balafre, *n.f.* Large scar on the face resulting from a sword slash.
Cicatrice, *n.f.* General term for a scar.

222.

Baille, *n.f.* Tub used on board ship.
Baquet, *n.m.* General term for a tub. Ex.: *Baquet de blanchisseuse*.
Cuve, *n.f.* Large tub or vat.
Tonneau, *n.m.* Special term sometimes used for a tub. Ex.: *Le tonneau de Diogènes*.

223.

Bain, *n.m.* Bath. The liquid or solution in which anything is bathed. Ex.: *Bain d'huile*.
Bath. Refers to the operation as a whole. Ex.: *Prendre un bain*.
Baignoire, *n.f.* The bath itself in which the operation is carried out. Ex.: *Baignoire en émail*.

224.

Baiser, *v.t.* To kiss ceremoniously other than the lips or face. Ex.: *Baiser le pied du Pape*.
Embrasser, *v.t.* To kiss. To embrace. Ex.: *Embrasser son enfant*.
Accoler, *v.t.* To kiss, at the same time throwing one's arms around the neck of the person kissed.
Donner l'accolade, *colloq.* The French custom of kissing, on each cheek, the recipient of any honour, decoration.

225.

Bassin, *n.m.* Large basin having steep sides and a flat bottom, and generally made of zinc.
Bol, *n.m.* Basin (china or earthenware) semi-spherical in shape, such as is used for making puddings.
Jatte, *n.f.* A small *bol*.
Cuvette, *n.f.* Basin made of enamel, zinc, earthenware, etc., such as a wash-hand basin.
Bassine, *n.f.* Large metal basin or pan for culinary purposes.

226.

Bastonnade, *n.f.* Old form of punishment by flogging prescribed in prisons, etc. Ex.: *Condamner à la bastonnade*.
Fouettement, *n.m.* The action of flogging with a whip. Also used figuratively in the sense of whipping or stinging. Ex.: *Fouettement du visage par la pluie*.
Fustigation, *n.f.* The action of flogging with a stick or rod. Fustigation.
Flagellation, *n.f.* Violent flogging with a stick, rod or whip. Flagellation. Denotes ignominy.

227.

Baril, *n.m.* Barrel, such as used for packing fish.
Barillet, *n.m.* Small barrel or keg for spirits.
Tonneau, *n.m.* Barrel, generally for containing beer.
Fût, *n.m.*, **Futaille,** *n.f.*, **Pièce,** *n.f.*, **Barrique,** *n.f.* These four words denote a wine barrel or cask having a certain capacity which, however, varies according to the district in which used.
Caque, *n.f.* Barrel for containing fish, gunpowder, grease, etc.

228.

Basting, *n.m.* Technical term for a plank roughly 2 inches thick by 6 inches wide.
Madrier, *n.m.* A large-sized plank.
Planche, *n.f.* Plank, generally speaking.
Ais, *n.m.* Thin board or plank cut to special dimensions for certain purposes. Ex.: *Les ais d'une cloison. Ais de relieur, de vitrier.*

229.

Balle, *n.f.* Ball (of a cartridge). Also a small playing ball. Ex.: *Balle de tennis.*
Bille, *n.f.* Ball (billiard). Ball bearings. Ex.: *Roulement à billes.*
Boule, *n.f.* Ball, generally speaking, especially that used when playing bowls or skittles. Ex.: *Boule de neige. Coffret en forme de boule.*
Boulet, *n.m.* Cannon ball.
Ballon, *n.m.* Large playing ball. A football.
Pelote, *n.f.* Large ball (of string, wool, etc.).
Peloton, *n.m.* Small ball (of thread, twine, silk, etc.).

230.

Barre, *n.f.* Bar, generally speaking. Ex.: *Barre de fer. Barres parallèles.*
Barreau, *n.m.* Small bar. Ex.: *Barreau de grille. Barreaux de chaise.* In legal parlance *barre* denotes the prisoners' bar or witness-box, *barreau* referring to lawyers. Ex.: *Paraître à la barre. Barre des témoins. L'éloquence du barreau.*

231.

Banqueroute, *n.f.* Culpable bankruptcy, attributable to mismanagement, incompetence, fraud, etc.
Faillite, *n.f.* Bankruptcy as a result of adverse circumstances.

232.

Bandage, *n.m.* Steel or solid rubber tyre.
Pneumatique, *n.m.* Pneumatic tyre.

233.

Balnéable, *adj.* Bathing. Refers to water suitable for bathing in. Ex.: *Eaux balnéables.*
Balnéaire, *adj.* Said of anything in connection with bathing. Ex.: *Station balnéaire.*

234.

Balle, *n.f.* Bale (of cotton, etc.).
Ballot, *n.m.* Small bale or bundle.

235.

Bâtiment, *n.m.* Building, generally speaking. Ex.: *Bâtiment de six étages.*
Bâtisse, *n.f.* Large building in brick or stone, uninteresting from an artistic point of view, such as a factory, barracks, etc.
Local, *n.f.* A building considered from the point of view of its situation, arrangement or purpose. Premises. Ex.: *Locaux insalubres.*
Édifice, *n.m.* Large or imposing building such as a cathedral.

236.

Bénévole, *adj.* Kind or gentle. Ex.: *Lecteur bénévole.*
Bienveillant, *adj.* Kind or well wishing. Ex.: *Accueil bienveillant.*
Bienfaisant, *adj.* Kind or well intentioned. Ex.: *Des soins bienfaisants.*
Bénin, *adj.* Kind, in the sense of good-natured. Ex.: *Caractère bénin.*

237.

Bêcher, *v.t.* To dig with a spade.
Creuser, *v.t.* To dig with any implement. Implies depth.
Piocher, *v.t.* To dig with a pick.
Retourner, *v.t.* To dig up in the sense of turning over.
Fouiller, *v.t.* To search for by digging.

238.

Bélandre, *n.f.* Dutch canal barge.
Chaland, *n.m.* Small canal or river barge.
Péniche, *n.f.* Barge of about 200 tons' capacity.

239.

Beau, *adj.* Handsome or good-looking.
Bellot, *adj.* Handsome or good-looking. Familiar term generally applied to children or young people. Ex.: *Qu'elle est bellotte!*

240.

Banlieue, *n.f.* Outlying suburbs.
Faubourg, *n.m.* Immediate suburbs.

241.

Bénéfice, *n.m.* Profit, generally in a pecuniary sense. Ex.: *Le bilan accuse des bénéfices considérables.* "Profit and loss" is, however, translated by *Profits et pertes.*
Profit, *n.m.* Profit in the sense of advantage. Ex.: *Tirer profit d'une affaire.*

242.

Bâtiment, *n.m.* A large ship. Ex.: *Bâtiment de guerre.*
Navire, *n.m.* Ship, generally speaking.

243.

Battre, *v.t.* To strike repeatedly and intentionally. To beat.
Frapper, *v.t.* To strike once. To hit.
Férir, *v.t.* To strike. This verb is now obsolete and only used in the expression *sans coup férir*. The past participle *féru* is, however, employed in a figurative sense as meaning "smitten". Ex. : *Il est féru de cette jeune fille.*

244.

Bâton, *n.m.* A rough stick used as a help when walking. Ex. : *L'aveugle se sert généralement d'un bâton.*
Canne, *n.f.* Walking-stick. Denotes a finished or ornamented article. Ex. : *Canne en bois de laurier.*

245.

Bâtir, *v.t.* To build. Denotes simply the work of building or causing to be built, without any technical consideration. Ex. : *Il s'est fait bâtir une maison près de la gare.*
Construire, *v.t.* To build. Implies the order or arrangement of the different materials used. Ex. : *La construction de la Tour Eiffel exigea des fondations spéciales.*
Édifier, *v.t.* To build anything of a monumental nature. The word is generally employed in a historical and absolute sense. Ex. : *Salomon édifia le Temple à Jérusalem.*

246.

Bésicles, *n.f.* Spectacles. The term strictly refers to the earliest glasses used and is now employed in an ironical sense only. Ex. : *Mettez vos bésicles.*
Lunettes, *n.f.* The general term for spectacles fitted with side pieces for fixing behind the ears.
Lorgnon, *n.m.* Spectacles without side pieces.
Face à main, *n.m.* Ladies' spectacles fitted with handle for holding in position.
Binocle, *n.m.* Double eye-glass. A *lorgnon*.

247.

Béret, *n.m.* Sailor's cap. Soft peakless cap, varying in shape, worn by children, students and certain infantry regiments.
Calot, *n.m.* Boat-shaped cap worn by certain regiments.
Bonnet de police, *n.m.* A *calot* worn with undress uniform.
Calotte, *n.f.* Skull cap.
Casquette, *n.f.* The ordinary cloth peaked cap worn by civilians.
Képi, *n.m.* Peaked military cap of special shape.

248.

Besogne, *n.f.* Work necessary or required to be done. Ex. : *J'ai une besogne urgente à faire.*
Travail, *n.m.* Work in general, from the point of view of the workman. Ex. : *Le travail c'est la santé.*

Labeur, *n.m.* Work, in the sense of toil or labour. Ex.: *Jouir du fruit de ses labeurs.*

Ouvrage, *n.m.* Work. Denotes strictly what is accomplished or produced by hand. Ex.: *Ouvrage de maçonnerie.*
Any literary work or production. Ex.: *Faire publier un ouvrage.*

Œuvre, *n.f.* Work. Denotes any literary or artistic production of merit. Ex.: *Les œuvres de Voltaire.* Deed or act. Ex.: *Œuvres de charité.* Work in the abstract. Ex.: *Se mettre à l'œuvre.*

Travaux, *n.m.* The whole of any work or works of a technical nature such as building, engineering, etc. Ex.: *Travaux de construction. Travaux publics.*

249.

Bercail, *n.m.* The fold, considered from without. Ex.: *Les moutons rentrent au bercail.*

Bergerie, *n.f.* The fold, considered from within. Ex.: *Les moutons sont dans la bergerie.*

250.

Béni, *pa. p.* Blessed by God or others. Refers to the blessing of persons only. Ex.: *Béni soit Dieu.*

Bénit, *pa. p.* Blessed by a religious ceremony. Refers to things only. Ex.: *Eau bénite.*

251.

Besace, *n.f.* Beggar's bag or wallet.

Bissac, *n.m.* Bag or wallet as carried by peasants, itinerant workmen, etc.

252.

Bévue, *n.f.* Mistake or error due to thoughtlessness, ignorance, inattention, etc. Blunder. Ex.: *Saluer un aveugle d'un coup de chapeau est une bévue.*

Erreur, *n.f.* Error or mistake, generally speaking. Ex.: *Vous faites erreur.*

Méprise, *n.f.* Error or mistake in the sense of misapprehension. Ex.: *Prendre au loin un mulet pour un cheval est une méprise.*

Gaffe, *n.f.* Familiar term for a blunder. Ex.: *Faire une gaffe.*

253.

Beaucoup, *adv.* Many. Ex.: *Raconter beaucoup d'histoires.*

Bien, *adv.* Many. Implies the addition of surprise, satisfaction, irony, etc. Ex.: *Voila bien des histoires!*

254.

Aventurier, *n.m.* Adventurer. One who lives by his wits or at the expense of others. Ex.: *L'aventurier tire profit de la crédulité des autres.*

Aventureux, *n.m.* Adventurous person. One whose character leads him to take risks or engage in hazardous enterprises. Ex.: *L'aventureux se lance où le prudent hésite.*

255.

Bijou, *n.m.* Personal jewel. A *bijou* is generally smaller and of less value than a *joyau*.
Joyau, *n.m.* Official or state jewel for ceremonial purposes. Ex. : *Les joyaux de la couronne.*

256.

Doit et avoir, *n.m.* The debit and credit sides of an account. Ex. : *Etablir un compte par doit et avoir.*
Débit et crédit, *n.m.* The amount or amounts with which a person's account is debited and credited respectively.

257.

Bestiaux, *n.m.* Cattle of all kinds considered individually. Ex. : *Mettre des bestiaux en pâture.*
Bétail, *n.m.* Cattle or livestock considered collectively. Ex. : *Le gros bétail comprend le cheval, le bœuf, le mulet, l'âne ; les moutons, les chèvres et les porcs constituent le menu bétail.*

258.

Betise, *n.f.* Foolishness as a result of ignorance or lack of intelligence. Ex. : *Dire des bêtises.*
Sottise, *n.f.* Foolishness resulting from wrong ideas or judgment. Ex. : *C'est une sottise de se croire infaillible en toutes choses.*

259.

Binette, *n.f.* Small hoe for weeding, etc.
Houe, *n.f.* Hoe.
Beuchon, *n.m.* Double-sided *binette*.
Binoche, *n.f.* Two-pronged hoe.
Sarcloir, *n.m.* Hoe for weeding crops.

260.

Blafard, *adj.* Pale in the sense of wan or sallow. Ex. : *Lueur blafarde. Teint blafard.*
Blême, *adj.* Pale or white as a result of fear, illness, etc. Ex. : *Visage blême.*
Hâve, *adj.* Pale (of faces). Denotes in addition a wasted or dismal appearance.
Pâle, *adj.* General term for "pale".

261.

Blâmer, *v.t.* To blame, generally speaking.
Reprendre, *v.t.* To blame, at the same time pointing out what is wrong. Ex. : *Il est du devoir des parents de reprendre leurs enfants quand ils ont tort.*
Gronder, *v.t.* To scold or chide.
Crier, *v.i.* To scold or grumble at loudly. Refers more to the noise made.

262.

Blé, *n.m.* Wheat or corn in general. Ex.: *Champ de blé. Epi de blé.*
Froment, *n.m.* Wheat, strictly speaking, as opposed to other cereals. Ex.: *Champ ensemencé de froment.*

263.

Se blottir, *v.r.* To crouch. Ex.: *Se blottir dans un coin.*
Se tapir, *v.r.* To crouch in an effort to hide oneself. Ex.: *Se tapir derrière une haie.*

264.

Bluter, *v.t.* To bolt or sift flour.
Tamiser, *v.t.* To sift, generally speaking.
Sasser, *v.t.* To sift ground material, such as flour, plaster, etc.
Cribler, *v.t.* To sift or screen coal, gravel, etc.
Passer à la claie, *colloq.* To sift sand, stones, etc., by means of a *claie* or large wirework sieve.

265.

Bienséance, *n.f.* Propriety of speech or conduct from a social point of view. Ex.: *Conduite contraire à la bienséance.*
Convenance, *n.f.* Established principles or customs regarding conduct or behaviour. Ex.: *Observer les convenances.*
Décence, *n.f.* Propriety or decency from a moral point of view.
Décorum, *n.m.* Propriety of conduct. Decorum. Implies a certain punctiliousness.

266.

Biffer, *v.t.* To cancel by crossing or striking out.
Effacer, *v.t.* To strike or cross out so as to render illegible. To efface.
Rayer, *v.t.* To cancel by a single stroke of the pen.
Raturer, *v.t.* To correct by crossing or striking out.

267.

Bigarreau, *n.m.* Red or white-heart cherry.
Cerise, *n.f.* Cherry.
Merise, *n.f.* The wild cherry.

268.

Blessure, *n.f.* Wound caused by a blow or injury. Ex.: *Sa blessure provient d'une chute.*
Plaie, *n.f.* A sore or breakage of the skin resulting from an injury or some internal disorder. Ex.: *La plaie provenant d'une brûlure est parfois très douloureuse.*
  Blessure and *plaie* are both used figuratively. Ex.: *L'alcoolisme est une des plus grandes plaies de l'humanité. Les blessures de l'amour propre.*

269.

Largeur, Laize, *n.f.* These two words both mean "width". *Laize* is, however, only used in connection with cloth.

270.

Bocage, *n.m.* Grove or small shady wood.
Bosquet, *n.m.* A clump of trees. A thicket.
Boqueteau, *n.m.* A small *bosquet* or thicket with undergrowth. A spinney.

271.

Bossu, *adj.* Humpbacked. Generally restricted to persons or animals. Ex.: *Le bison est bossu.*
Gibbeux, *adj.* Having a hump, protuberance, etc. Gibbous. Ex.: *Les montagnes donnent à la terre une apparence gibbeuse.*

272.

Étrange, *adj.* Strange, generally speaking. Ex.: *Une histoire étrange.*
Bizarre, *adj.* Strange in the sense of whimsical or fantastic. Ex.: *Avoir des idées bizarres.*
Baroque, *adj.* Strange in the sense of odd or peculiar as regards dress, style, etc. Ex.: *Costume baroque.*

273.

Bluette, *n.f.* Small spark, of short duration, such as given off by steel.
Étincelle, *n.f.* Spark from a fire, capable of igniting.
Flammèche, *n.f.* A small red-hot particle from a fire. A large spark.

274.

Bord, *n.m.* General term for the edge of any surface, etc. Ex.: *Les bords d'une table.*
Bordure, *n.f.* That which serves to mark or ornament an edge. An edging or border. Ex.: *Bordure de fleurs. Bordure de trottoir.*
Lisière, *n.f.* Edge or outskirts of a field, wood, etc. Ex.: *La lisière d'un bois.* Each of the two edges of a piece of cloth which determine its width.
Liséré, *n.m.* The edging or piping of cloth or clothing. Ex.: *Vêtement à liséré de soie.* The edge of tape, cloth, etc., differing in colour from the remainder of the piece. Ex.: *Ruban blanc à liséré rouge.*
Rive, *n.f.* The sloping edge or bank of a river, canal, etc. Ex.: *La rive droite de la Seine.*
Rivage, *n.m.* Water's edge or sea-shore. The word is used in connection with the sea or large rivers only. Ex.: *Gagner le rivage.*
Confins, *n.m.* Border or extreme limit. Confines. (The word is only used in the plural.) Ex.: *Les confins de la terre, de l'Europe.*
Berge, *n.f.* The raised bank, more or less inclined, of a canal or river. The word also denotes the road or path on the top of such bank. Ex.: *La berge d'un canal, d'un fleuve.*

275.

Boiter, *v.i.* To limp or be lame, generally speaking. Ex.: *Ce cheval boite.*
Clocher, *v.i.* To limp, causing the body to sway on both sides. The word is, however, employed in a figurative sense as indicating imperfection. Ex.: *Vers qui cloche.*

276.

Attendrissement, *n.m.* Momentary tenderness as a result of pity, compassion, etc. Ex. : *Larmes d'attendrissement.*
Tendresse, *n.f.* Characteristic tenderness. Denotes a natural disposition to be kind or affectionate. Ex. : *La tendresse d'une mère pour son enfant.*
Tendreté, *n.f.* Tenderness (of meat, vegetables, etc.).

277.

Borne, *n.f.* Limit beyond which it is impossible to go. Ex. : *Les bornes de l'esprit humain.*
Limite, *n.f.* Limit. That which one may or should not exceed. Ex. : *Limite de vitesse.*
Terme, *n.m.* Limit or extent to which one may go. Ex. : *Il faut mettre un terme à ces extravagances.*

278.

Boue, *n.f.* General term for the mud on roads, etc.
Fange, *n.f.* Liquid mud. Mire. Denotes something foul or unwholesome.
Crotte, *n.f.* Mud (when found on clothes, boots, etc.).
Limon, *n.m.* Mud carried along by rivers or streams.
Vase, *n.f.* Mud as found at the bottom of lakes, ponds and sometimes the sea.
Bourbe, *n.f.* Thick mud at the bottom of stagnant water.

279.

Bouffonnerie, *n.f.* Joke lacking refinement. Buffoonery.
Facétie, *n.f.* Facetious joke.
Plaisanterie, *n.f.* Harmless joke within the bounds of propriety. Ex. : *Il m'a raconté cela par plaisanterie.*

280.

Bougie, *n.f.* Wax (paraffin, stearine, etc.) candle.
Chandelle, *n.f.* Tallow candle, as used before the advent of the *bougie.*
Cierge, *n.m.* Church candle.

281.

Bossuer, Bosseler, *v.t.* These two words both mean "to dent". *Bossuer*, however, denotes a single large dent such as a hat might receive, whereas *bosseler* refers to the small dents usually found on silverware, etc.

282.

Botte, *n.f.* Top boot, reaching to the knee or above.
Bottine, *n.f.* Half or ankle boot.
Chaussure, *n.f.* Footwear, generally speaking. Ex. : *Marchand de chaussures.*

283.

Bouclier, *n.m.* General term for a shield. Ex.: *Bouclier de canon.*
Égide, *n.m.* Shield or protection. The word has a mythological origin and is only used figuratively. Ex.: *Se placer sous l'égide de quelqu'un.*
Écu, *n.m.* Warrior's shield bearing a coat of arms.
Écusson, *n.m.* Shield or escutcheon. (Heraldry.)

284.

Bougonner, Grommeler, *v.i.* To grumble or mutter discontentedly. *Bougonner* implies, however, that the action is more to oneself.
Grogner, *v.i.* To express one's discontent with a sort of growl.
Marmonner, Marmotter, *v.i.* To mutter between one's teeth in the sense of pronouncing indistinctly. To mumble.
Maronner, Gronder. To grumble in a general sense. *Maronner* is the familiar term.
Murmurer, *v.i.* To mutter or murmur.

285.

Bourg, *n.m.* Large compact village, almost a town, where the market for the district is held.
Bourgade, *n.f.* Large straggling village.

286.

Bourrasque, Rafale, *n.f.* Both these words mean "a squall", although *bourrasque* denotes more particularly a sudden gust of wind at sea.

287.

Bourse, *n.f.* Small handbag for containing money. Ex.: *Bourse de fantaisie.*
Porte-monnaie, *n.m.* Small purse, such as carried in the pocket. *Bourse* is invariably used in the figurative sense with reference to money. Ex.: *Avoir une bourse bien garnie.*

288.

Bouse, *n.f.* Ox or cow dung.
Fiente, *n.f.* Animal excrement in general.
Crotte, *n.f.* Term applied to the excrement of certain animals such as dogs, mice, hares, rabbits.

289.

Boussole, *n.f.* Magnetic compass.
Compas, *n.m.* Drawing compasses. Also used for the ship's compass.

290.

Boutique, *n.f.*, **Magasin, Débit,** *n.m.* Shop. A *boutique* is generally smaller than a *magasin*. A *débit* is a licensed shop (wine, tobacco, etc.)

291.

Branches, *n.f.* The individual branches of a tree.
Ramure, *n.f.*, **Branchage,** *n.m.* The branches, considered collectively, of a tree. *Ramure* applies more particularly to very tall or large trees.
Ramée, *n.f.* The leafy boughs or branches of a tree, forming a bower or arbour. Ex.: *Sous la verte ramée.*
Branches, with their leaves, cut from a tree and reserved for use as fuel or fodder.

292.

Branler, *v.t.* To shake or move from one side to the other. Ex.: *Branler la tête.*
"To shake the head" (negatively) is, however, translated by *Secouer la tête.*
Ébranler, *v.t.* To shake so as to cause to tremble or quiver. Ex.: *Le vent fait ébranler sa maison.*
Secouer, *v.t.* To shake energetically. Ex.: *Arbre secoué par le vent.* To shake off. Ex.: *Secouer la poussière de ses pieds.*
Agiter, *v.t.* To shake in order to stir up. Ex.: *Agiter une bouteille de médecine.*

293.

Boulon, *n.m.* Screwed bolt for engineering or constructional purposes.
Verrou, *n.m.* Door bolt.
Targette, *n.f.* Small door bolt.

294.

Bouffi, *adj.* Swollen in the sense of being puffy or bloated. Ex.: *Avoir des yeux bouffis.*
Boursouflé, *adj.* Swollen. Generally employed in connection with the skin. Ex.: *Visage boursouflé.*
Enflé, *adj.* Swollen or inflated as the result of internal pressure or disturbance. Ex.: *Avoir le bras enflé.*
Gonflé, *adj.* Swollen or inflated to an extreme degree. Ex.: *Un cadavre gonflé d'eau.*

295.

Livre, *n.m.* General term for a book.
Bouquin, *n.m.* Old or second-hand book of little value. The word is also employed as a familiar term for books in general. Ex.: *Aimer les bouquins.*

296.

Artificieux, *adj.* Crafty or cunning. Denotes the employment of skill or method for any purpose. Ex.: *Moyen artificieux.*
Astucieux, *adj.* Crafty or deceitful with intent to do harm. Ex.: *Adversaire astucieux.*
Fin, *adj.* Cunning in the sense of shrewd or artful. Ex.: *Jouer au plus fin.*
Finaud, *adj.* Cunning or artful beneath an appearance of simplicity. Ex.: *Paysan finaud.*

Rusé, *adj.* Crafty or cunning. Denotes a character addicted to deception or trickery. Ex.: *Une rusée commère.*
Malin, *adj.* Shrewd or artful. Implies an element of cleverness. Ex.: *Il est trop malin pour s'y laisser prendre.*

297.

Bout, *n.m.* The end of anything with regard to its length. Ex.: *Le bout d'un bâton.*
Extremité, *n.f.* The end, or part farthest from the centre of any surface, body, etc. Extremity.
Fin, *n.f.* The end. Refers to extent or duration only. Ex.: *La fin de la vie.*

298.

Briller, *v.i.* To shine in the sense of being bright. Ex.: *Les étoiles brillent.*
Luire, *v.i.* To shine by producing or giving out light. Ex.: *Le soleil luit.*
Reluire, *v.i.* To shine. Said of polished surfaces which reflect light. Ex.: *Toute surface polie reluit.*

299.

Briser, *v.t.* To break in small pieces or *débris*. Ex.: *Briser un verre.*
Casser, *v.t.* To break so as to render useless. Ex.: *Casser un carreau. Se casser le bras.*
Fracasser, *v.t.* To break noisily or violently. To shatter. Ex.: *Fracasser un bol.*
Concasser, *v.t.* To break up or crush (stones, coke, etc.).
Rompre, *v.t.* To break by bending. To snap. Ex.: *Rompre un roseau.* To break up or disintegrate. Ex.: *Rompre une assemblée. Rompre le pain.*

300.

Brasero, Brasier, *n.m.* Synonymous terms for a portable wood or coal fire such as used by contractors, etc. *Brasero*, however, strictly refers to the apparatus used in Spain instead of fixed fireplaces.
Braisière, *n.f.* Recipient for containing live *braise* or charcoal.

301.

Brigue, *n.f.* Intrigue or secret manœuvre on behalf of any person. Ex.: *S'appuyer sur la brigue pour son avancement.* Open manœuvre in the sense of canvassing, soliciting, etc. Ex.: *La brigue des votes.*
Cabale, *n.f.* Cabal or secret manœuvre against any thing or person. Ex.: *Monter une cabale contre une pièce de théatre.*
Intrigue, *n.f.* Secret manœuvre employed by one or more persons for any purpose. Intrigue.

302.

Complot, *n.m.* Secret arrangement between a number of persons for any criminal purpose. Plot. Ex.: *Tramer un complot.*
Conspiration, *n.f.* Secret arrangement between a large number of persons for any purpose generally directed against public or government affairs. Conspiracy.

Conjuration, *n.f.* Conspiracy, armed or otherwise, for the purpose of bringing about a revolution, etc., the conspirators having sworn not to betray their cause.

303.

Brillant, *n.m.* Brightness, with reference to light, metals, precious stones, etc. Ex.: *Le brillant de l'acier.* Also used figuratively. Ex.: *Discours qui a du brillant.*
Éclat, *n.m.* Brightness (of a fire, the sun, etc.). Brilliance in the sense of magnificence or splendour. Ex.: *L'éclat des cérémonies.*
Lustre, *n.m.* Brightness in the sense of being shiny. Lustre. Ex.: *Le lustre d'une fourrure.*

304.

Brouiller, *v.t.* To confuse or disarrange intentionally. Ex.: *Brouiller ses papiers.*
Embrouiller, *v.t.* To confuse or jumble. Generally used in a figurative sense. Ex.: *Embrouiller une question.*

305.

Burin, *n.m.* Chisel for cutting metal.
Bédane, *n.m.* Bolt or cross-cut chisel. Also a mortise chisel.
Ciseau. General term for a carpenter's chisel.
Tranche, *n.f.* Anvil chisel.

306.

Broc, *n.m.* Jug such as used for toilet purposes. A large wooden jug used by wine merchants.
Cruche, *n.f.* Earthenware jug or pitcher for water.
Cruchon, *n.m.* A small *cruche* or earthenware jug.

307.

Brocard, *n.m.* Gibe or taunt levelled at any class of people or at any individual person concerning his dignity or official position.
Lardon, *n.m.* Gibe or taunt of a personal nature. *Lardon* is more familiar than *brocard.*

308.

Broncher, Chopper, *v.i.* To stumble slightly. *Chopper* is the familiar term. Ex.: *Cheval qui bronche.*
Trébucher, *v.i.* To stumble to the extent of almost or completely losing one's balance.

309.

Arbuste, *n.m.* A bush or shrub. Ex.: *Le rosier et le chèvrefeuille sont des arbustes.*
Arbrisseau, *n.m.* Small tree capable of sheltering. Ex.: *L'aubépine et le lilas sont des arbrisseaux.*
Buisson, *n.m.* Clump of low bushes.

310.

Forêt, *n.f.* General term for a forest.
Futaie, *n.f.* Forest of lofty or full-grown trees.

311.

Bois, *n.m.* General term for a wood.
Broussaille, *n.f.* Undergrowth or scrub.
Taillis, *n.m.* A copse or wood composed of trees for periodical cutting.
Fourré, *n.m.* Thick wood, difficult to penetrate.

312.

Broyer, *v.t.* To crush or break up by grinding. Ex.: *Broyer des couleurs.*
Piler, *v.t.* To crush or break up by pounding or hammering. Ex.: *Piler des briques.*
Pulvériser, *v.t.* To reduce to powder. To pulverize.
Écraser, *v.t.* To crush in the sense of flattening. Ex.: *Écraser un ver.*
Triturer, *v.t.* To crush or grind to a fine powder. To triturate.

313.

Clairon, *n.m.* General term for a bugle.
Bugle, *n.m.* A bugle with keys like a cornet.

314.

Bruit, *n.m.* Noise in a general sense. Ex.: *Faire du bruit.*
Tapage, *n.m.* Great noise caused, strictly speaking, by knocking. The word is, however, used to denote a row of any kind. Ex.: *Un tapage infernal.*
Vacarme, *n.m.* Noise in the sense of din or uproar. Ex.: *Le vacarme des rues de Paris.*
Fracas, *n.m.* Noise caused by smashing, etc. A crash.
Tumulte, *n.m.* Noise caused by disorder, excitement, etc. Tumult.
Potin, Chahut, *n.m.* Slang expressions signifying a disturbance or uproar. A shindy.
Charivari, *n.m.* Strictly speaking, a disturbance made to express disapproval. The term is, however, generally employed to denote a row or hubbub of any description.
Tintamarre, *n.m.* Din or clatter. Implies the addition of disorder or confusion.

315.

But, *n.m.* Purpose or object. That which one aims at or strives for. Ex.: *Il l'a fait dans le seul but de vous être agréable.*
Dessein, *n.m.* Intention or design. Denotes the determination to attain any *but* or object. Ex.: *Il est parti dans le dessein de ne plus revenir.*
Vue, *n.f.* Object or view. Implies the wish that an effort will succeed in its purpose. Ex.: *Avoir quelque chose en vue.*

316.

Caboche, *n.f.* Large-headed nail.
Pointe, *n.f.* Small nail with parallel sides.
Clou, *n.m.* General term for a nail.
Semence, *n.f.* Brads or small tacks. Tin tacks.

317.

Cache-nez, *n.m.*   Large woollen wrap or muffler.
Fichu, *n.m.*   Large neckerchief worn by ladies.
Foulard, *n.m.*   Large silk neckerchief.
Cache-col, *n.m.*   Small neckerchief worn under the overcoat.

318.

Cacher, *v.t.*   To hide in a general sense. *Cacher un trésor.* The word is also used figuratively. Ex.: *Cacher la vérité.*
Céler, *v.t.*   To hide in the sense of keeping secret. Ex.: *Céler ses sentiments.*
Voiler, *v.t.*   To hide or conceal under cover of something else. Ex.: *Des nuages voilent le soleil.*
Recéler, *v.t.*   To hide in the sense of receiving and harbouring unlawfully. Ex.: *Recéler des bijoux volés. Recéler un déserteur.*

319.

Bicoque, *n.f.*   A miserable little house. A hovel. Ex.: *Quelle bicoque!*
Chaumière, *n.f.*   Cottage or small dwelling-place covered with *chaume* (thatched).
Maisonette, *n.f.*   Small house.

320.

Hiémal, *adj.*   Belonging to or concerning winter. Ex.: *Plante hiémale.*
Hivernal, *adj.*   Wintry. Ex.: *Temps hivernal.*
Hibernal, *adj.*   Taking place during winter. Hibernal. Ex.: *Travaux hibernaux.*

321.

Cabane, *n.f.*   Very small cabin or hut roughly built of poor materials. Ex.: *Cabane de berger.*
Baraque, *n.f.*   Hut such as used by soldiers, showmen, etc.
Baraquement, *n.m.*   Strictly speaking, a collection or group of huts. The word is, however, frequently employed to indicate a *baraque* or single hut.
Cahute, *n.f.*   Small wooden hut or cabin built of very rough materials.
Hutte, *n.f.*   Primitive hut such as used by savages.
Case, *n.f.*   A negro hut or cabin. Ex.: *La case de l'oncle Tom.*

322.

Cacheter, *v.t.*   To close by means of a seal. Ex.: *Cacheter une lettre.*
Clore, *v.t.*   To close permanently or for some time. Ex.: *Clore une séance. Clore une lettre.*
Fermer, *v.t.*   To close that which may be opened and closed alternatively. Ex.: *Fermer une porte, un livre.*

323.

Cadeau, Présent, *n.m.*   Present. A *cadeau* is less important or valuable than a *présent.*

324.

Cadre, *n.m.* General term for a frame. Ex.: *Le cadre d'un tableau.*
Encadrement, *n.m.* Strictly speaking, the framing, or placing in a frame, of anything. Ex.: *Encadrement d'un Corot.* The word also denotes the framework or border completely surrounding a window, carpet, etc. *L'encadrement d'une fenêtre.*

325.

Caducité, *n.f.* Decay or caducity.
Décrépitude, *n.f.* The last stages of decay. Decrepitude.
Vétusté, *n.f.* Decay as a result of old age. Ex.: *Tomber de vétusté.*

326.

Cahot, *n.m.* A jolt. Denotes any individual jerk or movement.
Cahotage, *n.m.* A jolting in the sense of a series or succession of jolts.
Cahotement, *n.m.* The action of jolting. Ex.: *Le cahotement d'une voiture.*

327.

Calme, *adj.* Calm. Denotes a relative condition, not necessarily permanent.
Tranquille, *adj.* Calm or tranquil by nature. Implies unchangeability.
Posé, *adj.* Calm in the sense of being staid. Refers to persons only.
Rassis, *adj.* Calm in the sense of being collected. (Said of persons.) Implies previous agitation or excitement.
Coi, *adj.* Tranquil or calm. Implies the absence of noise. The word is generally confined to the expressions: *Se tenir coi. Rester, demeurer coi.*

328.

Campagnard, *n.m.* Person who resides in the country.
Paysan, *n.m.* A peasant or rustic.

329.

Canari, *n.m.* The yellow canary bird belonging to the Canary Islands.
Serin, *n.m.* The general name for the canary family of birds.

330.

Capter, *v.t.* To captivate or win by loyal or underhand means. Implies intention. Ex.: *Il réussit à capter l'attention de son auditoire.*
Captiver, *v.t.* To captivate or win on merit, quality, etc., often unintentionally. Ex.: *Son charme nous captiva tous.*

331.

Casserole, *n.f.* General term for a saucepan.
Marmite, *n.f.* A large pot or saucepan with either two curved side handles or one over the top.
Caquerolle, *n.f.* A three-legged skillet or saucepan.
Cassotte, *n.f.* Small saucepan with a long handle, for drawing water.
Fait-tout, *n.m.* An earthenware or iron pot with side handles and a lid.

332.

Carrosse, *n.m.*   Large coach for family or ceremonial purposes.
Coche, *n.m.*   Travelling or stage coach.
Diligence, *n.f.*   The travelling coach which succeeded the *coche*.

333.

En cas, *prep. exp.*   In case of.   Refers to no specific eventuality.   Ex. : *En cas de danger tirer l'anneau.*
Au cas, Dans le cas, *prep. exp.*   In case.   These two expressions are synonymous and denote some special or particular event.   Ex. : *Au cas où il arriverait prevenez-moi.*

334.

Carrelet, *n.m.*   A plaice of the genus *platessa vulgaris*.
Plie, *n.m.*   General term for the plaice family of fishes.

335.

Canaille, *n.f.*   A vulgar or disreputable person of any class.   Ex. : *Celui qui vole son prochain est une canaille.*
Coquin, *n.m.*   A rogue or rascal.   Implies vulgarity.   (The term was originally applied, in this sense, to the lowest kitchen employees.)
Rogue, playfully speaking.   Ex. : *Mon coquin de fils.*
Polisson, *n.m.*   Blackguard or low fellow.   (The term was originally ascribed, in this sense, to vagabonds.)
A ragamuffin.   (Also frequently used, with reference to children, as term of endearment.   Ex. : *C'est un petit polisson.*)
A licentious individual.   A libertine.
Voyou, *n.m.*   A young street blackguard or ruffian.   A hooligan.
Goujat, *n.m.*   A low vulgar individual.   (Originally a soldier's servant.)
Fripouille, *n.f.*   Popular or familiar term for a *voyou* (q.v.).
Crapule, *n.f.*   A crapulous or thoroughly debauched person.
Misérable, *n.m.*   An unprincipled person.   A scoundrel or villain.
Pleutre, *n.m.*   A dastard or cad.
Vaurien, *n.m.*   A worthless fellow.
Arsouille, *n.m.*   A low crapulous cad.   This term is the worst of its kind which can be applied to a person.
Bandit, *n.m.*   A ruffian or vagabond (from *bandito*, the Italian for a bandit or robber).
Gredin, *n.m.*   A scamp or rascal.   Denotes a person without honour and unworthy of consideration.
Garnement, *n.m.*   A scapegrace or ne'er-do-well.
Scélérat, *n.m.*   A person who has committed, or is capable of committing, some serious crime.
Chenapan, *n.m.*   A thorough rogue or rascal.   A rapscallion.
Gueusard, *n.m.*   A blackguard or loafer.   Implies extreme poverty.

336.

Carreau, *n.m.*   Small pane of glass, strictly speaking, square, for windows, etc.   Ex. : *Casser un carreau.*

Vitre, *n.f.* Pane of glass, larger than a *carreau,* for doors, windows, etc. Ex. : *L'explosion fit trembler les vitres.*
Vitrail, *n.m.* Window of leaded (stained) glass, such as used in churches.
Vitrage, *n.m.* The glass windows, doors, etc., of a building, collectively speaking. Ex. : *Le vitrage d'un hotel.*
A glass partition.
Vitrine, *n.f.* The glass part of a shop window.

337.

Cadet, *adj.* The younger of two brothers or sisters. Ex. : *Frère cadet.*
The younger or youngest of all the brothers or sisters. Ex. : *C'est la sœur cadette de mes filles.*
The youngest of all the members of the family. Ex. : *L'enfant cadet d'une famille.* The word denotes rank or distinction.
Puisné, *adj.* Younger. Denotes order as regards birth. Ex. : *Mon frère puisné.*

338.

Cantatrice, *n.f.* A female professional vocalist possessing an excellent voice, good musical education, and a certain reputation.
Chanteuse, *n.f.* A female vocalist, not necessarily a *cantatrice.*

339.

Fripon, *n.m.* Rogue in the sense of a cheat or trickster. Ex. : *Un maître fripon.*
Rogue (said of a malicious or mischievous child). Ex. : *Ah ! le petit fripon !*
Escroc, *n.m.* A swindler or sharper.
Carottier (or **Carotteur**), *n.m.* A "wheedler" or "twister".
Filou, *n.m.* A cheat at gambling. Implies cleverness.
Tricheur, *n.m.* One who does not play fair with regard to games or unimportant things. A cheat.
Fourbe, *n.m.* A rogue or knave who resorts to treacherous means in order to deceive or cheat.

340.

Car, *conj.* For, when meaning "because". The word announces a reason or explanation, and often a development. Ex. : *Les jours sont courts car nous sommes au mois de décembre.*
Parce que, *conj.* Because. Unlike *car,* the term is used when replying to a question. Ex. : *Il n'a pu signer parce qu'il ne sait pas écrire. Pourquoi hésite-t-elle ? Parce qu'elle a peur de se tromper.*
A cause de, *prep. exp.* Because of. Ex. : *Il n'est pas venu à cause du mauvais temps.*

341.

Carcasse, *n.f.* The framework of, e.g. a lamp-shade, hat, etc.
Charpente, *n.f.* The wooden or metal framework (i.e. joists, beams, rafters) of a building.
Fuselage, *n.m.* The framework of an aeroplane.
Bâti, *n.m.* The framework or body of a machine. Ex. : *Bâti de métier.*

342.

Casque, *n.m.* Helmet, such as worn by soldiers, firemen, policemen, etc. Denotes a special head protection not necessarily corresponding to the remainder of the attire.

Heaume, *n.m.* Helmet, such as worn in the Middle Ages and generally forming part of a suit of armour.

343.

Canevas, *n.m.* Outline or groundwork of a painting, literary work, speech, etc.

Crayon, *n.m.* A light sketch, giving but a slight idea of any literary or other work.

Croquis, *n.m.* A rough sketch, hastily drawn.

Ébauche, *n.f.* A rough draft or outline of any literary or other work. Denotes an imperfect or unfinished stage.

Esquisse, *n.f.* A separate sketch made to serve as a plan for the main work.

344.

Chanteur, *n.m.* A male singer. Refers to the action of singing. Ex.: *Les chanteurs de l'Opéra.*

Chantre, *n.m.* A male church singer. Refers more to the profession or calling. The word is also used in connection with singing birds. Ex.: *Le rossignol est le chantre des bois.*

Chansonnier, *n.m.* Strictly speaking, a writer of songs or ballads. The word is, however, also used to denote a singer of comic or light songs.

345.

Capitonner, *v.t.* To stuff or pad furniture, etc., with (strictly speaking) waste silk, the padded part being afterwards cross-stitched. Ex.: *Fauteuil capitonné.*

Empailler, *v.t.* To stuff birds or animals for the purpose of preserving them.

Farcir, *v.t.* To stuff from a culinary point of view. Ex.: *Farcir une dinde.*

Bourrer, *v.t.* To ram a rifle, cartridge, etc., after having placed a *bourre* or wad.
To stuff or fill completely. Ex.: *Bourrer de tabac une pipe.*

Rembourrer, *v.t.* To stuff or pad furniture with hair, wool, etc.

Fourrer, *v.t.* To stuff or thrust in the sense of forcing into. Ex.: *Fourrer les mains dans ses poches. Fourrer son nez dans les affaires d'autrui.*

346.

Catir, *v.t.* To gloss by hot or cold pressing. Refers to cloth only.

Lustrer, *v.t.* To gloss or lustre, generally speaking. Ex.: *Lustrer une fourrure.*

Calandrer, *v.t.* To gloss or smooth cloth, paper, etc., by means of a *calandre* or roller press.

347.

Caution, *n.f.* Security or surety. A person who undertakes, on behalf of another, either to fulfil his pecuniary obligations or to make good any moneys, etc., entrusted to him and not accounted for, or to pay a certain sum or indemnity should he not carry out his agreement. Ex.: *Être caution de quelqu'un.*

Garant, *n.m.* One who guarantees, at his own risk, the carrying out of any agreement or the possession of any property, etc., sold or transferred. Ex.: *Le vendeur est garant envers l'acquereur de la propriété de la chose qu'il lui a vendue.*

Répondant, *n.m.* A person who guarantees another to be responsible for making good any loss, damage, etc., which the latter may cause third parties to suffer.

348.

Cave, *n.f.* An underground vaulted cellar.
Cellier, *n.m.* Cellar situated on the ground floor and generally with its entrance facing north in order to secure a cool temperature.

349.

Caverne, *n.f.* A cave or large vaulted opening.
Antre, *n.m.* A cave, such as might be inhabited by savages or other human beings. A den, figuratively speaking. Ex.: *Un antre de voleurs.*
Tanière, *n.f.* A cave inhabited by wild beasts. A den. Ex.: *La tanière de l'ours.* The expression *l'antre du lion* is, however, commonly employed.
Fosse, *n.f.* The den in an arena or zoological garden where wild animals are kept. Ex.: *La fosse aux lions.*

350.

Céder, *v.t.* To transfer property, etc., from one owner to another. Refers more to the giving up or handing over by the former owner. Ex.: *Céder un commerce.*
Transférer, *v.t.* To transfer, generally speaking.

351.

Cartel, *n.m.* Ornamented clock for hanging on the wall of a room.
Pendule, *n.f.* A house clock, such as placed on a mantelpiece.
Horloge, *n.f.* A station, church, or similar public clock. A grandfather's clock.

352.

Casse-tête, *n.m.* A club, such as used by savages. An early military weapon or club. A life preserver.
Massue, *n.f.* A club with one extremity, often spiked, heavier and larger than the other. The club used in gymnastics for swinging.
Mil, *n.m.* Synonymous term for the *massue* or club used in gymnastics.
Gourdin, *n.m.* A short thick club. A cudgel.
Trique, *n.f.* A thick stick.

Assommoir, *n.m.* Strictly speaking, any weapon used for stunning. A bludgeon. A loaded cane.

353.

Carier, *v.t.* To rot or decay with reference to teeth or bones.
Pourrir, *v.t.* To rot or decay (bodies, trees, wood, etc.). Also employed in a figurative sense. Ex.: *Société pourrie.*
Gâter, *v.t.* To rot or decay (meat, fruit, etc.). *Gâter* denotes a less advanced state of decay than that implied by *pourrir.*

354.

Carnassier, *adj.* Flesh eating. Said of animals which live exclusively on flesh or which prefer flesh to other forms of food.
Carnivore, *adj.* Flesh eating in addition to other forms of food. Carnivorous. Ex.: *L'homme est carnivore.*

355.

Cellule, *n.f.* Cell in a prison or monastery.
Cachot, *n.m.* A dark cell, generally underground. A dungeon.
Cabanon, *n.m.* A narrow dark cell or dungeon. A padded cell in a lunatic asylum.

356.

Ceinture, *n.f.* General term for a belt, sash, girdle, etc.
Ceinturon, *n.m.* Military sword belt.

357.

Cependant, Pourtant, *conj.* However. Yet. Still. These words affirm something contrary to what has previously been said or understood. *Pourtant,* however, denotes a stronger or more forceful affirmation than that expressed by *cependant.* Ex.: *Nous avions entendu qu'il était malade ; cependant, il travaille. Il est habile ; pourtant son adresse ne l'empêche pas de se tromper.*
Néanmoins, *adv.* Nevertheless. None the less. The word denotes an insistence on the second of two statements by merely restricting the first. Ex.: *Le forçat était poursuivi de près, il réussit néanmoins à se sauver.*
Toutefois, *adv.* However. Yet. Still. Denotes a departure or exception. Ex.: *Nous maintiendrons notre prix à condition, toutefois, que vous l'acceptiez par retour.*

358.

Certes, *adv.* Certainly. Denotes a definite and absolute affirmation or negation precluding any doubt, suspicion, etc. The word is generally employed in conjunction with the adverbs *oui* and *non.* Ex.: *Oui, certes. Non, certes.*
Certainement, *adv.* Certainly. Denotes a person's conviction or persuasion rather than his reasons for affirming or denying. Ex.: *Je ferai certainement ce que vous me demandez.*

359.

Cerveau, *n.m.* The brain, considered as the organ of thought. The mind or intellect. Ex. : *Avoir le cerveau dérangé.*
Cervelle, *n.f.* The brain. Denotes the matter or substance composing same. Ex. : *Se faire sauter la cervelle.*
Cervelet, *n.m.* The *cerebellum* or hind part of the brain, as opposed to the *cerebrum* or front and larger part.

360.

Cavité, *n.f.* Cavity or hollow. Denotes a fairly deep recess compared with its opening. Ex. : *Les cavités d'un rocher.*
Creux, *n.m.* Hollow. A shallow indentation on the surface of any body. Ex. : *Le creux de la main.*

361.

Cession, *n.f.* A gift in the sense of an assignment or a surrendering of property, etc. Ex. : *Cession de biens. Cession d'un droit.*
Concession, *n.f.* A gift or grant. A concession or something given completely and of one's own free will, and in the nature of a favour. Ex. : *Obtenir de l'État la concession d'une mine.*

362.

Chagrin, *n.m.* Sorrow or grief, generally the result of trouble, worry, etc. Denotes a state of mind not always apparent. Ex. : *La trahison de son ami lui fit beaucoup de chagrin.*
Douleur, *n.f.* Sorrow or grief. Acute mental suffering as the result of some specific adverse circumstance. Ex. : *La mort de son père le plongea dans la douleur.*
Tristesse, *n.f.* Sadness. Denotes a condition brought about by the continued remembrance of some great misfortune. Ex. : *Avoir l'âme remplie de tristesse.*

363.

Chambre, *n.f.* Room containing a bed. A bedroom. Ex. : *Chambre à coucher.* (*Chambre de débarras* is, however, an exception.)
Salle, *n.f.* Private room, such as a *salle à manger. Salle de bain.* A large public room or hall. Ex. : *Salle de spectacle. Salle de réception.*
Salon, *n.m.* Parlour or drawing-room.
Pièce, *n.f.* A term denoting a room of any description in a house. Ex. : *Maison de huit pièces.*

364.

Chanceler, *v.i.* To stagger or totter. Implies weakness or infirmity. Ex. : *Mur qui chancelle.*
Vaciller, *v.i.* To waver or be unsteady. Refers to anything not properly fixed. To vacillate. Ex. : *Lumière qui vacille.*
Tituber, *v.i.* To stagger in walking. To titubate. Ex. : *Ivrogne qui titube.*

365.

Chancir, *v.i.* To begin to turn mouldy. Denotes a commencement only. Ex.: *Confitures chancies.*
Moisir, *v.i.* To become mouldy. Denotes a more advanced stage.

366.

Chandelier, *n.m.* Large ornamental candlestick.
Bougeoir, *n.m.* Small portable candlestick for use in bedrooms, etc.
Girandole, *n.f.* Large ornamental candlestick with many stems or branches.

367.

Changeant, *adj.* Changeable as regards character or temper. Ex.: *Humeur changeante.*
Changeable or fickle with reference to the affections.
Inconstant, *adj.* Changeable or unsettled with reference to the weather. Ex.: *Temps inconstant.*
Changeable or fickle as regards the affections. Denotes that the person concerned was at one time well intentioned and implies disappointment, etc., for the person deceived.
Léger, Volage, *adj.* Fickle as regards the affections. Denotes a nature incapable of genuine or deep affection.

368.

Changer, *v.t.* To change in the sense of replacing one thing by another of a similar kind. Ex.: *Changer les fleurs dans un vase.*
To change money, notes, etc. Ex.: *Changer un billet de mille francs.*
v.i. To change or alter in appearance. Ex.: *Les enfants changent beaucoup au cours des premiers mois.*
Changer de, *v.i.* To change or replace something in connection with one's own person for something of the same kind. Ex.: *Changer de linge, d'avis, de domicile.*
Échanger, *v.t.* To exchange one thing for another. Ex.: *Échanger des prisonniers.*
Troquer, *v.t.* To barter or swop.
Permuter, *v.t., v.i.* To exchange situations or employment. To permute. Ex.: *Permuter des emplois. Permuter avec un collègue.*

369.

Chanson, *n.f.* A song in the sense of a ballad or ditty. Ex.: *Chanson bachique. Chanson d'amour.*
Chant, *n.m.* Song in the sense of vocal music. Singing. Ex.: *Leçon de chant.*
A song, i.e. the air or tune of any vocal music. Ex.: *Chants sacrés. Un chant à quatre voix.*

370.

Chapelain, *n.m.* Chaplain. A priest attached to a cathedral or private chapel.
Aumônier, *n.m.* Chaplain attached to, and strictly speaking, responsible for distributing the *aumône*, or alms, of any college, military or naval establishment, etc.

371.

Char, *n.m.* A four-wheeled cart or waggon. Ex.: *Char à foin*.
Chariot, *n.m.* A four-wheeled truck or trolley.
Charrette, *n.f.* A two-wheeled cart. Ex.: *Charrette à bras*.

372.

Change, *n.m.* Exchange with reference to banking, etc., operations only. Ex.: *Lettre de change. Le cours du change.*
Change (small money for large). *Monnaie* is, however, generally used in this sense. Ex.: *Donner de la monnaie.*
Changement, *n.m.* A change or substitution of one thing for another of a similar kind. Ex.: *Changement d'avis, de temps.*
A change in the sense of a transformation or conversion. Ex.: *Le froid produit le changement de l'eau en glace.*
A change in the sense of alteration. Ex.: *La colère opère souvent un changement dans les traits du visage.*

373.

Charrier, *v.t.* To carry or cart. Ex.: *Charrier du fumier.*
To carry along (of rivers, etc.). Ex.: *Ce fleuve charrie énormément de sable.*
Porter, *v.t.* To carry or take. Ex.: *Porter une lettre à la poste.*

374.

Châsse, *n.m.* A reliquary, originally in the form of a coffin, for the remains of saints.
Reliquaire, *n.m.* A reliquary, usually smaller than a *châsse*, for human or personal relics.

375.

Charbon, *n.m.* Any carbonized substance. Ex.: *Charbon de bois*. The word is, however, commonly used to denote coal. Ex.: *Marchand de charbon*.
Houille, *n.f.* Pit coal. Ex.: *Mine de houille*.

376.

Charge, *n.f.* Load. Denotes that which is carried or supported. Ex.: *La charge d'un pont, d'une colonne*.
Chargement, *n.m.* Strictly speaking, the loading of a cart, ship, etc. The word is, however, commonly used to denote the load or cargo itself. Ex.: *Bâteau avec un chargement de ciment*.

Faix, *n.m.* Heavy load or burden. Implies an accumulated weight liable to further increase. The word is generally employed in a figurative sense. Ex.: *Succomber sous le faix des responsabilités.*
Fardeau, *n.m.* A burden or load carried with or without difficulty. Ex.: *Porter un fardeau sur son dos.*

377.

Charge, *n.f.* A public position of some importance and carrying with it certain responsibilities. Ex.: *Charge de percepteur.*
Office, *n.m.* A permanent public position of importance. The term is now practically obsolete. Ex.: *L'office de chancelier.*

378.

Charlatanerie, *n.f.* The profession of a quack or charlatan. The act, speech or manner of a charlatan.
Charlatanisme, *n.m.* The character or nature of a charlatan or quack. Charlatanism. Ex.: *La médecine naquit avec un frère jumeau, le charlatanisme.*

379.

Charme, *n.m.* The hornbeam or yoke-elm tree.
Charmille, *n.f.* Dwarf hornbeam or yoke-elm.
A row or hedge of hornbeam.
Charmoie, *n.f.* Grove or plantation of hornbeam.

380.

Charme, *n.m.* An object credited with occult power. A charm.
Enchantement, *n.m.* The act of subjecting to magic power. Enchantment.
Ensorcellement, *n.m.* The act of bewitching or casting a spell. The state of being bewitched.
Maléfice, *n.m.* Witchcraft, from a moral or legal point of view. Ex.: *Les procès basés sur des accusations de maléfices ont été très nombreux.*
Sort, *n.m.* Magic spell. Ex.: *Jeter un sort sur quelqu'un.*
Sortilège, *n.m.* The exercise of occult power. Witchcraft or sorcery.
Conjuration, *n.f.* Warding off evil by occult means, or resorting to the latter, for the purpose of doing harm. Conjuration.

381.

Charnière, *n.f.* Hinge for a box, case, etc.
Gond, *n.m.* The fixed part of a door hinge on which the door itself turns.
Paumelle, *n.f.* That part of a hinge fixed to a window or light door, and which turns on the *gond* (q.v.).
Penture, *n.f.* The iron-work on a door for keeping the latter in position on its hinges.

382.

Châtaigne, *n.f.* General term for the fruit of any member of the chestnut family of trees.
Marron, *n.m.* Large kind of chestnut relished either roasted or as a sweetmeat. Ex.: *Marrons glacés.*

383.

Châtier, *v.t.* To correct carefully with the intention of eliminating the slightest imperfection. Ex. : *Auteur qui châtie son style.*
Corriger, *v.t.* To correct or put right. Ex. : *Corriger une dictée.*
Retoucher, *v.t.* To go over any work a second time with the intention of improving on the first effort. To touch up. Ex. : *Retoucher un tableau.*
Revoir, *v.t.* To re-examine any work with a view to improving, if necessary. To review. Ex. : *Revoir un manuscrit.*
Reviser, *v.t.* To re-arrange or amend that which has been reviewed.

384.

Forçats, *n.m.* Convicts, considered individually.
Chiourme, *n.f.* The whole of the convicts in any prison, penal establishment, etc. Ex. : *Garde-chiourme.*

385.

Chaud, *n.m.* Heat in an absolute sense and independent of any body in which it may be found. Ex. : *Il fait chaud. Avoir chaud.*
Chaleur, *n.f.* Heat communicated by a fire, the sun, etc. The term denotes a relative degree of heat. Ex. : *Chaleur tropicale. La chaleur du soleil.*

386.

Chauffer, *v.t.* To communicate heat or warmth to any body by means of a fire, etc. Ex. : *Chauffer un lit.*
Échauffer, *v.t.* To produce heat or warmth in any body by rubbing, movement, etc. Ex. : *On s'échauffe en courant.*
Réchauffer, *v.t.* To warm or heat again. To warm up. Ex. : *Réchauffer un mets.*

387.

Chemin, *n.m.* General term for a road leading from one place to another.
Route, *n.f.* A high or main road, larger and more important than a *chemin*, linking two towns together. Ex. : *Route nationale.*
Voie, *n.f.* A road in government or official language. Ex. : *Voie publique.* The word is also used to denote an old Roman road or *via.*

388.

Chiquer, *v.t.* To chew tobacco.
Mâcher, *v.t.* To chew food, etc.

389.

Chirurgique, *adj.* Surgical in the sense of being connected with the art. Ex. : *Revue chirurgique.*
Chirurgical, *adj.* Surgical. Denotes a relationship with actual surgery. Ex. : *Opération chirurgicale.*

390.

Chuchoterie, *n.f.* A whispered conversation or discussion.
Chuchotement, *n.m.* The act of whispering. A whisper.

391.

Cheveux, *n.m.* The hairs of the head considered individually. Ex.: *Avoir des cheveux épars.*
Chevelure, *n.f.* The hairs of the head considered collectively. A head of hair. Ex.: *Avoir une belle chevelure.*
Poils, *n.m.* Hairs on the breast, arms, etc.
Crin, *n.m.* Hair from the mane or tail of a horse. Horse-hair.

392.

Chicane, *n.f.* Wrangling or quibbling. Chicanery.
Chicanerie, *n.f.* Any individual quibble or pettifogging trick.

393.

Chicanier, *n.m.* A person who resorts to quibbling or wrangling.
Chicaneur, *n.m.* A person who is by nature a quibbler or wrangler.

394.

Cher, *adv.* Dear or dearly. Refers to the *complément* or object in a sentence. Ex.: *Aujourd'hui nous payons cher le beurre.*
Chèrement, *adv.* Dear or dearly. Refers to the subject of a sentence. Ex.: *Ce soldat a vendu chèrement sa vie.*

395.

Choisir, *v.t.* To choose (that which is considered best). Implies the exercise of freedom or liberty in choosing. Ex.: *Choisir un chapeau.*
Faire choix. To choose. Denotes merely a selection or distinction. Ex.: *J'ai fait choix d'un homme pour ce travail.*
Opter, *v.i.* To choose. Denotes the obligation to decide on one of two things, it being impossible to have them both. Ex.: *Opter entre deux propositions.*

396.

Choquer, *v.t.* To knock together. To strike against. Ex.: *Choquer des verres les fait tinter.*
Heurter, *v.t.* To knock together or collide violently. Ex.: *En heurtant des verres on risque de les briser.*
In a figurative sense *choquer* means to shock or offend lightly. *Heurter* means to outrage or offend deeply. Ex.: *Paroles qui choquent le bon sens. Absurdité qui heurte la raison.*

397.

Choir, *v.i.* To fall. Implies a blow or shock, coupled with the idea of toppling over. The infinitive and past participle are the only forms now used and the word is generally employed in a figurative sense. Ex.: *Manœuvre pour faire choir le ministère.*
Échoir, *v.i.* To fall (to the lot of). Ex.: *Cela lui échut en partage.*
To fall (or become) due. Ex.: *Le paiement de cette traite échoit demain.*
Déchoir, *v.i.* To fall figuratively in the sense of waning or declining. Ex.: *Homme dont la réputation commence à déchoir.*

Tomber, *v.i.* To fall in a general sense. Implies a sudden heavy fall from a certain height, without the idea of toppling over. Ex.: *Tomber de son cheval.*
To fall into decay. Ex.: *Ce château tombe en ruines.*
To fall in the sense of happening or taking place at a certain time. Ex.: *Cette année Noël tombe un dimanche.*
Dégringoler, *v.i.* To fall or tumble down. Ex.: *Dégringoler d'une échelle.*

398.

Chouette, *n.f.* Owl of the genus *Strix.*
Chat-huant, *n.m.* Screech-owl.
Effraie, n.f. Barn owl.
Hibou, *n.m.* Owl of the family *Strigidæ.* (*N.B.—Hibou* is the general term employed.)

399.

Chrétienté, *n.f.* Christianity, i.e. the whole body of Christians. Christendom.
Christianisme, *n.m.* Christianity, i.e. the Christian religion.

400.

Cintrer, *v.t.* To construct or bend in the form of an arch or curve. Ex.: *Cintrer une poutre.*
Courber, *v.t.* To bend, not necessarily in an exact geometrical curve. Ex.: *Courber un bâton.*
Recourber, *v.t.* To bend round or back. Denotes a more extended operation than that expressed by *courber.* Ex.: *Recourber une barre de fer pour en faire un crochet.*
Ployer, *v.i.* To bend slightly. Implies resistance on the part of the object bent. Ex.: *Le plomb est un metal qu'on ploie facilement.*
To bend in the sense of yielding or giving away. Ex.: *Poteau qui ploie sous sa charge.*
Plier, *v.i.* To bend, generally, what is intended to be bent. Ex.: *Plier les genoux, les coudes.*

401.

Cime, *n.f.*, **Sommet,** *n.m.* The top or highest point of any natural body, such as a mountain, tree, etc. *Cime,* however, denotes that the body terminates more or less in a peak or point, whereas the use of *sommet* is unrestricted.
Comble, *n.m.* The top of any building, etc., i.e. its covering or roof. Ex.: *Comble à pignons. De fond en comble.*
Faîte, *n.m.* The top or highest part of a *comble* (q.v.). A roof top.
Sommité, *n.f.*, **Haut,** *n.m.* The top or upper part of any body considered in an abstract sense. Ex.: *La sommité d'une tour.*

402.

Clerc, *n.m.* A clerk in a lawyer's, notary's, solicitor's or similar office. Ex.: *Clerc d'huissier. Clerc de notaire.*
Employé aux écritures, *n.m.* Clerk. Refers generally to those employed in private business houses.

Commis, *n.m.* Clerk, strictly speaking, in a public or government office. Denotes a certain responsibility. Ex.: *Premier commis. Commis des douanes.*

403.

Cligner, *v.t.* To wink. *Cligner l'œil.*
To gaze with half-closed eyes. To screw up the eyes. Ex.: *La lumière du soleil fait cligner les yeux.*
Clignoter, *v.i.* To close and open the eyes rapidly and repeatedly. To blink.

404.

Clabauder, *v.i.* To bark for no reason, or give tongue falsely, with reference to hounds.
Aboyer, *v.i.* To bark, with special reference to large dogs.

405.

Civière, *n.f.* Term applied to the various kinds of litters or stretchers used for transporting stones, barrels, statues in a procession, coffins, etc.
Brancard, *n.m.* A stretcher for carrying wounded, sick, etc.

406.

Citoyen, *n.m.* Citizen, i.e. one entitled to the privileges or rights of a city. A freeman.
Concitoyen, *n.m.* A fellow-citizen.
Citadin, *n.m.* A citizen in the sense of a city or town resident.

407.

Cinquante, *adj.* Fifty.
Cinquantaine, *n.f.* About or approximately fifty. Ex.: *Il y avait une cinquantaine de personnes à la séance.*
The age of fifty. Ex.: *Atteindre la cinquantaine.*

408.

Clabaudage, *n.m.* Brawling, i.e. the actual noise itself.
Clabauderie, *n.f.* A brawl. Refers to the event.

409.

Cri, *n.m.* A cry or shout. Ex.: *Pousser des cris.*
Criaillerie, *n.f.* Bawling or shouting in an abusive manner.
Crierie, *n.f.* Bawling or shouting. Refers more to the jarring effect on the ear.

410.

Clair, *adv.* Clearly. Refers to the *complément* or object in a sentence. Ex.: *Je vois clair dans l'affaire.*
Clairement, *adv.* Clearly. Refers to the subject of a sentence. Ex.: *Je vois clairement où il veut en venir.*

411.

Créancier, Créditeur, *n.m.* Creditor. *Créancier* is the general term, the word *créditeur* being more restricted to accountancy.

412.

Climatérique, *adj.* Relating to or concerning climate. Ex.: *Étude climatérique d'un pays.*
Climatique, *adj.* Climatic. Refers to the climate itself. Ex.: *Influence climatique.*

413.

Clientèle, *n.f.*, **Achalandage,** *n.m.* Custom or goodwill of any business or establishment.
Pas de porte, *n.m.* The right to the name and mark of any business, included in the *fonds de commerce* (q.v.).
Fonds de commerce, *n.m.* A business or establishment sold as a going concern. A *fonds de commerce* includes generally the *clientèle* or *achalandage*, the *pas de porte*, the *droit au bail* (lease), and the *marchandises* or stock in trade.

414.

Cloche, *n.f.* Large bell (in a tower or elsewhere).
Clochette, *n.f.* Small hand-bell. Ex.: *Clochette de messe.*
Bourdon, *n.m.* Great bell. Ex.: *Le bourdon de Notre-Dame.*
Sonnette, *n.f.* A door bell. Ex.: *Tirer la sonnette.*
Sonnerie, *n.f.* A bell capable of ringing continuously. Ex.: *Sonnerie électrique.*
Grelot, *n.m.* A small bell attached to a dog's collar or horse's harness.
Sonnaille, *n.f.* Bell hung round a cow's or sheep's neck.
Carillon, *n.m.* A peal of bells.

415.

Clocher, *n.m.* Steeple or bell tower.
Clocheton, *n.m.* Small bell tower. Bell turret.

416.

Clos, *n.m.* Cultivated land surrounded by hedge or wall.
Closeau, *n.m.* Small *clos* (q.v.).
Closerie, *n.f.* Small piece of land with a house and surrounded by a hedge or wall.

417.

Cobaye, *n.m.* The cavy or guinea-pig class of quadruped.
Cochon d'Inde, *n.m.* The domesticated guinea-pig.

418.

Cocasse, *adj.* Comical or funny in aspect, i.e. tending to be ridiculous. Ex.: *Il est cocasse avec ce chapeau.*
Drôle, *adj.* Droll or funny in the sense of being odd or strange. Ex.: *Une drôle d'idée.*
Drolatique, *adj.* Funny or humorous, i.e. intended to amuse. Ex.: *Une histoire drolatique.*

Plaisant, *adj.* When placed after the noun, *plaisant* means "humorous" or "amusing". If placed before, the word corresponds to "ridiculous". *Un homme plaisant* amuses with his humour, etc.; *un plaisant homme* is merely ridiculous.

Risible, *adj.* Laughable or causing laughter.

419.

Coaguler, *v.t.* To separate the solid matter of any substance from its liquid solution. To coagulate. Ex.: *Coaguler le sang.*

Congeler, *v.t.* To solidify a liquid by means of a low temperature. To congeal. Ex.: *L'alcool ne se congèle qu'à une température très basse.*

Figer, *v.t.* To thicken or partially solidify when cooling. Ex.: *Le beurre fondu se fige en refroidissant.*

Cailler, *v.t.* To curdle or form into clots. Ex.: *La présure caille le lait.*

420.

Clouer, *v.t.* To fasten with nails. To nail.

Clouter, *v.t.* To stud or adorn with nails. Ex.: *Clouter une porte.*

421.

Clown, *n.m.* The English type of circus clown.

Bouffon, *n.m.* A clown of the fool or jester type. A buffoon.

Paillasse, *n.m.* A clown or knockabout comedian, of Italian origin. A Merry Andrew.

Pitre, *n.m.* A clown or fool of the juggler's-assistant type.

Saltimbanque, *n.m.* A clown whose performance includes acrobatic tricks, feats of strength, juggling, etc.

422.

Cent, *adj.* A hundred.

Centaine, *n.f.* About one hundred. Ex.: *Trajet d'une centaine de kilomètres.*

423.

Clarté, *n.f.* Light in the sense of a medium which renders it possible to see clearly and distinctly. Ex.: *Lire à la clarté d'une lampe. La clarté du jour.*

Lumière, *n.f.* Light. That by which objects are rendered perceptible to the eye. Ex.: *La lumière electrique. Lampe qui donne beaucoup de lumière.*

Lueur, *n.f.* A faint light. A glow or glimmer. Ex.: *La lueur d'un incendie.*

Clair, *n.m.* Light, with reference to the moon. Moonlight. Ex.: *Un beau clair de lune.* "The light of the moon" is translated *la lumière de la lune.*

Jour, *n.m.* Light as opposed to darkness or night. Ex.: *Il fait jour.*

Luminade, *n.f.* Light (artificial). Used only in the expression *Pêche à la luminade.*

424.

Cocher, *n.m.* Driver of a coach or carriage.
Conducteur, *n.m.* Motor-bus driver (the conductor of a bus or tram is called the *receveur*). Cattle driver.
Chauffeur, *n.m.* Motor-car driver.
Mécanicien, *n.m.* Railway-engine driver.
Wattman, *n.m.* Electric tram or train driver.
Charretier, *n.m.* Driver of a *charrette* or cart.
Voiturier, *n.m.* General term for a cart or van driver.

425.

Coin, *n.m.* A corner, i.e. the interior or exterior point formed by the junction of two lines. Ex.: *Le coin de la rue.*
Recoin, *n.m.* A secluded corner. A nook or cranny. Ex.: *Chercher dans tous les coins et recoins.*
Encoignure, *n.f.* A corner, i.e. the recess formed by the junction of two walls, etc.

426.

Col, *n.m.* A long and narrow mountain pass.
Défilé, *n.m.* A military term for a narrow pass necessitating its negotiation in single file.
Détroit, *n.m.* A strait or narrow marine passage. The term is, however, sometimes used in connection with a pass on land.
Gorge, *n.f.* A gorge or narrow pass between hills or mountains.
Pas, *n.m.* A special name for a strait or marine passage, and certain mountain passes. Ex.: *Le Pas de Calais.*

427.

Colis, *n.m.* Package or parcel intended for despatch by an established means of transport. Ex.: *Colis postal.*
Paquet, *n.m.* General term for a package, bundle or parcel. Ex.: *Faire un paquet de vieux vêtements.*

428.

Collecte, Quête, *n.f.* Both these words mean "a collection", made church or elsewhere. *Quête*, however, denotes a collection made for charitable purposes. *Collecte* refers more to the actual collecting.

429.

Collègue, *n.m.* Colleague or one who is associated with others having the same duties, sharing the same responsibilities, etc. (other than partners in business).
Confrère, *n.m.* "Confrère" or person who follows the same profession as another, or who is a member of the same society, corporation, etc

430.

Asbeste, *n.f.* Asbestos, generally speaking.
Amiante, *n.m.* A white flexible variety of asbestos. Amianthus.

431.

Amidon, *n.m.* Starch before being mixed with boiling water.
Empois, *n.m.* Starch, i.e. the jelly or paste prepared ready for use.

432.

Cognée, *n.f.* An axe in the form of a *coin* or wedge, such as used for felling trees.
Hache, *n.f.* General term for an axe.

433.

Colère, *n.f.* General term for anger.
Courroux, *n.m.* Poetic or expressive term denoting the wrath of some important or superior person. Ex. : *Le courroux de Dieu.*
Emportement, *n.m.* A sudden fit of anger. Rage.

434.

Colère, *adj.* Choleric. Denotes a custom or habit.
Colérique, *adj.* Choleric. Refers to the disposition to be irascible.
Coléreux, *adj.* Choleric in the sense of being easily or readily angered.

435.

Colorer, *v.t.* To colour in the sense of giving (generally a single) colour to anything. Ex. : *Colorer en rouge. Colorer son style.*
Colorier, *v.t.* To colour, i.e. to apply colours to. Ex. : *Colorier un dessin.*

436.

Col, *n.m.* The collar of a coat or similar garment.
Collet, *n.m.* A large cloth collar worn by ladies for protection against cold.
Collerette, *n.f.* Small fancy collar, usually made of lace and worn with a bodice or blouse.
Collier, *n.m.* A horse's or dog's collar.
Faux-col, *n.m.* The detachable linen collar worn with a tie.

437.

Couleur, *n.f.* Colour, i.e. the particular impression conveyed to the eye. Ex. : *La couleur de ce manteau est trop vive.*
  Couleur is used figuratively in connection with style or expression.
Coloris, *n.m.* Colour or colouring. Denotes the resultant effect of any choice or arrangement of colours. Ex. : *Le coloris d'un tableau.* Figuratively, *coloris* is used in connection with thoughts or imagination. Ex. : *Le style est le coloris des idées.*

438.

Combattre, *v.t.* To fight in the sense of battling with. Ex. : *Combattre un incendie, la maladie, ses ennemis.*
Se battre, *v.r.* To fight. Refers more to the actual fighting. Ex. : *Se battre dans la rue. Se battre à l'épée.*

439.

Collectionner, *v.t.* To collect (stamps, medals, autographs, etc.).
Quêter, *v.t.* To collect money in a church or elsewhere.
Rassembler, *v.t.* To collect (troops, one's strength or ideas, papers, etc.).
Recueillir, *v.t.* To collect (information, votes, etc.).
Réunir, *v.t.* To collect or gather friends, proofs, etc.
Percevoir, *v.t.* To collect public taxes.

440.

Comestible, *adj.* Eatable, i.e. suitable for food. Edible. Ex. *Champignons comestibles.*
Mangeable, *adj.* Eatable, with reference to the quality or condition of any food. Ex.: *Les produits comestibles ne sont pas toujours mangeables.*

441.

Commande, *n.f.* An order for goods, etc., to be delivered against payment. (The term *ordre* is also employed in this sense.)
Commandement, *n.m.* An order or command, such as given by a superior to a subordinate. Command in the sense of supreme control over any naval or military force.
Ordre, *n.m.* Order in the sense of bidding or instruction. Ex.: *Donner des ordres à quelqu'un. Jusqu'à nouvel ordre.*
Order, i.e. endorsement on any bill, letter of exchange, etc. Ex.: *Billet à ordre.*

442.

Comme, Que, *adv.* How. Denotes to what degree and refers to the object in a sentence or to the circumstances connected therewith. Ex.: *Voyez comme cette bague brille ! Que c'est gentil de votre part de venir !*
Comment, *adv.* How. Denotes in what manner and refers to the subject in a sentence. Ex.: *Vous verrez comment je m'y prendrai. Vous savez comme il l'aime ; il ne sait comment le prouver.*

443.

Commencement, Début, *n.m.* Commencement or beginning. *Commencement* refers more to the beginning of any duration or extent measured by time, and also presents the idea of the whole. *Début* merely denotes the beginning of anything from the point of view of progress or continuation. Ex.: *Le commencement du travail a eu lieu l'année dernière, mais dès le début on s'est heurté à des difficultés.*

444.

Comprendre, *v.t.* To understand. Implies a complete knowledge in detail and as a whole. Ex.: *Son raisonnement est difficile à comprendre.*
Entendre, *v.t.* To understand in the sense of gathering or making out. Ex.: *Je n'entends pas l'affaire ainsi.*

Saisir, *v.t.* To grasp the meaning of. Ex.: *Je ne saisis pas très bien ce qu'il veut dire.*

Savoir, *v.t.*, **Connaître**, *v.t.* To understand in the sense of having a knowledge of. Ex.: *Savez-vous conduire une auto ? Il ne connait pas un mot de français.*

445.

Concerner, Regarder, Toucher, *v.t.* These three verbs all signify " to concern ", but to varying degrees. *Concerner* denotes a closer relationship than that expressed by *regarder*, while *toucher* marks an even more direct connection.

446.

Complaire, *v.i.* To please. Denotes the desire and, consequently, the effort to give pleasure. Ex.: *Chercher à complaire à quelqu'un.*

Plaire, *v.i.* To please without, however, striving to do so. Ex.: *Elle plaisait à tout le monde par son amabilité.*

447.

Complexion, *n.f.* Mental constitution resulting from character or disposition of the mind.

Constitution, *n.f.* Natural physical condition of a body. Constitution.

Naturel, *n.m.* Mental disposition towards good or evil.

Tempérament, *n.m.* Character or disposition, with special reference to any particular trait or quality.

448.

Commencer à, *v.i.* To commence. Implies that the action will continue for some time or will increase or develop progressively. Ex.: *Les enfants commencent à parler vers la deuxième année.*

Commencer de, *v.i.* To commence. Denotes an action limited as regards duration. Ex.: *Orateur qui commence de parler.*

449.

Communier, *v.i.* To communicate, i.e. to receive the Holy Communion.

Communiquer, *v.i.* To communicate in a general sense.

450.

Compétiteur, *n.m.* Competitor. Implies a competition not always open or declared.

Concurrent, *n.m.* Competitor. Denotes simultaneous competition and a frank desire to beat on merit.

451.

Comparer à, Comparer avec, *v.t.* When used in the sense of comparing one thing with another similar, the addition of *à* to the verb *comparer* implies a brief or hasty comparison. For example, the sentence *comparer une copie à un tableau* means merely to ascertain that one is more or less valuable than the other. *Comparer* *une copie avec un tableau* denotes, however, a more detailed or thorough comparison with a view to establishing the resemblance, relative merit, etc. *Comparer à* also means "to compare" in the sense of likening to. Ex.: *On compare la mort à une porte par laquelle nous devons tous passer tôt ou tard.*

Collationner, *v.t.* To compare a document with the original or with another (true) copy.

452.

Complainte, *n.f.* Complaint, generally unfounded, and wearying or annoying in effect. Ex.: *Cessez vos complaintes.*

Plainte, *n.f.* Complaint with reason, or considered so. Ex.: *Donner à quelqu'un un sujet de plainte.*

In legal parlance *complainte* signifies an action against a person who prejudices another's right of possession, usufruct, etc., whereas *plainte* is the general term denoting an accusation or charge. Ex.: *Porter plainte.*

Doléance, *n.f.* A complaint, generally of a wearisome nature, and usually in connection with small unimportant things.

453.

Concile, *n.m.* Church council assembled for the purpose of deciding questions of ecclesiastical doctrine or discipline. Ex.: *Concile œcuménique. Le Concile du Vatican.*

Conseil, *n.m.* Council (town, military, etc.). Ex.: *Conseil municipal. Conseil d'État.*

454.

Conciliant, *adj.* Conciliatory by nature or disposition Ex.: *Humeur conciliante.*

Conciliateur, *adj.* Conciliatory. Refers to the act of conciliating. Ex.: *Paroles conciliatrices.*

455.

De condition, De qualité, *adj. exp.* *Un homme de condition* is a man who occupies a high rank by reason of his wealth, social position, profession, etc., whereas *un homme de qualité* is of noble birth, his rank not being due to possible wealth or other considerations.

456.

Conduire, *v.t.* To lead or conduct. Implies authority or control, the word referring to either beings or things. Ex.: *Conduire une dame, un aveugle, un orchestre.*

Guider, *v.t.* To lead or guide in the sense of showing the way or directing. The word is only used in connection with persons. Ex.: *Aveugle qui se guide à l'aide d'un bâton. Il n'était guidé que par son intérêt.*

Mener, *v.t.* To lead or be at the head of. Implies vigour or enthusiasm on the part of the leader. Ex.: *Les événements nous mènent presque toujours. Mener la danse.*

To lead, with reference to one's life. Ex.: *Mener une vie heureuse.*

457.

Conférer, Déférer, *v.t.* *Conférer* means to confer or bestow any title, office, etc., on a person called to succeed as a matter of course, whereas *déférer* refers to something out of the ordinary, such as the creation of a new title or office, a reward for merit, etc.

458.

Confiance, *n.f.* Confidence in the sense of trust, reliance, or firm belief in oneself or in others. Ex. : *Avoir confiance en quelqu'un. Digne de confiance.*
Confidence, *n.f.* Confidence, i.e. privacy or intimacy. Ex. : *Faire une confidence à quelqu'un.*

459.

Confidemment, *adv.,* **En confidence,** *adv. exp.* Confidentially, i.e., not to be revealed. The former marks the action, the latter the manner.
Confidentiellement, *adv.* Confidentially. Refers to what is not intended to become public or official.

460.

Conjuré, *n.m.* Conspirator. The word merely indicates that a person is a conspirator by reason of his oath. (See Group 302.)
Conjurateur, *n.m.* Conspirator. Denotes action or organization.

461.

Connaître, *v.t.* To know in the sense of having a knowledge of. Ex. : *Connaître plusieurs langues étrangères. Connaître Londres.*
To know, i.e. be acquainted with a person or a thing. Ex. : *Il ne connaît pas votre mari. Je ne connais pas la maison dont vous parlez.*
To know in the sense of suffering or meeting with. Ex. : *Connaître le malheur.*
To know, i.e. to admit or recognize. Ex. : *Ne pas connaître de maître.*
Savoir, *v.t.* To know how to do a thing. Ex. : *Savoir nager. Savoir conduire une auto.*
To have a knowledge of. Ex. : *Savoir l'anglais* (or *connaître l'anglais*).
To know in the sense of having experience. Ex. : *Savoir commander.*
To know (by heart or from memory). Ex. : *Savoir son rôle.*
A good rule to remember in connection with these two verbs is that *connaître* invariably requires a *complément direct* or object, whereas *savoir* may be followed immediately by *que* or another verb. In this connection it is interesting to note that expressions such as "to know how to dance" may either be translated by *connaître la danse* or *savoir danser.*

462.

Congratulations, Compliments, *n.m.*, **Félicitations,** *n.f.* *Congratulations* means "congratulations", strictly speaking, of a deeper or more sincere kind than those expressed by *félicitations* or *compliments*. The word is, however, now almost obsolete, *félicitations* and *compliments* being used instead. The former denotes a genuine participation in another's happiness, *compliments* denoting rather the manner in which the congratulations are addressed. Ex.: *Lettre de félicitations. Adresser des compliments à quelqu'un.*

463.

Conjoint, *n.m.* A legal term denoting the husband or wife, that is to say, the partner of a married person. Ex.: *Droits du conjoint survivant.*

Mari, *n.m.* Husband. The word merely indicates the state of marriage. Ex.: *Le mari doit protection à sa femme.*

Époux, *n.m.* Husband, i.e. his wife's partner in marriage. *Époux* is more intimate than *mari*, the latter word being generally restricted to everyday conversation.

464.

Consacrer, *v.t.* To consecrate in the sense of devoting or employing. Ex.: *Consacrer tout son temps à l'étude.*
To consecrate, i.e. to dedicate, by means of a religious ceremony, to the service of God. Ex.: *Consacrer une église, un calice, un cimetière.* To consecrate the eucharistic elements.

Sacrer, *v.t.* To consecrate. Special term used only in connection with the consecration of a bishop or the coronation of a king, emperor.

465.

Conserver, *v.t.* To keep, at the same time taking precautions to prevent deterioration, damage, loss in value, etc. Ex.: *Conserver des viandes, sa santé, sa fortune.*

Garder, *v.t.* To keep, i.e. to desire not to give. Ex.: *Je veux garder ce livre en mémoire de mon frère.* "To keep silence" is translated by *garder le silence.*

Retenir, *v.t.* To keep or retain, i.e. to desire not to return. Ex.: *Il a retenu l'argent que nous lui avions prêté.*

Entretenir, *v.t.* To keep in the sense of maintaining. Ex.: *Entretenir une maison en bon état. Entretenir une armée.*

Tenir, *v.t.* To keep (house, a shop, an inn, one's word, etc.). Ex.: *Tenir maison, un magasin, sa parole.*
To keep in a certain state or condition. *Tenir une porte fermée. Tenir la gauche.*

Faire, *v.t.* To keep in the sense of making or compelling. Ex.: *Faire attendre quelqu'un.*

466.

Confus, *adj.* Confused. Refers to the state only. Ex. : *Je suis confus de ma sottise involontaire.*
Confondu, *adj.* Confused by reason, i.e. rendered so. Refers to the action of confusing. Ex. : *L'accusé fut confondu par un témoignage inattendu.*
Interdit, *adj.* Confused in the sense of being reduced to silence or of losing one's presence of mind. Ex. : *Elle resta interdite devant l'accueil qu'on lui fit.*
Interloqué, *adj.* Suddenly confused or disconcerted. Denotes great surprise. Ex. : *Il était interloqué par la réplique.*

467.

Constant, Fidèle, *adj.* Faithful in friendship or affection. *Fidèle*, however, presupposes a promise or duty to remain faithful.

468.

Considérable, *adj.* Large or big. Implies consideration or worthiness of note. Ex. : *Des travaux considérables.*
Grand, *adj.* Large or big. Refers merely to the size or extent of the thing in question. Ex. : *Une grande maison.*
Important, *adj.* Large or big. Denotes a possible effect or consequence. Ex. : *Passer une commande importante.*

469.

Consolant, *adj.* Consoling by nature or disposition. Ex. : *Ami consolant.*
Consolateur, *adj.* Consoling. Denotes actual consolation. Ex. : *Paroles consolatrices.*

470.

Consommer, *v.t.* To consume. Denotes use, necessity or usefulness. Ex. : *Une armée en guerre consomme beaucoup d'aliments en conserve.*
Consumer, *v.t.* To consume in a harmful or destructive sense. Ex. : *Incendie qui consume trois maisons.*

471.

Contrée, *n.f.* Country from the point of view of aspect, natural resources or division of the globe. Ex. : *Contrée sauvage.*
Pays, *n.m.* Country, with reference to the inhabitants or their morals. Ex. : *Pays civilisé.*
Campagne, *n.f.* Country, as opposed to the town. Ex. : *Vivre à la campagne.*

472.

Contrefaçon, *n.f.* Forgery or fraudulent imitation in general. Denotes either the act of forging or the counterfeited article. Ex. : *Contrefaçon d'une marque de fabrique. Contrefaçon littéraire.*
Contrefaction, *n.f.* The act of forging or counterfeiting public or government property. Ex. : *Contrefaction des monnaies.*

473.

Contribution, *n.f.* Government tax, i.e. the amount which each taxpayer is called upon to pay. Ex. : *Contributions directes, indirectes.*
Imposition, *n.f.* The levying or assessment of a tax or duty. The word sometimes refers to the tax itself which, strictly speaking, is the *impôt* (q.v.). Ex. : *Imposition des nouveaux droits.*
Impôt, *n.m.* Tax, i.e. the tax itself or the obligation to pay same. Ex. : *Impôt sur le revenu.*
Taxe, *n f.* Tax levied, e.g. on certain foodstuffs, theatres, clubs, motor-cars, etc.
Droit, *n.m.* Duty or dues. Ex. : *Droits de douane. Droits d'octroi. Droits d'entrée.*
Cote, *n.f.* " Direct " or personal tax on property. Ex. : *Cote mobilière.*

474.

Continuation, Suite, *n.f. Continuation* denotes generally the continuation of any work commenced by somebody else, whereas *suite* signifies the continuation of one's own effort. *Continuation* may, furthermore, refer to the actual continuation, or act of continuing, any work, *suite* indicating the work done to complete the task. Ex. : *La mort de l'auteur a empêché la publication de la suite de ses articles dont la continuation a été entreprise par un ami.*

475.

Continuer, *v.t.* To continue. Denotes merely an increase in extent or duration.
Poursuivre, *v.t.* To continue in the sense of persevering or progressing along preconceived lines. *Poursuivre* is only used with reference to one's own work or plan. Ex. : *Il poursuivit son discours.*

476.

Continuer à, Continuer de, *v.i. Continuer à* refers to an action which is indefinite or of which the end is not immediately anticipated. Ex. : *Continuer à bien se porter. Continuer de* denotes an action which is either limited or of short duration. Ex. : *Continuer d'écrire une lettre commencée.*

477.

Contredire, *v.t.* To contradict inadvertently or without knowing, i.e. in the sense of saying something which happens to be in contradiction to what has already been said. Ex. : *On peut se contredire sans le savoir.*
Dédire, *v.t.* To contradict knowingly or deliberately. To disavow or gainsay.
Démentir, *v.t.* To contradict or deny in the sense of declaring a statement to be untrue or unfounded. Ex. : *La nouvelle fut démentie par les journaux.*

478.

Conter, *v.t.* To tell or relate familiarly or for the purpose of amusing. Ex. : *Conter une histoire.*
Raconter, *v.t.* To tell or relate with the intention of instructing or imparting information. Ex. : *Racontez-moi les détails de la fête.*
Relater, *v.t.* To relate or describe. Denotes a description in the nature of a report or statement. Ex. : *Relater un fait.*
Narrer, *v.t.* To relate or narrate. Refers to the style or manner in which a fact, etc., is related.

479.

Contexture, Texture, *n.f.* The arrangement or interweaving of the parts forming a whole. Texture. The words are generally used in a figurative sense, *contexture* denoting something more complicated than that expressed by *texture*. Ex. : *Contexture des os. La texture d'une pièce de théatre.*
Tissu, *n.m.*, **Tissure,** *n.f.* *Tissu* denotes the actual tissue or fabric itself, whereas *tissure* refers to the manner in which it is woven. Ex. : *La tissure du tissu cellulaire est lâche.*

480.

Contenance, *n.f.*, **Maintien,** *n.m.* The former denotes moral bearing or countenance under exceptional circumstances, whereas *maintien* applies to general or customary moral bearing, i.e. good education, dignity of character, etc. Ex. : *Perdre contenance.*
Port, *n.m.* Physical bearing and carriage. Ex. : *Avoir un port de reine.*
Prestance, *n.f.* Physical bearing. The term is only used with reference to a noble or dignified appearance. Ex. : *Homme d'une belle prestance.*
Représentation, *n.f.* Dignified or imposing appearance becoming persons holding a high rank or position.

481.

Contemplateur, *adj.* Contemplative. Denotes active or actual contemplation. Ex. : *Un regard contemplateur.*
Contemplatif, *adj.* Contemplative (by nature or disposition). Ex. : *Esprit contemplatif.*

482.

Convier, *v.t.*, **Inviter,** *v.t.* To invite. *Convier* refers to more familiar or intimate gatherings, whereas *inviter* denotes politeness or a certain amount of ceremony. Ex. : *Être convié à une fête de famille. Elle est invitée au bal.* In the substantive sense the term *invité* is generally used in preference to *convié.* Ex. : *J'attends mes invités.*

483.

Convoi, Enterrement, *n.m.*, **Funérailles, Obsèques,** *n.f.* "A funeral" may be translated, in a general sense, by each of these words. However, strictly speaking, *convoi* refers to the funeral procession or those composing same. Ex. : *Être au convoi*. *Enterrement* denotes the actual interment or graveside ceremony. Ex. : *Aller à un enterrement*. *Funérailles* refers more to the ceremony or pomp displayed at a funeral, whilst *obsèques* denotes the respect shown by those present.

484.

Contradiction, *n.f.* Contradiction, i.e. the act of contradicting. Ex. : *Avoir l'esprit de contradiction*.
Contredit, *n.f.* Contradiction. Refers to the words used to contradict. Ex. : *Sans contredit*. (This expression is commonly employed to mean "unquestionably" or "indisputably".)

485.

Convulser, *v.t.* To convulse or contract convulsively.
Convulsionner, *v.t.* To produce or occasion a convulsive movement.

486.

Coquelicot, *n.m.* The wild or field poppy.
Pavot, *n.m.* The cultivated poppy from which opium is obtained.

487.

Conduit, *n.m.*, **Conduite,** *n.f.* *Conduit* denotes an individual pipe installed for conveying gas, water, etc., whereas *conduite* refers to an installation or arrangement of pipes for ensuring the distribution of a gas or liquid in several directions.

488.

Coque, *n.f.* The shell of an egg.
Coquille, *n.f.* The shell of a snail, nut, or univalve shell-fish.
Coquillage, *n.m.* Synonym for *coquille* with regard to shell-fish, except that *coquillage* implies something more complicated or varied, especially when used in the plural. Ex. : *Fleurs faites de coquillages*. The word is also often used to denote the fish itself inside a shell. Ex. : *Manger des coquillages*.
Écaille, *n.f.* Each of the two parts of the shell of a bivalve. Ex. : *Écaille d'huitre, de moule*.

489.

Corbeille, *n.f.* Basket with either very small side handles or none at all.
Panier, *n.m.* Basket with a handle over the top.
Corbillon, *n.m.* Small basket in which bread is baked.
Manne, *n.f.* Large basket, varying in shape, and used for carrying fruit, crockery, etc. Hamper.

490.

Corde, *n.f.* Cord or rope in a general sense.
Cordage, *n.m.* A quantity or cord or rope. Implies various kinds or sizes.
Cordon, *n.m.* Small cord or rope for ringing a bell, opening a door, etc.
Cordelière, *n.f.* Fancy cord or girdle for, e.g., a dressing-gown.

491.

Cordonnier, *n.m.* A boot and shoe maker or repairer. Implies workmanship of a certain quality or standard.
Bottier, *n.m.* A bootmaker who specializes in making *bottes* or top-boots.
Savetier, *n.m.* A boot mender who does rough repairs. A cobbler.

492.

Correct, *adj.* Correct or right in the sense of complying with all the rules. Ex.: *Une phrase correcte. Un dessin correct.*
Exact, *adj.* Correct or right in the sense of being accurate or true. Ex.: *Un compte exact. Ce thermomètre n'est pas exact.*

493.

Correctif, *adj.* That which is capable of correcting. Corrective. Ex.: *Châtiments correctifs.*
Correctionnel, *adj.* Law term relating to correction or the punishment for misdemeanour. Ex.: *Peine, chambre correctionnelle.*

494.

Corsaire, Forban, Pirate, *n.m.* *Pirate* is the general term for "pirate". *Forban* denotes a pirate or sea robber proscribed by all countries and having the right to no flag whatever.
A *corsaire* is a pirate or corsair formerly commissioned by a country to make war on an enemy's mercantile marine.

495.

Cortège, *n.m.* Procession other than of a military or religious nature. Ex.: *Cortège funèbre. Cortège carnavalesque.*
Défilé, *n.m.* Military procession or march past. Denotes the procession itself.
Procession, *n.f.* Religious procession.
Défilement, *n.m.* Military procession or marching past. Refers to the act of marching or filing off.

496.

Côte, *n.f.* A hill in the sense of an inclined road. Ex.: *Monter une côte.*
Colline, *n.f.* A hill, i.e. an elevated mass of land, less in height than a mountain.
Coteau, *n.m.* The slopes or sides of a *colline*. Ex.: *Coteaux boisés.*

497.

Cou, *n.m.* The neck of human beings or animals.
Col, *n.m.* The neck of a bottle or similar receptacle.

498.

Couard, *n.m.* Coward. The word, though strictly referring to animals who, from fear, keep their tail between their legs, is, however, applied comparatively to human beings.
Lâche, *n.m.* Coward. Denotes lack of courage in the face of danger.
Poltron, *n.m.* Coward, or one who betrays fear in presence of danger and runs away.

499.

Coucher, *v.i.* To sleep. Refers to the habit of going to bed. Ex.: *Il couche chez ses parents.*
Dormir, *v.i.* To sleep. Denotes actual slumber. Ex.: *Le bruit de l'usine m'empêche de dormir.*
S'endormir, *v.r.* To fall asleep or go to sleep.

500.

Couler, *v.i.* and *v.t.* General term meaning "to flow". Ex.: *Le Rhône coule plus rapidement que la Seine. Faire couler le sang.*
Découler, *v.i.* To flow. Denotes the downward course or direction. Ex.: *Sang qui découle d'une blessure.*
Écouler, *v.t.* To drain off or make flow away. Ex.: *Faire écouler l'eau d'un réservoir.*

501.

Couleuvre, *n.f.*, **Serpent,** *n.m.* A *serpent* is a poisonous snake, a *couleuvre* being of the harmless variety.

502.

Corridor, *n.m.* The main passage or corridor in a house, hotel, etc., leading to the various rooms.
Couloir, Passage, *n.m.* A passage, generally smaller than a corridor, leading from one room to another. The term *passage* is not, however, often used in this sense.

503.

Contusion, *n.f.* A bruise or contusion.
Bleu, *n.m.* Familiar term for a bruise which leaves a black or blue mark.
Meurtrissure, *n.f.* A bruise or contusion which either breaks the skin or leaves a livid mark.

504.

Coupe, *n.f.* A large cup with a stem and made of precious metal, china, etc., for ceremonial, presentation or ornamental purposes.
Tasse, *n.f.* An ordinary drinking cup without a stem.

505.

Couper, *v.t., v.i.* General term meaning "to cut". Ex.: *Couper du pain, des cartes, du fil. Couteau qui coupe bien.* (*N.B.*—*Se couper au doigt* means "to cut one's finger", whereas *se couper le doigt* means "to cut off one's finger".)

Trancher, *v.t.* To cut off completely. Ex.: *Trancher la tête à quelqu'un.* To cut in slices, slabs, etc. Ex.: *Trancher du pain, du marbre.*

Tailler, *v.t.* To cut for the purpose of imparting a certain form or shape. To carve. Ex.: *Tailler du bois, de la pierre.*

Retrancher, *v.t.* To cut off figuratively in the sense of suppressing or doing away with. Ex.: *Retrancher une dépense.*
To cut off in the sense of separating from. Ex.: *Retrancher des branches d'un arbre.*

Découper, *v.t.* To cut out, such as a design, etc. Ex.: *Découper une image.*

506.

Couple. *Couple* is feminine when the two things or beings forming the couple are connected accidentally or considered so. In this sense the word is generally confined to animals or things. Ex.: *Une couple de bœufs. Une couple de serviettes. Couple* in the masculine gender denotes, as regards human beings, a couple united by marriage, affection or interest, whereas, in the case of animals, the male and female are implied, or else a suitability for acting or working together. Ex.: *Un couple d'amis. Un couple de pigeons. Un couple de chevaux attelés à une voiture.*

507.

Coupler, *v.t.* To couple in the sense of linking or joining together. Ex.: *Roues couplées.*

Accoupler, *v.t.* To arrange in couples. Ex.: *Colonnes accouplées. Accoupler des bœufs.*
To couple for breeding purposes. To pair.

508.

Cour, *n.f.* Law court higher or more important than a *tribunal.* A High Court. Ex.: *Cour de Cassation.*

Tribunal, *n.m.* The ordinary law or police court. Ex.: *Tribunal de première instance.*

509.

Courbe, *adj.* Bent naturally. Implies that the article has never been straight. Ex.: *Bâton courbe.*

Courbé, *adj.* Bent artificially. Refers to something which originally straight. Ex.: *Barre courbée.*

Recourbé, *adj.* Bent round or back. (See Group 400.)

510.

Couverture, *n.f.* That part of a roof which actually "covers" or protects, e.g. slates, tiles, etc.

Toit, *n.m.* Roof, considered as a part of a building. Ex.: *Le toit d'une maison.*
Toiture, *n.f.* Roof or roofing. Refers to the various materials (rafters, laths, slates, etc.) employed. Ex.: *Cette toiture est en mauvais état.*

511.

Couvrir, *v.t.* General term for "to cover". Ex.: *Couvrir une statue, un livre.*
To cover (expenses, outlay, etc.) Ex.: *Couvrir ses frais.*
To cover in the sense of travelling. Ex.: *Couvrir cinq kilomètres en une heure de marche.*
Recouvrir, *v.t.* To cover completely so as to hide from view. Ex.: *La neige recouvre l'herbe.*

512.

Cracher, *v.i.* General term meaning "to spit".
Crachoter, *v.i.* To spit frequently.

513.

Crainte, Peur, Frayeur, Épouvante, *n.f.,* **Effroi,** *n.m.* A series of words indicating fear or fright. *Crainte* denotes fear inspired by something which may be harmful or otherwise. Ex.: *La crainte de mal faire rend souvent maladroit.* *Peur* indicates fear as the result of some danger, etc., often imaginary. Ex.: *Le gros chien fit peur à l'enfant.* *Effroi* denotes fright in the presence of real danger. *Frayeur* means "a fright", i.e. extreme fear either momentary or without grounds. *Épouvante* is fright which causes one to flee terrified. Ex.: *Frapper d'épouvante.* (See Group 82.)

514.

Crasse, *n.f.* Dirt accumulated gradually on the skin, clothes, etc.
Saleté, *n.f.* Dirt in a general sense. Ex.: *Maison pleine de saleté.* The word also means "dirtiness". Ex.: *La saleté des rues.*
Immondice, *n.f.* Unwholesome dirt. Filth. The word is generally used in the plural. Ex.: *Les immondices des rues.*

515.

Cravache, *n.f.* A riding-whip.
Fouet, *n.m.* A whip with a lash.

516.

Créance, *n.f.* Firm belief or reliance in general. Denotes the state. Ex.: *Bruit qui trouve créance.*
Croyance, *n.f.* Belief or opinion regarding anything in particular. Ex.: *Je n'ai aucune croyance en cette histoire.*
Religious belief. Ex.: *La croyance des juifs.*

517.

Crever, *v.t.* To burst or break open. Ex.: *Crever un sac.*
Éclater, *v.i.* To burst with a report. To explode.

518.

Cric, Vérin, *n.m.* A *cric* is a jack usually operated by a rack and pinion. A *vérin* is a screw-jack.

519.

Crouler, *v.i.*, **S'écrouler,** *v.r.* To fall in the sense of collapsing. Denotes violence or noise. *S'écrouler* is more precise, *crouler* being especially used figuratively. Ex. : *La maison s'est écroulée pendant la tempête. Fortune qui croule.*

S'ébouler, *v.r.* To fall to pieces, or crumble away. Ex. : *Cette falaise s'éboule lentement.*

S'affaisser, *v.r.* To give way or collapse, strictly speaking, beneath a load.

S'effondrer, *v.r.* To collapse. Implies a giving way underneath.

520.

Croûte, *n.f.* The crust of a loaf as opposed to the crumb.
Croûton, *n.m.* The crusty end of a loaf.

521.

Croissance, *n.f.* Growth, i.e. the act of growing. Ex. : *Observer la croissance d'un arbre.*

Cru, *n.m.* Growth, i.e. the amount or extent grown. Ex. : *Le cru d'un arbre dans une année.*

Crue, *n.f.* The ultimate or full growth. Ex. : *Cet arbre a pris toute sa crue.*

522.

Dague, *n.f.*, **Poignard,** *n.m.* *Dague* denotes the early dagger of Spanish or Italian origin. *Poignard* is the term employed nowadays.

523.

Dans, En, *prep.* *Dans* is used before words denoting some definite or precise circumstance, *en* only being employed before words taken in a vague or general sense. For this reason *dans* takes the article before the noun which it precedes, whereas *en* does not. Ex. : *Je l'ai vu dans une colère terrible. Être en colère. Conduire en prison. Renfermer dans la prison de la Santé.* *Dans* is used before names of towns and *en* before names of countries. Ex. : *Dans Paris. En Angleterre.* (As regards French departments *dans* is employed together with the article. Ex. : *Dans la Somme.* The same may be said of corresponding counties, etc., in other countries. Ex. : *Sa ville natale se trouve dans le Kent.*) When speaking of towns it should be noted that the expression, e.g. "in Paris", can and is more often translated by *à Paris*, the use of *dans* denoting, on the other hand, actual location within the town itself. Ex. : *Il est à Paris depuis deux ans. Il se promène dans Paris tous les jours.* *Dans* is furthermore used to express the time or date on which an event takes place, *en* indicating the duration. Ex. : *Il partira dans deux heures pour un voyage qu'il compte faire en trois jours.*

524.

Débit, *n.m.* Output or capacity of any source or mechanical apparatus. Ex. : *Débit horaire d'une pompe, d'une rivière.*
Rendement, *n.m.* Output of a factory, mine, etc. Ex. : *Il est satisfait du rendement de l'usine.*

525.

Don, *n.m.* A voluntary gift or grant. Refers to the actual thing given. Ex. : *La France a reçu un don généreux pour la restauration du château de Versailles.*
Gift in the sense of a natural advantage. Ex. : *Le don de la parole.*
Donation, *n.f.* The act of giving (law term). Ex. : *Donation entre vifs.*
Dation, *n.f.* Legal term signifying a giving of something, other than money, in payment of a debt. Ex. : *Dation en paiement.*

526.

Débris, *n.m.* Detached fragmentary remains which may sometimes be used again. Ex. : *Débris d'un naufrage, d'une fortune, d'un vase.*
Décombres, *n.m.* Mingled building remains or rubbish for removal.
Déchets, *n.m.* Waste material from any process treated to form another but inferior product. Ex. : *Déchets de coton, de soie.*
Chutes, *n.f.* Waste material which "falls" during any process or treatment. Ex. : *Chutes de sciage.*

527.

Davantage, *adv.* More. The word denotes a superiority the result of a general comparison and is employed in an absolute sense. Ex. : *Il est fort mais son frère l'est davantage.*
Plus, *adv.* More. *Plus* is used when making a direct or definite comparison and, unlike *davantage*, is followed by *que*. Ex. : *Il est plus fort que son frère. Elle est plus qu'heureuse.* When denoting a superiority expressed by a number, *plus* is followed by *de* instead of *que*. Ex. : *J'ai fait ce voyage plus de vingt fois.*
Encore, *adv.* More. Implies an additional quantity and not necessarily a comparison. Ex. : *Nous n'avons pas suffisamment d'hommes ; il faut nous en envoyer encore.*

528.

Décaper, *v.t.* To clean the surface of metals.
Nettoyer, *v.t.* General term meaning "to clean".
Décrotter, *v.t.* To clean footwear, i.e. to remove the dirt.
Cirer, *v.t.* To clean boots or shoes, i.e. to polish them.
Curer, *v.t.* To clean out a canal, ditch, or other watercourse.
Écurer, *v.t.* To clean or wash dishes, kitchen utensils, etc.
To clean out a well or a port.
Dégraisser, *v.t.* To clean cloth, strictly speaking, to remove stains or grease. *Nettoyer* is, however, commonly used in this sense. Ex. : *Nettoyage à sec.*

Décrasser, *v.t.* To clean by removing accumulated dirt. Ex.: *Décrasser un fusil.*
Récurer, *v.t.* To clean by rubbing. To scour.

529.

Déceler, *v.t.* To reveal or disclose in the sense of pointing out what has been hidden or kept secret. Ex.: *Cette lueur décèle un incendie. Déceler un crime.*
Dévoiler, *v.t.* To reveal by removing that which either completely hides anything or prevents it from being properly seen or understood. Ex.: *Dévoiler un mystère.*
Découvrir, *v.t.* To reveal or point out to others what they themselves do not perceive. Ex.: *Il découvrit à la police le complot.*

530.

Décès, *n.m.* Death, in legal parlance or phraseology. Ex.: *Le médecin n'a pu que constater le décès.*
Mort, *n.f.* General term for "death", denoting the cessation of life. Ex.: *Être sur son lit de mort.*
Trépas, *n.m.* Death. The word is a poetic term denoting the passing from one life to another.

531.

Déclamer, *v.t.* To recite poetry, etc., with suitable voice inflexion. Ex.: *Déclamer des vers.*
Réciter, *v.t.* To recite or repeat what has been learnt. Ex.: *Réciter sa leçon.*

532.

Déclin, Déclinement, *n.m.* *Déclin* denotes the actual decline, *déclinement* indicating the preliminary approach.

533.

Déconvenue, *n.f.* Mishap denoting disappointment. Ex.: *Il ne voulait pas me parler de sa déconvenue.*
Malencontre, *n.f.* An unexpected and embarrassing mishap.
Mésaventure, *n.f.* Mishap or misadventure with a humorous element.

534.

Découler, *v.i.* To spring or proceed from. Implies a direct relationship. Ex.: *De la cupidité découle la plupart des crimes.*
Dériver, *v.i.* To be derived from in, strictly speaking, an indirect manner. Ex.: *Mot qui dérive du grec.*
Emaner, *v.i.* To proceed or emanate from. Denotes a continuous stream or supply. Ex.: *La lumière émane du soleil.*
Procéder, Provenir, *v.i.* To proceed or come from. *Procéder* refers more to the intellect, *provenir* to the senses. Ex.: *Maladie qui procède d'un accident. Ces fleurs proviennent de mon jardin.*

535.

Décrier, *v.t.* To cry down or bring into disrepute a person's honour or reputation.
Décréditer, *v.t.* To discredit completely. Ex.: *Décréditer un honnête homme.*
Discréditer, *v.t.* To discredit in the sense of attacking or lowering a person's commercial reputation. Ex.: *Discréditer un négociant.*
Dénigrer, *v.t.* To disparage (talent, merit, value, etc.). Ex.: *Dénigrer un artiste.*

536.

De bon gré, *adv. exp.* Without obligation.
De bonne volonté, *adv. exp.* Without aversion.
De bon cœur, *adv. exp.* Willingly or with affection.
De bonne grâce, *adv. exp.* Amiably or politely.

537.

Dans l'idée, *colloq.* (To have) an idea. Denotes belief or conviction. Ex.: *J'ai dans l'idée qu'il pleuvra demain.*
Dans la tête, *colloq.* (To have) a mind. Implies will or intention. Ex.: *Il a dans la tête de rester.*

538.

Décroissance, *n.f.* Decrease as opposed to increase. Ex.: *La décroissance de la mortalité d'un pays.*
Décroissement, *n.m.* Progressive or gradual decrease. Ex.: *Le décroissement de la lune, des jours.*

539.

Dédain, *n.m.* Disdain or contempt by reason of a high idea of one's own importance.
Mépris, *n.m.* Disdain or contempt for what is considered in itself unworthy of esteem.

540.

Dédale, Labyrinthe, *n.m.* *Dédale* is generally employed in a figurative or comparative sense to express something very intricate, *labyrinthe* being more often reserved to denote some material labyrinth such as a building or plantation. Ex.: *Le dédale des lois. Le Vatican est un véritable labyrinthe.*

541.

Dédommagement, *n.m.* The action of indemnifying for loss or damage. Implies an approximate indemnification. Ex.: *Il a reçu une forte somme en dédommagement de l'accident.*
Indemnité, *n.f.* Indemnity considered equal to the amount of loss sustained. Ex.: *Il a reçu une indemnité de 500,000 francs.*

542.

Défaut, Manque, *n.m.*, **Faute,** *n.f.* *Manque* denotes merely the absence or lack of anything ; *défaut* the lack of that which is required to complete. *Faute* implies the deficiency as a result of what is lacking. Ex. : *Sa conduite indique un manque d'éducation. Le défaut d'argent l'a empêché de continuer ses études. Il a été acquitté faute de preuves.*

543.

Défaut, *n.m.* Fault or defect in the character of a person or the quality of a thing. An imperfection.

Défectuosité, *n.m.* Defect or imperfection, smaller or less important than a *défaut*. The word also denotes the state of that which is defective or imperfect.

Vice, *n.m.* Flaw or defect seriously affecting the nature or quality of a thing. Ex. : *Vice de construction.*

544.

Défiance, Méfiance, *n.f.* *Méfiance* denotes complete mistrust as a result of habit or instinct ; *défiance* a partial mistrust inspired by circumstances, experience, etc.

545.

Défoncer, *v.t.* To break open by knocking out the bottom of, e.g. a barrel, a case, etc.

Enfoncer, *v.t.* To break in, e.g. a door, cupboard, etc., i.e. to smash the panels.

Fracturer, *v.t.* To break or force open (locks, doors).

546.

Dégât, *n.m.* Damage caused either by the destruction of useful things or by their deterioration. Ex. : *L'orage a causé de grands dégâts.*

Avarie, *n.f.*, **Dommage,** *n.m.* See *Avarier, endommager.* (See Group 202.)

547.

Dégénération, *n.f.* Degeneration, i.e. the act of degenerating.

Dégénérescence, *n.f.* The state of that which has been degenerating for some time and which continues to do so. Degeneracy.

548.

Degré, *n.m.*, **Marche,** *n.f.* The steps of any stairway. *Degré* refers to the height or interval between each, *marche* being the usual term employed to denote where the feet are placed. Ex. : *S'asseoir sur les marches d'un escalier.*

Marchepied, *n.m.* The step of a carriage or other vehicle.

Échelon, *n.m.* The step or rung of a ladder.

Pas, *n.m.* A step taken when walking.

Seuil, *n.m.* The step or threshold of a door. (*Pas* is also used in this sense.)

549.

Décamper, *v.i.*   To go away hurriedly. To clear off.
Déguerpir, *v.i.*   To clear off, leaving one's belongings behind.

550.

Déguiser, *v.t.*   To disguise in any manner so as to render unrecognizable.
Travestir, *v.t.*   To disguise by wearing clothes other than those which one is accustomed to wear.

551.

Déguster, *v.t.*   To taste, i.e. to drink slowly in order to appreciate the quality of a liquid. Ex.: *Déguster du vin.*
Goûter, *v.t.*   To taste, i.e. to eat or drink a small quantity in order to test the quality. Ex.: *Goûtez ce vin et dites-moi ce que vous en pensez.*

552.

Dehors, *n.m.*   Outside, i.e. the immediate surroundings. Ex.: *Bruit qui vient du dehors.*
Extérieur, *n.m.*   The visible exterior or outside of anything. Ex.: *L'extérieur de ce chateau est très beau.*

553.

Dedans, *n.m.*   The space inside anything. Ex.: *Le dedans d'une maison.*
Intérieur, *n.m.*   The visible interior or inside. Ex.: *L'intérieur de cette cathédrale est plus intéressant que l'extérieur.*

554.

Au dehors, En dehors, Au dedans, En dedans, *adv. exp.,* **Hors,** *prep.*
Au dehors and *au dedans* denote the state of being outside and inside respectively; *en dehors* and *en dedans* implying movement from the inside or the outside as the case may be. Ex.: *Votre frère vous attend au dehors. Porte qui s'ouvre en dedans.* The same may be said of the prepositional expressions *en dehors de* and *hors de*, the former implying movement from the inside to the outside whereas the latter merely indicates the relative situation and is especially used figuratively. Ex.: *Il est allé en dehors de la ville. Sa maison est située hors de la ville. Être hors d'haleine.*

555.

Délibérant, *adj.*   Deliberative, i.e. having authority to deliberate. Ex.: *Assemblée délibérante.*
Délibératif, *adj.*   Deliberative or pertaining to deliberation. Ex.: *Voix délibérative.*
Délibératoire, *adj.*   Having a deliberative style or form. Ex.: *Forme délibératoire.*

556.

Délié, *adj.*   Thin or slender in the sense of being drawn out such as a thread or wire.
Grêle, *adj.*   Thin or slender. Implies the addition of weakness. Ex.: *Des jambes grêles.*

Maigre, *adj.* Thin as opposed to fat.
Mince, *adj.* Thin as opposed to thick.

557.

Délivrer, Livrer, *v.t. Livrer* means to deliver simply, such as goods. *Délivrer* implies a certain obligation or formality in connection with the delivery or issue. Ex.: *Délivrer un passeport, des billets.*

558.

Définitivement, *adv.,* **En définitive,** *adv. exp. Définitivement* is the everyday term, *en définitive* being reserved for use in connection with legal matters. Ex.: *Gagner un procès en définitive.*

559.

Demeure, *n.f.* Residence. Word used in everyday language to indicate where one is established. Ex.: *Fixer sa demeure quelque part.*
Domicile, *n.m.* Residence. Legal term denoting a person's official residence for business, legal or other purposes. Ex.: *Élire domicile.*
Résidence, *n.f.* Residence (of a certain size or importance).

560.

Demeurer, *v.i.* To continue to remain. Denotes generally a longer duration than that implied by *rester.* Ex.: *Sa santé demeure précaire.*
Rester, *v.i.* To remain, contrary to that which changes place or position. Ex.: *Il restera à Paris encore un mois.*

561.

Demeurer, Habiter, Loger, Vivre, *v.i. Demeurer* meaning "to live" refers to the street, district, etc., wherein one's residence is situated. *Habiter* refers more to the residence itself, while *loger* indicates the actual part of the house, etc., occupied. *Vivre* denotes the manner of living. Ex.: *Demeurer à la campagne. Habiter une villa. Loger au deuxième. Vivre de ses rentes.*

562.

Demi, *n.m.* Half, with reference to arithmetical calculations. Ex.: *Dix moins un demi.*
 adv. Half, i.e. incompletely or insufficiently. Ex.: *Viande à demi-cuite. Homme à demi-mort.*
Moitié, *n.f.* The half of the whole of anything. Moiety. Ex.: *Perdre la moitié de sa fortune.*
Mi, *adj. inv.* Half, i.e. mid or midway. Ex.: *A mi-chemin. A mi-côte.* Half, i.e. partly or in part. Ex.: *Tissu mi-soie.*

563.

Démonstration, Protestation, *n.f.,* **Témoignage,** *n.m.* A *démonstration* is an outward sign of any feeling genuine or pretended, a *protestation* being an assurance of the same. A *témoignage* is a mark or proof generally shown by acts, of any feeling which really exists.

564.

Démontrer, *v.t.* To show by demonstration.
Montrer, *v.t.* To show, i.e. to expose to view.
Indiquer, *v.t.* To show or point out. To indicate directly.
Désigner, *v.t.* To show or indicate by means of a sign.
Marquer, *v.t.* To mark or distinguish anything from amongst other things.

565.

Dénégation, *n.f.* A denial with regard to the manner or circumstances in which it is made.
Déni, *n.m.* Denial. Denotes the actual denial itself.
Reniement, *n.m.* A denial in the sense of a disavowal.
Négation, *n.f.* A denial or refusal. Ex.: *Répondre par une négation.*

566.

Dénier, Renier, Nier, *v.t.* To deny. See the substantive forms (*dénégation, reniement,* and *négation* respectively) of these verbs which are dealt with in Group 565. (See also Group 477.)

567.

Denrées, *n.f.* Produce obtained from the land for trading purposes.
Marchandises, *n.f.* Manufactured goods in general.
Subsistances, *n.f.* A country's products or its land produce from the point of view of supplies.
Vivres, *n.m.* Food already prepared for consumption.

568.

Dental, *adj.* Pertaining to the teeth with reference to pronunciation. Ex.: *Consonne dentale.*
Dentaire, *adj.* Dental, from the point of view of anatomy. Ex.: *Nerfs dentaires.*

569.

Dentier, *n.m.* A set of false teeth.
Denture, *n.f.* A person's natural teeth.

570.

Dénué, *pa. p.* Completely deprived of. Devoid. Ex.: *Une nouvelle dénuée de fondement.*
Dépourvu, *pa. p.* Deprived of what is necessary. Ex.: *Armée dépourvue de munitions.*
Dépouillé, *pa. p.* Deprived or stripped of that which forms a large or important part. Ex.: *Arbre dépouillé de ses feuilles.*
Privé, *pa. p.* Deprived of what is considered a natural possession. Ex.: *L'homme, privé d'air, ne peut pas exister.*

571.

Déballer, *v.t.* To unpack a *balle* (bale or bundle).
Dépaqueter, *v.t.* To unpack a *paquet* (packet or parcel)

572.

Déparier, *v.t.* To remove one of two forming a pair. Ex. : *Déparier des gants.*

Dépareiller, *v.t.* To spoil a pair or set by either removing or replacing by something different. Ex. : *Dépareiller un service à thé.*

573.

Départir, *v.t.* To distribute or share out. Implies an action by somebody in authority. Ex. : *Départir des faveurs.*

Partager, *v.t.* To divide into portions to be shared. Ex. : *Partager un gâteau.*

Répartir, *v.t.* To apportion or allot for distribution. Ex. : *Répartir les contributions.*

574.

Dépasser, *v.t.* To exceed or go beyond, generally in a material or physical sense. Ex. : *Cet arbre dépasse tous les autres. Dépasser le but.*

Surpasser, *v.t.* To exceed or go beyond, morally or figuratively speaking. To surpass. Ex. : *Le résultat surpasse l'attente.*

Outrepasser, *v.t.* To exceed or overstep. Implies excess or an action worthy of blame. Ex. : *Outrepasser ses pouvoirs.*

575.

Dépêcher, Hâter, Presser, *v.t.* These three words mean " to hurry " or " to hasten " in various ways. *Hâter* denotes diligence more or less sustained : *presser* implies an unrelaxed effort. *Dépêcher*, activity and despatch.

576.

Dépens, *n.m.* Expenses, generally of a legal nature. Ex. : *Être condamné aux dépens.*
Expense in the sense of detriment. Ex. : *S'enrichir aux dépens d'autrui.*

Dépense, *n.f.* Expense or expenditure. Ex. : *Ces travaux ont occasionné une grande dépense d'argent et de temps.*

Frais, *n.m.* General term for " expenses ". Ex. : *Frais de déplacement.*

Déboursé, *n.m.* Expense or disbursement.

Débours, *n.m.* Commercial term for incidental expenses in connection with a transport or carriage account.

577.

Déperdition, Perte, *n.f.* *Perte* is the general term for " loss ", *déperdition* denoting a diminution or partial loss. Ex. : *Déperdition de chaleur.*

578.

Dix, *adj.* Ten (exactly).

Dizaine, *n.f.* About ten. Ex. : *Casser une dizaine d'œufs.*

579.

Dépeuplement, *n.m.*, **Dépopulation**, *n.f.* *Dépopulation* denotes the act of depopulating ; *dépeuplement*, the result.

580.

Déplaisant, *adj.* Unpleasant in the extreme. The word is especially used in a moral sense. Ex. : *Manières déplaisantes.*
Malplaisant, *adj.* Unpleasant, i.e. insufficiently pleasant or agreeable.

581.

Depuis, Dès, *prep.* *Depuis,* meaning " from ", is used in connection with order or distance ; *dès* refers to time or extent. Ex. : *Depuis le premier jusqu'au dernier. Depuis Paris jusqu'à Londres. Dès le commencement. Il est aveugle dès son enfance.*
(*N.B.*—*Depuis* is, however, always used when translating "from ... to ". Ex. : *Depuis le commencement jusqu'à la fin.*)

582.

Dépurer, Épurer, Purifier, *v.t.* *Purifier* is the general term. *Épurer* means to purify (or refine in the case of metals, etc.) to a greater degree than that expressed by *purifier*, while *dépurer* denotes complete or perfect purification, the term being generally reserved for use in connection with chemistry.

583.

Déraisonnable, *adj.* Partially or momentarily without reason.
Irraisonnable, *adj.* Totally devoid of reason.

584.

Dérégler, *v.t.* To put out of order. Refers to the consequent irregular movement. Ex. : *Avoir l'estomac déréglé.*
Détraquer, *v.t.* To put out of order. Ex. : *Détraquer une montre.*

585.

Dérober, Voler, Détrousser, Dévaliser, Chiper, *v.t.* *Voler* is the general term meaning " to thieve " or " to steal ". *Dérober* means to steal furtively, while *détrousser* is used in connection with travellers only. *Dévaliser* signifies to rob a person of his effects. *Chiper* is the familiar term corresponding to " pinch " in English.

586.

Désabuser, *v.t.* To undeceive or disabuse of that which has created false hopes or ideas. Ex. : *Je dois vous désabuser sur son caractère.*
Détromper, *v.t.* To undeceive by simply explaining an error.

587.

Débarquer, Désembarquer, *v.t.* *Débarquer* means to disembark or unload on arrival at a ship's destination ; *désembarquer,* to disembark before the commencement or completion of the journey.

588.

Déserteur, Transfuge, *n.m.* The *déserteur* merely abandons his post. The *transfuge* does more ; he goes over to the enemy.

589.
Déshabiller, *v.t.* To undress completely.
Dévêtir, *v.t.* To undress partially, i.e. to remove top or outer garments.

590.
Désoccupé, *adj.* Unoccupied in the sense of having time to spare, or nothing much to do.
Inoccupé, *adj.* Unoccupied, i.e. having nothing whatever to do.
Désœuvré, *adj.* Unoccupied, i.e. not doing, nor wishing to do, anything.

591.
Destin, *n.m.* Destiny, or that which regulates or governs the future.
Destinée, *n.f.* Destiny, or fate, as ordained by the *destin* (q.v.).
Sort, *n.m.* Fate or lot. Implies a certain element of chance and generally refers to any individual circumstance. Ex. : *Se plaindre de son sort.*

592.
Déterrer, Exhumer, *v.t.* *Déterrer* is the everyday term meaning "to disinter" or "exhume". *Exhumer* implies a certain solemnity, or an act ordered by some authority.

593.
Deuxième, Second, *adj.* As a general rule *deuxième* may be used when referring to the second of more than two ; *second*, when there are two only. Strictly speaking, however, the former indicates a chance or arbitrary classification whereas the latter denotes the natural or rightful place. *Second* also calls to mind the *premier*, or that which it follows. Ex. : *Il était deuxième sur la liste. L'habitude est une seconde nature.*

594.
Devancer, *v.t.* To precede or go before. Denotes an advantage obtained. Ex. : *Je croyais être le premier mais vous m'avez devancé.*
Précéder, *v.t.* To precede or go before. Denotes merely the order or position. Ex. : *Lisez le chapitre qui précède.*

595.
Devancier, Prédécesseur, *n.m.* *Prédécesseur* denotes a predecessor in any office or official position, whereas *devancier* applies to a predecessor in any unofficial career or following, such as an artist, author, etc.

596.
Devant, *prep.* Before, i.e. opposite or in front of. Ex. : *Elle aime rester devant la fenêtre. Sa maison est devant la gare.*
Avant, *prep.* Before. Denotes priority of time or order. Ex. : *Avant la fin du mois. Sa maison est avant la gare* (i.e. before one gets to the station).

597.
Dévotion, *n.f.* Devotion of a religious nature. Piety.
Dévouement, *n.m.* Devotion in the sense of affection or devotedness.

598.

Directif, *adj.* Serving to direct without actually doing so. Directive.
Dirigeant, *adj.* Directing. Denotes actual direction.

599.

Diffamatoire, *adj.* Likely or intended to defame. Defamatory. Ex. : *Discours diffamatoire.*
Diffamant, *adj.* Actually defaming.
Diffamable, *adj.* Capable of being defamed.

600.

Différend, *n.m.* Difference, i.e. contention or dispute. Ex. : *Vider un différend.*
Différence, *n.f.* Difference in the sense of variation or dissimilarity.

601.

Difficile, Difficultueux, *adj.* *Difficile* refers to the action ; *difficultueux*, to the character or nature. *Un homme difficile* is difficult to get on with. *Un homme difficultueux* makes or exaggerates difficulties.

602.

Discrétion, *n.f.* Discretion, i.e. the avoidance of saying or doing anything likely to displease or harm another.
Réserve, *n.f.* Reserve, i.e. prudence or fear of compromising oneself. Ex. : *Se tenir sur la réserve.*
Retenue, *n.f.* Discretion or reserve. Denotes control of oneself in order to avoid becoming too involved in any matter.

603.

Disette, Famine, *n.f.* *Disette* indicates the dearth of food in a country or district, *famine* denoting the result and considered as a national calamity.

604.

Déjoindre, Disjoindre, *v.t.* *Disjoindre* indicates the commencement of the act of separating ; *déjoindre* denotes complete separation.

605.

Dissension, *n.f.*, **Dissentiment,** *n.m.* *Dissension* (dissension) indicates variance or contention brought about by *dissentiment* (dissent) which is merely difference of opinion.

606.

Distance, *n.f.*, **Éloignement,** *n.m.* *Distance* indicates the space separating one thing from another. *Éloignement* denotes the same space considered as placing one object at a distance from another. Ex. : *La distance de Paris à Calais est de 300 kilomètres. L'éloignement de la gare m'oblige de partir de bonne heure pour prendre le train.*

607.

Diurne, *adj.* Daily, i.e. performed in twenty-four hours. Ex.: *Mouvement diurne de la terre.*
Day or diurnal, as opposed to night. Ex.: *Oiseau diurne.*
Journalier, *adj.* Daily, i.e. happening or recurring every day. Ex.: *Nos besoins journaliers.*
Quotidien, *adj.* Daily, as opposed to any other period. Quotidian. Ex.: *Publication quotidienne.*

608.

Docte, *adj.* Learned, generally as regards ancient history, literature, etc.
Erudit, *adj.* Learned. Denotes the possession of much knowledge gained by book study. Erudite.
Savant, *adj.* Learned. Implies a scientific application of the knowledge acquired.

609.

Docteur, Médecin, *n.m.* *Docteur* is the more modern term which has generally superseded *médecin*. French army doctors are, however, invariably styled *médecins militaires*.

610.

Dominant, Dominateur, *adj.* *Dominant* denotes the state or condition of that which dominates; *dominateur* refers more to the act of dominating. Ex.: *Esprit dominant. Ton dominateur.*

611.

Douceâtre, *adj.* Sweetish, i.e. not over sweet. Ex.: *Un fruit douceâtre.*
Doucereux, *adj.* Insipidly sweet. Ex.: *Vin fade et doucereux.*

612.

Douceur, Mansuétude, *n.f.* *Douceur* is the general term for "gentleness". *Mansuétude* denotes gentleness considered either as a Christian virtue or an inherent quality.

613.

Douter, *v.i.* To doubt or be doubtful of. Ex.: *Je ne doute pas de sa probité.*
Se douter, *v.r.* To doubt in the sense of suspecting. Ex.: *Il s'est douté de l'autenticité du tableau.*

614.

Droiture, *n.f.* Straightforwardness (of heart, morals, etc.).
Rectitude, *n.f.* Straightforwardness, with reference to the mind, judgment or intelligence.

615.

Durant, *prep.* During, when meaning throughout. Ex.: *Ils n'habitent Paris que durant l'hiver.*
Pendant, *prep.* During, i.e. at a certain moment within a given period. Ex.: *La maison s'est écroulée pendant la nuit.*

616.

Durcir, *v.i.*, **Endurcir**, *v.t.* *Durcir* simply means to harden or become hard; *endurcir* denotes a gradual or progressive hardening. Ex. : *Le beurre durcit au froid. Le travail manuel endurcit le corps.*

617.

Éclair, *n.m.*, **Foudre**, *n.f.* An *éclair* is merely the visible flash accompanying lightning; *foudre* is the electrical discharge.

618.

Écarter, *v.t.* To push aside. Ex. : *Écarter les branches d'un arbre.*
Éloigner, *v.t.* To remove with the intention of keeping at a distance. Ex. : *Éloigner une chaise du feu.*
Détourner, *v.t.* To divert or cause to deviate. Ex. : *Détourner le cours d'une rivière.*

619.

Mettre à l'écart, *colloq.* To put or lay aside with the intention of recovering later.
Mettre au rancart, *colloq.* To lay aside in the sense of discarding.

620.

Échapper à, *v.i.* To escape from in the sense of getting out of or extricating oneself from. Ex. : *Échapper à une difficulté.*
Échapper de, *v.i.* To escape from, i.e. to get away from. Ex. : *Échapper de prison.*
Réchapper, *v.i.* To escape, with an effort, from great danger. Ex. : *Réchapper de la mort.*

621.

S'enfuir, *v.r.*, **Fuir**, *v.i.* To flee or take to flight. Denotes haste in order to avoid being caught. Ex. : *Elle s'est enfuie de la maison paternelle. Fuir devant l'ennemi.*
S'évader, *v.r.* To take to flight furtively. To slip away.
S'esquiver, *v.r.* To slip away quietly or skilfully.
Se sauver, *v.r.* To flee or run away unharmed from any danger, etc. Ex. : *Il s'est sauvé à la nage.*
Se dérober, *v.r.* To retire or withdraw quietly. Denotes a wish to avoid. Ex. : *Se dérober à une réunion.*

622.

Éclaircir, *v.t.* To enlighten, i.e. to make clear any question, doctrine, etc., which has remained obscure.
Éclairer, *v.t.* To enlighten the mind or reason. Ex. : *Éclairer le peuple, c'est le moraliser.*

623.

Éconduire, *v.t.* To conduct or show off the premises in the sense of dismissing or refusing. Ex. : *Éconduire un prétendant.*
Conduire, *v.t.* To conduct or show to any place. Ex. : *Conduisez votre ami à sa chambre.* (See also Group 456.)

624.

Économe, *adj.* Economical with reference to persons. Thrifty. Ex.: *Ménagère économe.*
Économique, *adj.* Economical as applied to things. Ex.: *Système économique de chauffage.*

625.

Écorcher, *v.t.* To rub off the skin to a greater extent than that implied by *érafler*. Ex.: *Ronces qui écorchent les mains.*
Érafler, *v.t.* To remove a very small portion of the skin. To graze. Ex.: *La balle lui a éraflé la peau.*

626.

S'égratigner, *v.r.* To scratch oneself as with a nail or a pin.
Se gratter, *v.r.* To scratch oneself in order to relieve an itching.
Griffer, *v.t.* To scratch with the claws or nails.

627.

Écrin, *n.m.* A case for rings, jewellery and similar articles.
Étui, *n.m.* A case for, e.g., a hat, musical instrument, spectacles, revolver, field-glasses, etc.

628.

Écriteau, *n.m.* A notice on a board, card, etc., for fixing anywhere.
Affiche, *n.f.* A notice or advertisement intended to be stuck or otherwise fastened to a wall, hoarding, etc. Poster.
Avis, *n.m.* Notice, i.e. the actual information such as contained in an *affiche*, newspaper, etc.
Avertissement, *n.m.* An *avis* or notice intended as a warning.
Placard, *n.m.* Placard containing written or printed information of any kind for conveyance to the public.
Pancarte, *n.f.* A large *placard*.
Réclame, *n.f.* Advertisement of any kind.

629.

S'écrier, *v.r.* To cry in the sense of exclaiming. Ex.: "*C'est honteux !*" *s'écriait-il.*
Crier, *v.t.* To cry out, i.e. to shout. Ex.: *Crier "Au feu !"*.
  v.i. To cry out or utter a cry. Ex.: *Crier de douleur.*
  v.t. To cry publicly, i.e. to hawk. Ex.: *Crier des journaux.*
Se récrier, *v.r.* To cry out or exclaim in wonder, surprise, anger, etc. Ex.: *Tout le monde s'est récrié contre le nouvel impôt.*
Pleurer, *v.i.* To cry, i.e. to weep. Ex.: *Pleurer de joie.*

630.

Écume, *n.f.* Froth or foam with reference to the sea, human beings, or animals. Ex.: *L'écume des flots, d'un cheval.*
  Scum. Ex.: *La fermentation produit de l'écume.* The word is also used figuratively in this sense. Ex.: *L'écume de la société.*
Mousse, *n.f.* Froth, with reference to beer, milk or cream.

631.

Écumant, Écumeux, *adj*. *Écumant* denotes the action; *écumeux* the state or condition. Ex.: *La mer écumante. Un cheval écumeux.*

632.

Éducation, *n.f.* Moral education or upbringing.
Instruction, *n.f.* Education received at school, college, etc.

633.

Effaré, *adj*. Visibly scared or frightened. Ex.: *Avoir l'air effaré.*
Effarouché, *adj*. Scared or frightened from some outside cause. Ex.: *Le gibier fuit effarouché au bruit du fusil.* (See Group 513.)

634.

Effectivement, *adv.*, **En effet**, *adv. exp.* *Effectivement* refers to facts, and may be translated by "in reality", "really" or "actually". Ex.: *Les marchandises sont effectivement parties.* *En effet* refers more to ideas and can be rendered by "indeed", "in fact" or "as a matter of fact". Ex.: *En effet, je l'ai vu hier.*

635.

S'efforcer, *v.r.* To try or endeavour. Implies a concentrated effort either physical or otherwise. Ex.: *Il s'efforça de soulever la pierre.*
Tâcher de, Tâcher à, *v.i.* To try or endeavour. Denotes perseverance or sustained action. *Tâcher de* is used when the action is merely considered difficult, *tâcher à* being reserved for cases either involving a great effort or denoting an attempt at something impossible. Ex.: *Demain vous tâcherez de venir plus tôt. Ils tâchèrent pendant longtemps à mettre le moteur en marche.*
Essayer, *v.t.* To try or test. Ex.: *Essayer un vêtement, ses forces.*

636.

S'effriter, *v.r.* To fall to dust. Ex.: *Cette statue s'effrite.*
S'émietter, *v.r.* To crumble. Ex.: *Ce gâteau est trop sec; il s'émiette.*

637.

Effronté, Éhonté, Impudent, *adj*. These three words denote varying degrees of impudence or shamelessness. *Effronté* is stronger than *impudent*, while *éhonté* denotes a total lack of moral sentiment.

638.

Effusion, *n.f.*, **Épanchement**, *n.m.* *Effusion*, in a figurative sense, denotes a more violent or passionate outpouring than that expressed by *épanchement*.

639

S'égarer, *v.r.* To go astray, i.e. to wander unintentionally and momentarily from the right path. Ex.: *Il s'est égaré pendant la nuit.*
Se fourvoyer, *v.r.* To go astray in the sense of deliberately taking the wrong path through ignorance, thoughtlessness, etc. Ex.: *Le guide s'est fourvoyé, et nous aussi.*

640.

Égoïste, Personnel, *adj.* *Égoïste* denotes a greater selfishness than that implied by *personnel.* Ex. : *L'homme personnel rapporte tout à lui ; l'homme égoïste pense à lui et veut que tout le monde y pense.*

641.

Élaguer, *v.t.* To lop off the useless or superfluous branches of a tree.
Émonder, *v.t.* To prune or trim small trees, a vine, etc.

642.

Élan, Élancement, *n.m.* *Élan* refers more to the nature of any yearning or rapture ; *élancement,* to the movement itself. Ex. : *Un élan de pitié. Les élancements de l'esprit vers la vérité.*

643.

Hausser, *v.t.* To raise or lift up. Ex. : *Hausser le bras.*
Rehausser, *v.t.* To raise or increase that which has either sunk or is already high. Ex. : *La rareté d'un article ne fait que rehausser sa valeur.*
Exhausser, *v.t.* To increase in height by addition. Ex. : *Exhausser un mur.*
Lever, *v.t.* To lift up or place in an upright position that which is low or lying down. Ex. : *Lever les mains, une statue.*
Relever, *v.t.* To restore to its original position that which has sunk or fallen. Ex. : *Relever un enfant tombé par terre.*
Soulever, *v.t.* To raise or lift a short distance, or from off the ground. Ex. : *Soulever un poids, un rideau.*
Élever, *v.t.* To lift or raise to a high or prominent position. To elevate. Ex. : *Élever la voix, des obstacles, un tableau, un monument, la température, quelqu'un au ministère.*

644.

Éloge, *n.m.* Praise in the sense of eulogy or a panegyric. Denotes generally a reference to some specific quality. Ex. : *Faire l'éloge de quelqu'un.*
Louange, *n.f.* Praise in the sense of honour or tribute due to merit. The word denotes praise given in a vague or general manner. Ex. : *Chanter les louanges de Dieu.*

645.

Épouser, *v.t.*, **Se marier,** *v.r.* To marry, i.e. to become the husband or wife of a person. Ex. : *Il a épousé sa cousine.*
Marier, *v.t.* To marry in the sense of giving or joining in marriage. Ex. : *Il a marié sa fille à un industriel.*

646.

Embêter, *v.t.* To annoy in the sense of bothering or being a nuisance.
Ennuyer, *v.t.* To annoy, i.e. to bore or importune.
Gêner, *v.t.* To annoy, i.e. to hinder or get in the way.
Contrarier, *v.t.* To annoy in the sense of vexing or provoking.

647.

Embrassade, *n.f.*, **Embrassement,** *n.m.* *Embrassade* denotes merely an embrace considered apart from any possible feeling. *Embrassement* implies accompanying affection or tenderness.

648.

Embrun, *n.m.* Mist or fine spray blown from waves by the wind.
Bruine, *n.f.* Mist in the sense of very fine rain.
Brume, *n.f.* Mist or sea fog.
Brouillard, *n.m.* General term for fog.

649.

Éloigné, *adj.* Distant. The word expresses the situation of anything at a great distance from something else. Ex.: *Une ville éloignée d'une autre. Récit éloigné de la vérité.*
Lointain, *adj.* Distant. The term merely gives an idea as to locality. Ex.: *Pays lointain.*
Distant, *adj.* Distant, i.e. at a distance. Refers to time or space. Ex.: *Villages distants l'un de l'autre de 10 kilomètres.*

650.

Émoi, *n.m.*, **Émotion,** *n.f.* *Émoi* denotes the state of mind. *Émotion* is the manifestation, generally more or less apparent, of such a state. Ex.: *Mettre en émoi. La nouvelle lui causa une grande émotion.*

651.

Émousse, *adj.* Blunt, with reference to instruments for cutting. Ex.: *Couteau émoussé.*
Contondant, *adj.* Blunt, i.e. having no edge, such as a bar of iron.

652.

Empêchement, Obstacle, *n.m.* An *empêchement* is that which hinders or prevents the commencement of any movement or action; an *obstacle* is an obstacle encountered after a start has been made.

653.

Emplir, *v.t.* To fill (completely) that which is intended to contain liquid, etc. Ex.: *Emplir d'eau un vase.*
Remplir, *v.t.* To refill or fill entirely that which is only partially filled. To fill up. Ex.: *Remplir un verre.*
To fill, i.e. to place a number or quantity of things in any space, etc. Ex.: *Remplir de livres un rayon.*
To fill, figuratively speaking. Ex.: *Remplir une fonction.*
To fill in or up any form, document, etc.
Combler, *v.t.* To fill in any hollow, thereby destroying its existence. Ex.: *Combler un fossé.*

654.

Empreindre, Imprimer, *v.t.* *Imprimer,* meaning to imprint or impress, is more commonly used than *empreindre.* Ex. : *On imprime un mouvement, des sensations, des principes,* etc. *Leurs pas étaient empreints sur la sable.*

655.

Émule, *n.m.* One who competes with the same chances, capabilities, etc.

Émulateur, *n.m.* One who endeavours to attain the higher position, rank, etc., held by another. An emulator.

656.

Enceindre, *v.t.* To surround closely so as to form a limit. Ex. : *Enceindre une ville de murailles.*

Enclore, *v.t.* To enclose on all sides in order to prevent entrance. Ex. : *Enclore une propriété.*

Entourer, *v.t.* To surround in the sense of occupying the surrounding space. Ex. : *L'ennemi entoura la ville.*

Environner, *v.t.* *Environner* has the same meaning as *entourer* except that the surrounding space occupied is more outlying.

Cerner, *v.t.* To surround in the sense of investing or hemming in.

657.

Enchérir, Renchérir, *v.t.* *Enchérir* means to increase the price, degree, amount, etc., of anything. *Renchérir* denotes either an increase concerning that which is already high, dear, excessive, etc., or an element of excess or daring with regard to the action itself. Ex. : *La pénurie fait enchérir le prix des vivres. Il exagère, mais son frère renchérit encore.*

658.

Encore, Aussi, *adv.* *Encore,* meaning "also" or "as well", refers more to quantity or amount ; *aussi* denotes similarity or comparison. Ex. : *Non seulement savant, il est encore artiste. Il est aussi artiste que savant.*

659.

Endroit, Lieu, Emplacement, Parages, *n.m.*, **Place,** *n.f.* *Lieu* denotes any place or space in its entirety ; *endroit* marks either a particular spot or a part of any space. *Place* implies occupation. Ex. : *Paris est un lieu renfermant de ravissants endroits. Rangez ce livre à sa place.* An *emplacement* is the place or site with reference to any building existing or proposed, or which has disappeared. *Parages* means "place" in the sense of "way" or "parts". Ex. : *Nous sommes heureux de vous revoir dans ces parages.*

660.

Artistement, *adv.* With art, i.e. skilfully or dexterously.
Artistiquement, *adv.* With art, i.e. artistically.

661.

Ayant droit, Ayant cause, *n. m.* *Ayant droit* denotes the party interested in any matter and who can only act in his own name, whereas *ayant cause* means an assign or person to whom certain rights have been assigned and who can therefore act either in his own name or that of the person whom he represents.

662.

Emporter, Remporter, *v.t.* In the sense of taking or winning, *emporter* merely denotes the obtaining of that which is offered as a prize, reward, etc., whereas *remporter* implies an additional element of rivalry or competition.

663.

Enfermer, Renfermer, *v.t.* *Renfermer* denotes a closer or more wilful confinement than that implied by *enfermer*. Ex.: *Enfermer un prisonnier. Renfermer un lion dans une cage.* *Renfermer* also means to confine again. Ex.: *Renfermer un prisonnier qui s'était évadé.*

664.

Écurie, Étable, *n.f.* An *écurie* is a stable for horses. An *étable* is a stable or shed for cattle.

665.

Enjoué, *adj.* Merry or cheerful, with reference to disposition or character.
Gai, *adj.* Gay or merry, with reference to mood or temper.
Gaillard, *adj.* Gay or merry. Denotes boisterousness or unrestraint.

666.

Enluminer, *v.t.* To illuminate books, manuscripts, etc.
Illuminer, *v.t.* To illuminate a building, statue, etc.

667.

Ennuyeux, Ennuyant, *adj.* *Ennuyeux* means annoying by nature or disposition. *Ennuyant* is used in connection with some particular instance or occasion.

668.

Énoncé, *n.m.*, **Énonciation,** *n.f.* An *énoncé* is the actual statement or declaration made. An *énonciation* is the act of declaring or stating.

669.

S'informer de, *v.r.* To enquire, i.e. to ask for information regarding anything.
S'enquérir de, *v.r.* To enquire after. Denotes a more thorough or complete enquiry than that implied by *s'informer*. Ex.: *S'enquérir de la santé de quelqu'un.*

670.

Enfin, *adv.* At last. After all. Ex.: *Enfin, vous voilà! Enfin, cela ne le regarde pas.*
À la fin, *adv. exp.* In the end. Refers to the actual end of any action, etc. Ex.: *L'ennemi capitula à la fin.*

Finalement, *adv.* Finally. Ex.: *Nous avons dû, finalement, y renoncer.*
En fin de compte, *adv. exp.* All things considered. Ex.: *En fin de compte, je préfère rester.*
A la longue, *adv. exp.* In the end, i.e. in the long run. In time. Ex.: *Vous vous y habituerez à la longue.*

671.

Engloutir, *v.t.* To swallow up in the sense of overwhelming or devouring. Ex.: *Le tremblement de terre engloutit une ville entière.*
Engouffrer, *v.t.* To swallow up as in a gulf, abyss or other opening. Ex.: *Tous les jours le Métro engouffre sa proie humaine.*

672.

Enregistrer, *v.t.* To register luggage, etc.
Charger, Recommander, *v.t.* To register a letter or parcel.
Inscrire, *v.t.* To register or enter in a register.
Immatriculer, *v.t.* To enrol or register in a *matricule* which is an official list of patents, *huissiers*, military recruits, etc.

673.

Ensanglanté, *adj.* Covered with blood from any source.
Sanglant, *adj.* Bloody or bleeding, i.e. covered with one's own blood.
Sanguinolent, *adj.* Medical term used to denote any substance or matter containing blood.
Sanguin, *adj.* Relating to, or abounding with blood. Sanguine.

674.

Ensemble, *adv.* Together, i.e. in the same place. Ex.: *Les employés lurent ensemble l'affiche sur la grève.*
A la fois, *adv. exp.* Together, i.e at the same time. Ex.: *Grâce à la téléphonie sans fil les nouvelles peuvent être annoncées à tous les pays à la fois.*

675.

S'ensuivre, *v.r.* To follow logically or as a result. Ex.: *Malgré cela, il ne s'ensuit pas que vous ayez raison.*
Suivre, *v.t.* General term meaning "to follow". Ex.: *Suivre une procession, un régime.*

676.

Entendre, Ouïr, *v.t.* Ouïr denotes a more vague or indistinct hearing than that implied by *entendre*. Ex.: *Nous avons entendu le rossignol aujourd'hui. J'ai ouï dire qu'il était mort.*

677.

Entériner, Ratifier, *v.t.* *Ratifier* is the ordinary term meaning "to ratify". *Entériner* means to ratify legally any deed, etc., the validity of which depends on such ratification.

678.

Enterrer, Inhumer, Enfouir, Ensevelir, *v.t.* To bury. *Enterrer* may be used in connection with animals or things, as well as human beings; *inhumer* is only employed with regard to the latter and denotes, in addition, a certain ceremony accompanying the burial. *Enfouir* means to bury for the purpose of hiding or concealing. Ex.: *Enfouir un trésor*. *Ensevelir*, strictly speaking, denotes the action of enshrouding or laying out for burial, but is also employed in the elevated style for the burial of persons. In addition the word means "to bury under". Ex.: *Le pompier fut enseveli sous les ruines de la maison*. (See also Group 483.)

679.

Entêté, *adj.* Obstinate on any particular occasion as a result of opposition or preconceived opinion.
Têtu, *adj.* Obstinate by nature or disposition. Denotes a total disregard for the opinion of others or a high idea of one's own.
Opiniâtre, *adj.* Obstinate. Indicates a wilful character incapable of giving way.
Obstiné, *adj.* Obstinate or stubborn, and yielding only with difficulty.

680.

Entièrement, *adv.*, **En entier,** *adv. exp.* *Entièrement* modifies the action expressed by the verb; *en entier* refers to the object in a sentence. Ex.: *Je suis entièrement de votre avis. Malgré la longueur du rapport il le lut en entier.*

681.

Envers, *prep.* Towards or to, in a moral sense. Ex.: *La gratitude d'un enfant envers ses parents.*
Vers, *prep.* Towards, i.e. in the direction of. Ex.: *Il leva les yeux vers le tableau.*

682.

Gravir, *v.t.* and *i.*, **Grimper,** *v.i.* *Gravir* means "to climb", generally by walking, and implies an effort. *Grimper* denotes a more natural action such as that performed by plants, animals. Ex.: *Gravir une côte. Grimper sur un arbre.*

683.

Épave, *n.f.*, **Naufrage,** *n.m.* *Épave*, meaning a wreck, is used in a wider sense than *naufrage*, which applies only to shipwrecks. Ex.: *Épave d'une fortune, d'une armée.*

684.

Épée, *n.f.* A two-edged straight sword.
Sabre, *n.m.* A single-edged curved sword, such as used in the army.
Glaive, *n.m.* The name given to the type of two-edged sword used by the Greeks and Romans, or during the Middle Ages. The word is also used to denote the sword in a figurative sense. Ex.: *Le glaive de la justice.*
Espadon, *n.m.* A large two-handed sword used in the Middle Ages.

685.

Épreuve, *n.f.*, **Essai,** *n.m.* An *épreuve* is a test as to the quality of anything. An *essai* denotes a test or trial as to fitness for use. Ex.: *Faire l'épreuve d'une chaudière* means to test a boiler under pressure. *Faire l'essai d'une chaudière* denotes a trial with a view to ascertaining general suitability when working.

686.

Équarrir, *v.t.* To square, i.e. to form or cut to right angles. Ex.: *Équarrir une poutre.*
Carrer, *v.t.* To square in the sense of giving a square form to. Ex.: *Carrer un bloc de marbre.*

687.

Errer, *v.i.* To wander in the sense of deviating from a definite or pre-arranged route. Ex.: *On erre quand on perd son chemin.*
To wander, figuratively speaking. Ex.: *Laisser errer ses pensées, son imagination.*
Vaguer, *v.i.* To wander aimlessly or for no fixed purpose.

688.

Escadre, *n.f.* Fleet squadron under the command of a vice-admiral.
Escadron, *n.m.* A military squadron (cavalry, infantry, etc.).
Escadrille, *n.f.* A small squadron of light naval units. Ex.: *Escadrille de torpilleurs.*
A squadron of aeroplanes.

689.

Esclandre, Scandale, *n.m.* *Scandale* denotes the actual scandal itself. *Esclandre* refers more to the result or effect of a scandal.

690.

Escompte, *n.m.* Discount for cash payment.
Remise, *n.f.* Trade discount or allowance.

691.

Espérance, *n.f.*, **Espoir,** *n.m.* *Espérance* denotes the state of a soul constant in hope. *Espoir* refers more to that which is desired and therefore denotes hope of a more definite nature. Ex.: *L'espérance est une vertu théologale. Maladie qui ne laisse pas d'espoir.*

692.

Escarbille, Cendre, *n.f.*, **Fraisil, Mâchefer,** *n.m.* *Cendres* is the general term for cinders (or ash). An *escarbille* is a half-burnt cinder found in a furnace, and a *fraisil* the same as found in a forge. *Mâchefer* is coal slag or dross.

693.

Escargot, *n.m.* General term for a "snail". The word is invariably used with reference to the edible variety.
Limace, *n.f.* Large red or black naked snail, or slug.

Limaçon (or **Colimaçon**), *n.m.* A snail with a helical-shaped shell.
Loche, *n.f.* Small grey naked snail, or slug.

694.

Escarpolette, Balancoire, *n.f.* Although both these words are commonly used to denote a swing, *escarpolette* is the correct term in this sense. A *balancoire* is, strictly speaking, a see-saw.

695.

Étain, Fer-blanc, *n.m.* *Étain* is pure tin ; *fer-blanc* is tin plate or thin iron sheet coated with tin.

696.

Étalage, *n.m.* Shop window, i.e. what is displayed therein. Ex.: *Aller voir les étalages.*
Devanture, *n.f.* A shop front as a whole, including the window.
Vitrine, *n.f.* A shop window in which goods are displayed. Ex... *Regarder dans une vitrine.*

697.

Étoile, *n.f.*, **Astre,** *n.m.* Both these words are commonly used to denote a star ; an *astre* is, however, any heavenly luminous body, and may therefore refer to the sun or the moon.

698.

Étude, *n.f.*, **Bureau,** *n.m.* *Bureau* is the general term for an office. A solicitor's, notary's or similar government official's office is, however, invariably known as an *étude*.

699.

Éveiller, Réveiller, *v.t.* *Éveiller* means "to awake" naturally, i.e. when a person has slept sufficiently. *Réveiller* implies a sudden or unexpected awakening. Ex.: *Il s'éveille toujours à six heures. L'explosion réveilla tout le quartier.*

700.

Excès, *n.m.* Excess, i.e. the difference between two unequal quantities. Ex.: *Deux est l'excès de douze sur dix.*
Excess in the sense of immoderation. Ex.: *Des excès de table, de vitesse.*
Excédent, *n.m.* Excess beyond what is due or necessary. Ex.: *L'excédent d'une somme après les dépenses.*

701.

Étourdi, *adj.* Thoughtless. Denotes a vivacity which prevents the use of common sense.
Écervelé, *adj.* Hare-brained, i.e. incapable of acting intelligently.
Insouciant, *adj.* Thoughtless in the sense of being heedless or unconcerned.

702.

Excepté, *prep.* Except or excepting. Implies an exception resulting from difference or nonconformity. Ex. : *Ils sont tous reçus à l'examen, excepté mon frère.*

Hors, Hormis, *prep.* Except. Merely denotes exclusion. Ex. : *Il a vendu toutes ses maisons hors deux.* (It is to be noted, however, that such expressions as *hors ligne, hors concours,* imply an exception for some special reason.)

Sauf, *prep.* Except. Save. Denotes a reserve. Ex. : *Bureau ouvert tous les jours sauf le dimanche.*

703.

Envoyer, Expédier, *v.t.* Envoyer is the general term meaning "to send". *Expédier* strictly means to send by any means of despatch or transport. Ex. : *Envoyer des renforts au secours d'une armée. Expédier des marchandises en grande vitesse.*

704.

Exposé, *n.m.* Simple statement or account, precise, and containing but the bare facts. Ex. : *Il nous fit un exposé de la situation.*

Exposition, *n.f.* Detailed statement or account. Ex. : *L'exposition d'une doctrine.*

Déclaration, *n.f.* A statement of a formal nature. Declaration. Ex. : *Faire une déclaration devant témoins.*

Relevé de compte, *n.m.* Statement of account. The single word *relevé* is often employed in this sense.

État, *n.m.* Statement, i.e. information arranged in the form of a list, table, or return. Ex. : *État de frais.*

705.

Désespérance, *n.f.*, **Désespoir,** *n.m.* *Désespérance* and *désespoir* are the antonyms of *espérance* and *espoir* respectively. (See Group 691.)

706.

Fabrique, *n.f.*, **Manufacture,** *n.f.* *Fabrique* meaning a factory, refers more to the work actually done therein, or to the industrial element. *Manufacture* has reference to the kind of goods manufactured, and is especially used to describe a government establishment.

707.

Face, Façade, *n.f.* *Face* merely denotes the front, rear, or any side of a building, etc. A *façade* is the front of a large building, the word implying structural ornamentation or decoration. Ex. : *Peindre les quatre faces d'une maison. La façade d'une cathédrale.*

708.

Face, *n.f.* Face. The term is either used in a familiar sense or when speaking or writing in an elevated style. Ex. : *Avoir la face tuméfiée. La face du Seigneur.*

Visage, *n.m.* Face. Refers more to the expression portrayed. Ex.: *Visage rayonnant de joie.*
Figure, *n.f.* Face, with reference to its physiological form or appearance. Ex.: *Une jolie figure.*
Minois, *n.m.* Face, i.e. its general look or appearance. Ex.: *Un minois intelligent.* The word is mostly used as a slang term for the face generally.

709.

Façons, Manières, *n.f. Façons,* meaning "ways" or "manners", implies affectation. *Manières* indicates something more natural. Used in the singular and meaning "style" or "manner", these two words are synonymous.

710.

Fade, *adj.* Having but little taste, i.e. dull or flat.
Insipide, *adj.* Having no taste at all. Insipid.

711.

Fainéant, Paresseux, *adj. Paresseux* denotes laziness which is not necessarily habitual, and may only be exceptional. *Fainéant* (literally "do nothing") indicates extreme laziness unrelieved by any activity.

712.

Il faut, Il est nécessaire, *colloq.* "It is necessary" or "it must". *Il faut* is stronger than *il est nécessaire* and indicates an absolute necessity.

713.

Famélique, *adj.* Distressed or suffering as a result of hunger.
Affamé, *adj.* Famished.

714.

Falot, Fanal, *n.m.,* **Lanterne,** *n.f. Lanterne* is the general term for a lantern. A *falot* is a large lantern formerly suspended from a pole, or carried, and since replaced by the street lamp. A *fanal* is a lantern generally used as a signal such as on ships, locomotives, etc.

715.

Fatal, *adj.* Fatal, i.e. decreed by fate. Ex.: *Une fatale erreur.*
Funeste, *adj.* Fatal in the sense of being baleful or disastrous. Ex.: *Une passion funeste.*

716.

Fébrile, Fiévreux, *adj. Fiévreux* refers to actual fever. *Fébrile* means "feverish" in a figurative sense. Ex.: *Région fiévreuse. Impatience fébrile.*

717.

Fête, *n.f.* A public or religious holiday.
Vacances, *n.f.* Holiday from the point of view of suspension of work or occupation. Ex.: *Partir en vacances. Vacances de Noël.*

Congé, *n.m.* Holiday. Refers to the duration of same. Ex.: *Avoir un mois de congé.*
Jour férié, *n.m.* Holiday, i.e. a day set apart by law for the celebration of some event. Ex.: *Le lundi de Pentecôte est un jour férié.*
Permission, *n.f.* Leave of absence. Furlough.

718.

Feuillé, Feuillu, *adj.* An *arbre feuillé* is a tree having leaves. An *arbre feuillu* is a tree having many leaves.

719.

Fier, Orgueilleux, *adj.* *Fier* implies a sentiment not altogether unworthy. *Orgueilleux* denotes disdainful pride or inordinate self-esteem. Ex.: *Il est fier du succès de son fils. La fortune l'a rendu très orgueilleux.*

720.

Filateur, Fileur, *n.m.* A *filateur* is the owner of a spinning mill, a *fileur* being a person who actually spins.

721.

Fixage, *n.m.*, **Fixation**, *n.f.* *Fixage* means the act of fixing in a material sense. Ex.: *Fixage d'une console à un mur.* *Fixation* denotes a fixing in the sense of determining or establishing. Ex.: *Fixation des impôts.* A fixing bath for photographic purposes is a *bain de fixage*.

722.

Fonte, Fusion, Refonte, *n.f.* *Fusion* is the act of casting or melting; *fonte*, the result. Ex.: *La fonte des métaux. Métal en fusion.* *Refonte* denotes the recasting or melting down of any object or article. Ex.: *La refonte des cloches, des monnaies.*

723.

Feu, Défunt, *adj.* Late or deceased. *Feu* is generally used in connection with distinguished persons. Ex.: *Feu le pape. Son oncle défunt.*

724.

Se fier, *v.r.* To trust in, or rely on to a certain extent. Ex.: *Homme à qui on peut se fier.*
Se confier à, *v.r.* To trust in without reserve, in the sense of confiding in a person. Ex.: *Je me confie à vous.*
Se confier en, *v.r.* To trust in entirely, i.e. to have complete confidence in every respect. Ex.: *Se confier en Dieu.*

725.

Format, *n.m.* Size (of a book, sheet of paper, etc.).
Grandeur, *n.f.* Relative size. Magnitude. Ex.: *Grandeur d'un parc.*
Grosseur, *n.f.* The size of anything having volume. Ex.: *La grosseur d'un diamant.*
Size, i.e. thickness. Ex.: *La grosseur d'un arbre, d'une colonne.*

Dimensions, *n.f.* Size, i.e. dimensions. Ex.: *Dimensions d'une cour.*
Pointure, *n.f.* Size (of boots, collars or gloves).
Encolure, *n.f.* Size of the collar band on a shirt.

726.

Fortuné, *adj.* Fortunate, i.e. favoured by fortune. Ex.: *Événement fortuné.*
Heureux, *adj.* Fortunate, i.e. lucky. Ex.: *Etre heureux au jeu, en affaires.*

727.

Fourché, *adj.* Forked artificially.
Fourchu, *adj.* Forked naturally. Ex.: *Arbre fourchu.*

728.

Fourmiller, *v.i.* To swarm or abound. Refers to the quantity. Ex.: *L'esplanade fourmille de monde.*
Grouiller, *v.i.* To swarm in the sense of being alive with. Denotes the movement. Ex.: *Étang grouillant de poissons.*

729.

Fourreau, *n.m.* A sheath or cover for anything long and slender, such as a sword, umbrella, etc.
Gaîne, *n.f.* A sheath or case for, generally speaking, cutting instruments. Ex.: *Gaîne de couteau, de ciseaux.*

730.

Four, Fourneau, *n.m.*, **Fournaise,** *n.f.* *Four* and *fourneau* refer to industrial furnaces, *four* applying generally to metallurgy except in the case of a blast furnace which is a *haut fourneau. Fournaise* is the biblical or poetic expression. Ex.: *Fournaise ardente.*

731.

Frais, *n.m.* Freshness or coolness. Refers to the place where found. Fresh air. Ex.: *Mettre quelque chose au frais.*
Fraîcheur, *n.f.* Freshness in an abstract sense. Ex.: *La fraîcheur du matin.*

732.

Fleuve, *n.m.*, **Rivière,** *n.f.* A *fleuve* is generally larger or more important than a *rivière*, and in any case flows direct into the sea.

733.

Vague, Onde, Lame, Ondulation, *n.f.*, **Flot, Raz de Marée,** *n.m.* *Vague* denotes a greater disturbance than that implied by the term *flot* and refers more to waves which form near the shore. Ex.: *Les vagues se brisent contre les rochers. Flots écumeux. Vague* also denotes a wave in the sense of a rush or spell. *Vague de chaleur. Onde* marks the undulatory movement of flowing water, also a sound, electric or similar kind of wave. Ex.: *Le vent fait des ondes sur les rivières. Onde hertzienne.* A *lame* is a wave whose summit breaks into foam, a *raz de marée* being a tidal wave. *Ondulation* means an undulation, i.e. a wave-like form or movement. Ex.: *Théorie des ondulations. Ondulation Marcel.*

734.

Filou, Larron, Voleur, *n.m.* *Voleur* is the general term for a thief. A *larron* is one who steals furtively. *Filou* denotes skill or cleverness and is the French for "pickpocket". (See Group 585.)

735.

Fondement, *n.m.* Foundation, i.e. substructure or masonry up to the level of the ground.
Fondation, *n.f.* Foundation. Refers to the work, such as excavation, pile driving, etc., necessary for the *fondement*.

736.

Forfait, Crime, Délit, *n.m.* *Forfait* denotes a worse or bigger crime than that expressed by the word *crime*. A *délit* is an offence against the laws of a country.

737.

Fourbe, *n.f.* Cheating. Knavery. Denotes custom or habit. Ex.: *Sa fourbe est bien connue.*
Fourberie, *n.f.* Cheating or knavery. Refers to any individual act. Ex.: *Une fourberie grossière.*

738.

Frimas, *n.m.* Hoar frost. Frozen dew.
Givre, *n.m.* The thin coating of ice which forms in small particles on trees, telegraph wires, etc., during winter.
Gelée, *n.f.* Frost, i.e. the severe weather which is the cause. Ex.: *Une forte gelée.*
Verglas, *n.m.* The thin coating of ice formed from freezing rain and which covers the roads, pavements, etc.

739.

Fugitif, Fuyard, *n.m.* *Fugitif* is the ordinary term for "fugitive" A *fuyard* is one who has been put to flight or who is pursued.

740.

Frissonner, *v.i.* To shiver or shudder. Denotes an independent or outside cause. Ex.: *Frissonner de froid, horreur, fièvre,* etc.
Frémir, *v.i.* To quiver, more as a result of one's own feelings. Ex.: *Frémir de joie, colère, indignation,* etc.
Grelotter, *v.i.* To shiver or shudder with cold. *Grelotter* denotes a more permanent shivering than that expressed by *frissonner.*

741.

Froid, *n.m.* Cold in an absolute sense. Ex.: *Il fait froid. Avoir froid.*
Froidure, *n.f.* Coldness (of the air, atmosphere, or climate).
Froideur, *n.f.* The state or quality of that which is cold. Denotes a relative absence of heat. Ex.: *La froideur du marbre.* Coldness, figuratively speaking. Ex.: *La froideur d'un accueil.*

742.

Funèbre, *adj.* Funeral, i.e. forming part of the actual funeral itself. Ex.: *Oraison, convoi, honneurs,*funèbres.* In a figurative sense the word means "funereal", i.e. dismal or mournful. Ex.: *Des idées funèbres.*
Funéraire, *adj.* Funeral. Refers to anything appertaining thereto. Ex.: *Drap, urne, frais funéraires.*

743.

Fureur, Furie, *n.f. Fureur* denotes fury which may be controlled or contained, whereas *furie* indicates visible or physical fury. *Fureur* furthermore implies an element of exaltation, passion, etc. Ex.: *Un accés de fureur. Aimer à la fureur. Les fureurs de la guerre. La furie de la tempête, des vagues. Un lion en furie.*

744.

Furieux, Furibond, *adj. Furieux* refers more to some specific act of fury or rage. *Furibond* indicates fury or the inclination to be furious. Ex.: *La tempête furieuse. Des regards furibonds. Homme furibond.* (It is to be noted, however, that the meaning of these two words is often interchanged, *furieux* denoting the disposition to be furious, *furibond* expressing extreme or violent fury.)

745.

Gardien de la paix, Agent de police, Sergent de ville, Garde champêtre, Gendarme, *n.m. Agent de police* is the general term for the French equivalent of an English policeman. In Paris an *agent de police* is called a *gardien de la paix*, and in the provinces, a *sergent de ville*. These expressions are, however, rarely employed for ordinary purposes, the French town policeman being best known everywhere as an *agent*. A *garde champêtre* is a rural policeman whose chief duty is the protection of land or property. A *gendarme* is a member of the *Gendarmerie Nationale*, a corps of armed police (mounted and unmounted) distributed throughout the land generally.

746.

Gaucherie, *n.f.* Awkwardness, i.e. lack of gracefulness.
Maladresse, *n.f.* Awkwardness or clumsiness on a particular occasion. Ex.: *La maladresse du chirurgien coûta la vie à son paiient.*
Malhabileté, *n.f.* Awkwardness or clumsiness, i.e. want of skill or tact.
Impéritie, *n.f.* Unskilfulness through want of experience.

747.

Gazon, *n.m.*, **Pelouse, Herbe,** *n.f.* *Herbe* is the general term for "grass". *Gazon* denotes the short cut grass on a well-kept lawn. Turf. A *pelouse* is a lawn or grass plot. (The word *gazon* is also often used in this sense.)

748.

Geindre, *v.i.* To moan or whine without reason.
Gémir, *v.i.* To moan or groan under oppression, affliction, etc. Ex.: *Gémir de douleur.*

749.

Gens, Personnes, Peuple. *Gens* refers to people or persons in general, except when preceded by an adjective. *Personnes* denotes individual persons having no relationship other than the group or assembly which they happen to form. Ex.: *Les gens disent qu'il ne reviendra plus. Il n'y avait que quatre personnes au salon. Peuple* means the people of a country or nation as distinguished from the rulers. Ex.: *Le peuple romain. Le bas peuple.*

750.

Futur, A venir, *adj.* Future. *Futur* as an adjective denotes something more certain or immediate. *A venir* refers to the distant future.

751.

Gager, Parier, *v.t.* *Gager* means, strictly speaking, to leave the *gage* or stakes with a third party pending the result of the bet. *Parier* denotes a bet made directly between two persons. For ordinary purposes, however, the two words are synonymous, no distinction whatever being made.

752.

Gibet, *n.m.*, **Potence,** *n.f.* *Potence* denotes the actual gallows used for hanging. *Gibet* is used in a wider sense, the word covering, in addition, the contrivance for exposing hanged criminals, the spot whereon the gallows is erected, and even the cross as an instrument of capital punishment.

753.

Glouton, *n.m.* Glutton. One who eats to excess.
Goinfre, *n.m.* Glutton. The word denotes, in addition, repulsive manners at table.
Gourmand, *n.m.* Gormandiser. A person who is fond of eating a great deal.
Goulu, *n.m.* Glutton. Denotes greediness or avidity.

754.

Gouttière, Nochère, *n.f.*, **Cheneau, Ruisseau,** *n.m.* *Gouttière, cheneau* and *nochère* denote various types of roof gutters. A *gouttière* is usually made of zinc and suspended under the edge of the roof. A *cheneau* is larger than a *gouttière* and generally forms part of the roof itself. A *nochère* consists of boards nailed together at right angles. A *ruisseau* is a street gutter.

755.

Grève, *n.f.* Beach or seashore of a sandy, stony or rocky nature.
Plage, *n.f.* Seashore. Refers to the stretches of sand usually frequented by visitors. Ex. : *Aller à la plage.*

756.

Grâce, *n.f.* Mercy in the sense of pardon or forgiveness. Ex. : *Grâce ! Grâce ! Demander grâce.*
Merci, *n.f.* Mercy, meaning power. Ex. : *Etre à la merci de quelqu'un.*
Miséricorde, *n.f.* Mercy, i.e. the virtue of forbearance or compassion. Ex. : *La miséricorde divine.*

757.

Grave, *adj.* Serious, i.e. having far-reaching consequences. Ex. : *Un grave accident.*
Grave or serious as regards the mind or understanding. Ex. : *Un grave magistrat.*
Sérieux, *adj.* Serious, as opposed to frivolous. Ex. : *Avoir un air sérieux.*
Serious, i.e. sincere or genuine. Ex. : *Une affaire sérieuse.*

758.

Se griser, S'enivrer, Se soûler, *v.r.* *Se griser* and *s'enivrer* both mean to drink to the extent of affecting the senses. *Se griser* denotes, however, a partial, and *s'enivrer* a total intoxication. *Se soûler* means "to get drunk", i.e. to drink as much as possible.

759.

Guenilles, *n.f.*, **Loques,** *n.f.*, **Haillons,** *n.m.* Synonymous terms for "rags" in the sense of old worn-out garments. Ex. : *Mendiant en guenilles.*
Chiffons, *n.m.* General term for "rags". Pieces of rag. Ex. : *Marchand de chiffons.*
Lambeaux, *n.m.* Rags, i.e. torn pieces of cloth. Tatters. Ex. : *Ses vêtements furent déchirés en lambeaux.*
Oripeaux, *n.m.* Rags, i.e. old or worn-out finery.
Drilles, *n.f.* Rags used for the manufacture of paper.

760.

Cure, *n.f.* Cure, i.e. the means employed or treatment followed. Ex. : *Faire une cure.*
Guérison, *n.f.* Cure, i.e. the final restoration to health. Ex. : *L'on désespérait de sa guérison.*

761.

Guetter, *v.t.* To watch in the sense of waiting for. Ex. : *Chat qui guette une souris.*
Veiller, *v.t.* To keep watch. To be on the watch. Ex. : *Veillez à ce qu'il ne se sauve pas.*

Épier, *v.t.* To watch, i.e. to observe secretly. To spy upon. Ex.: *Épier les mouvements de quelqu'un.*

Surveiller, *v.t.* To watch over or supervise. Ex.: *Surveiller des travaux.*

762.

Grief, *n.m.* Complaint. Refers to the cause thereof. Ex.: *Exposer ses griefs.*

Plainte, *n.f.* Complaint, i.e. the act of complaining. Ex.: *Porter plainte.*

Réclamation, *n.f.* A complaint in the sense of a claim or objection. Ex.: *Faire une réclamation.*

763.

Habit, *n.m.* Evening dress.
Jaquette, *n.f.* Morning coat.
Veste, *n.f.* Jacket such as worn by tradespeople, grooms, etc.
Veston, *n.m.* The jacket of a lounge suit.
Vareuse, *n.f.* Military or naval undress tunic or jacket.

764.

Hâbleur, Fanfaron, Vantard, Craqueur, *n.m.* A *hâbleur* is a person who boasts continually for no purpose. A *fanfaron* (or *vantard*) is a braggart whose object is self-aggrandizement. *Craqueur* is the familiar term for a boaster.

765.

Haleine, *n.f.,* **Souffle,** *n.m.* *Haleine* denotes the breath which leaves the lungs naturally; *souffle,* that which is expelled with an effort. Ex.: *Retenir son haleine. Etre à bout de souffle.*

766.

Hâtif, *adj.* Early or precocious. Denotes a rapid advance towards maturity.

Précoce, *adj.* Precocious. Indicates the state of early maturity.

767.

Heure, *n.f.* Time, i.e. the particular time of day as indicated by the clock. Ex.: *Quelle heure est-il?*

Temps, *n.m.* Time in the sense of duration, opportunity, or an allotted period. Ex.: *Il est temps de partir. Si j'ai le temps je viendrai demain.*

768.

Huit, *adj.* Eight (exactly).
Huitaine, *n.f.* About eight. Ex.: *Passer une huitaine de jours à la campagne.* (The expression *huitaine de jours* is commonly used to denote a week.)

769.

Humidifier, Humecter, Mouiller, Tremper, *v.t.* These words indicate the act of wetting to various degrees. *Humidifier* means "to damp" or "moisten"; *humecter*, "to wet slightly"; *mouiller*, "to wet thoroughly"; *tremper*, "to soak". The latter term implies immersion.

770.

Hymen, Hyménée, *n.m.* *Hymen*, in a figurative and poetic sense, refers only to actual marriage or union. *Hyménée* denotes marriage with its attendant circumstances, results, etc., i.e. the state of marriage. Ex. : *Allumer le flambeau de l'hymen. Un heureux hyménée.*

771.

Identique, *adj.* The very same, i.e. not differing in any way. Identical.
Conforme, *adj.* Conformable, or having the same form.
Pareil, *adj.* The same as regards quality, characteristics, etc., though not necessarily identical.
Semblable, *adj.* Similar, i.e. having qualities, etc., which bear comparison.
Ressemblant, *adj.* Resembling, i.e. having the same appearance.
Similaire, *adj.* Having the same nature. Homogeneous.

772.

Ignare, *adj.* Ignorant, i.e. illiterate or lacking education.
Ignorant, *adj.* Ignorant or illiterate. The word also means "ignorant" in the sense of being unaware or uninformed.

773.

Imaginer, *v.t.* To imagine in the sense of supposing or conceiving. Ex. : *Je ne peux imaginer rien de plus extraordinaire.*
S'imaginer, *v.r.* To imagine, i.e. to believe or be persuaded. Ex. : *Le fou s'imaginait être un roi.*

774.

Immeuble, Immobilier, *adj.* *Immeuble* is the term used to describe real estate, i.e. the actual property itself. Ex. : *Biens immeubles. Immobilier* refers to anything connected with real estate. Ex. : *Vente, succession immobilière.*

775.

Immodéré, *adj.* Immoderate; lacking moderation. Ex. : *Un luxe immodéré.*
Démesuré, *adj.* Inordinate, i.e. exceeding just proportions. Ex. : *Ambition démesurée.*
Excessif, *adj.* Excessive. Implies a tendency to be harmful or prejudicial. Ex. : *Vitesse excessive.*
Outré, *adj.* Violently exaggerated. Ex. : *Opinions outrées.*

Désordonné, *adj.* Inordinate. Denotes unrestraint. Ex.: *Passion désordonnée.*

Déréglé, *adj.* Intemperate. Denotes irregularity. Ex.: *Une vie déréglée.*

776.

Imprévu, *adj.* Unforeseen. Not reckoned on. Ex.: *Accident imprévu.*

Inopiné, *adj.* Unexpected, i.e. not imagined or thought of. Ex.: *Il fut étonné de l'arrivée inopinée de son oncle.*

Inattendu, *adj.* Unexpected. Denotes an element of surprise. Ex.: *Recevoir une visite inattendue.*

777.

Immédiatement, Incessamment, *adv.* *Immédiatement* admits of no delay whatever. *Incessamment* has the same meaning but is also used as denoting "very shortly". Ex.: *Les marchandises partiront incessamment.*

778.

Inclinaison, *n.f.* Inclination, i.e. deviation from the horizontal or perpendicular. Ex.: *Angle d'inclinaison.*

Inclination, *n.f.* Inclination in the sense of disposition or taste. Ex.: *Suivre son inclination.*

779.

Indication, *n.f.* Indication, i.e. the act of indicating or pointing out.

Indice, *n.m.* Indication in the sense of a sign or token.

780.

Induire à, Induire en, *v.t.* *Induire à* means "to lead" or "to induce" but merely denotes the attempt. *Induire en* means to actually lead or induce, whether intentionally or otherwise. Ex.: *Induire à mal faire. Induire en erreur.*

781.

Incurable, Inguérissable, *adj.* *Incurable* means "incurable" in the sense that the disease or complaint, although curable, has so far resisted all remedies. *Inguérissable* denotes a complaint for the cure of which there is no hope.

782.

Inénarrable, *adj.* That cannot be explained or related. Ex.: *Beauté inénarrable.*

Indicible, *adj.* That cannot be suitably described. Unspeakable. Ex.: *Douleur indicible.*

Inexprimable, *adj.* That cannot be sufficiently expressed or depicted. Ex.: *Un charme inexprimable.*

783.

Invitation, Invite, *n.f.* *Invitation* is the general term for an invitation. Ex.: *Envoyer une invitation à dîner.* An *invite* is an invitation in the sense of a call or inducement. Ex.: *Ce beau temps est une invite à la promenade.*

784.

Ivre, Soûl, *adj.* *Ivre* denotes that the senses are affected ; the word is therefore best rendered in English by "intoxicated ". *Soûl* indicates the state of having drunk to the extent of completely losing one's senses. "Drunk" is the exact equivalent. (See also Group 758.)

785.

Jaillir, Rejaillir, *v.i.* *Jaillir* means to gush or spout out in a single flow or direction. *Rejaillir* implies a rebound or a gushing in all directions. Ex. : *Source qui jaillit de la terre. Son sang rejaillit sur nous.*

786.

A jamais, Pour jamais, *adv. exp.* *À jamais* is vague and indefinite when compared with *pour jamais*. The former expression allows a hope in the distant future which *pour jamais* definitely excludes, and may therefore be used in an augmented form, e.g. *à tout jamais, au grand jamais*. Ex. : *Il est parti à jamais. La mort les a réunis pour jamais.*

787.

Jeter, Lancer, *v.t.* *Jeter* is the general term meaning "to throw". *Lancer* denotes the addition of force, and therefore corresponds to the English expression "to fling". Ex. : *Jeter quelque chose à terre, quelqu'un en prison. Lancer des pierres.* (*N.B.—Jeter* also means "to throw away". Ex.: *Jeter une pomme gâtée.*)

788.

Joint, *n.m.*, **Jointure,** *n.f.* *Joint* refers more to the place where a joint is made. *Jointure* denotes generally the arrangement or composition of a joint. Ex. : *Faire un joint dans un parquet. La jointure du coude.*

789.

Jour, *n.m.* Day considered as a division of time. Ex. : *Le mois de juin a trente jours.*
Journée, *n.f.* Day. Refers to the duration of a day's occupation or to what is accomplished during that period. Ex. : *La loi sur la journée de huit heures. Cet ouvrier termine sa journée à six heures.*

790.

Juron, *n.m.* Oath in the sense of a curse or swear word. Refers to expressions such as those frequently employed. Ex. : *Lâcher un juron.*
Jurement, *n.m.* An unnecessary oath used in ordinary conversation. Ex. : *Proférer des jurements.*
Serment, *n.m.* An oath sworn solemnly before a witness on some special occasion. Ex. : *Prêter serment.*

791.

Lâcher, Relâcher, *v.t.* *Lâcher*, meaning "to release" or "let go", denotes suddenness with regard to the movement. *Relâcher* means "to let go" or "release" in the sense of granting full liberty or relaxing. Ex.: *Lâcher un prisonnier* (i.e. allow him to escape). *Relâcher un prisonnier* (i.e. restore him his liberty and rights). *Relâcher la discipline.*

792.

Lacs, *n.m.* A snare or trap consisting of a slip-knot for game.
Lacet, *n.m.* A small *lacs*.
Rets, *n.m.* A net for ensnaring or trapping.
Piège, *n.m.* General term for a trap for catching animals, birds, etc. Certain traps have special names, e.g. *ratière, souricière*. The word is also that employed when referring figuratively to a trap. Ex.: *Se laisser prendre au piège.*
Traquenard, *n.m.,* **Traquet,** *n.m.* Trap for noxious animals.
Trappe, *n.f.* Trap comprising a trap-door over a pit or other opening.

793.

Laiton, Cuivre jaune, Airain, *n.m. Laiton* and *cuivre jaune* are synonymous terms for "brass", *cuivre jaune* merely denoting the distinction between the alloy and pure copper (*cuivre rouge*). *Airain* means copper or its alloys, brass, bronze, etc., the term being reserved for poetic use. Ex.: *Statue, âge d'airain.*

794.

Se lancer, S'élancer, *v.r. S'élancer* denotes a greater or more violent effort and calls to mind the commencement of the act. *Se lancer* simply means "to spring" or "rush" and presupposes less reflection or forethought. Ex.: *Il s'élança de sa chaise. Se lancer dans l'eau.*

795.

Langue, *n.f.* Language or tongue, i.e. the words employed by any nation or country for the purpose of expressing itself. Ex.: *La langue française.*
Language, *n.m.* Language, i.e. the manner or style of expressing oneself generally or on particular occasions. Ex.: *Language grossier, incorrect, poétique.*
Language in the sense of system or arrangement of signs as a means of expression. Ex.: *Le language des fleurs, des yeux.*

796.

Largesse, Libéralité, *n.f. Largesse* means more than *libéralité*. For example, *Faire des largesses* means "to be very liberal".

797.

Larmes, *n.f.*, **Pleurs**, *n.m.* Larmes merely denotes the liquid secreted by the eye glands. Pleurs (only used in the plural) refers to tears shed under the influence of sorrow. Ex. : *Elle le supplia les larmes aux yeux. La fumée acre me fit venir des larmes. Essuyez ces pleurs, le mal n'est pas irréparable.*

798.

Las, *adj.* Tired in the sense of being weary. Denotes lassitude. Ex. : *Être las de la vie. Je suis las de vous voir ici.*
Fatigué, *adj.* Tired, i.e. fatigued. The word is more often than not used in a physical sense. Ex. : *Cheval fatigué. Avoir les yeux fatigués par une lumière trop vive.*

799.

Lavage, Lavement, *n.m.* Lavage is the general term for "washing"; lavement is only used in connection with church ceremony. Ex. : *Le lavage d'un plancher. Lavement des mains, des pieds.*

800.

Lésine, Lésinerie, *n.f.* Lésine means "stinginess" considered as an imperfection. A *lésinerie* is any individual act of stinginess.

801.

Léger, *adj.* Light as opposed to heavy. Ex. : *Légère comme une plume.*
Leste, *adj.* Light in the sense of being nimble or brisk. Ex. : *Danseuse très leste.*

802.

Légèrement, *adv.*, **À la légère**, *adv. exp.* In a material sense *légèrement* denotes the degree or extent, whereas *à la légère* indicates the manner or style. Ex. : *Se blesser légèrement. Être vêtu à la légère.* Figuratively speaking, *légèrement* denotes inconsideration or want of reflection, while *à la légère* means "after the fashion of those who act lightly". Ex. : *Agir légèrement. Parler à la légère.*

803.

Levant, Est, Orient, *n.m.* Est is the general term for "east". Ex. : *Le vent souffle de l'est.* Orient is used more in connection with geography and, as in English, is written with a capital letter when meaning "The East". Ex. : *L'orient est en feu ; le soleil se lève. L'extrême Orient.* Levant calls to mind the rising of the sun. Ex. : *Cette pièce est exposée au levant.*

804.

Liège, *n.m.* Cork, i.e. the substance obtained from the tree and used for various purposes. Ex. : *Ceinture en liège.*
Bouchon, *n.m.* Cork for bottles, etc. The word is more correctly rendered in English by "stopper" (*boucher*, "to stop up"), as a *bouchon* may be made of cork, glass, or rubber.

805.

Lier, *v.t.* To fasten in the sense of binding or tying with a view to preventing movement or action. Ex.: *Lier les mains avec une corde.*

Attacher, *v.t.* To fasten by any means. Ex.: *Attacher avec de la ficelle, un clou, une épingle,* etc.
To tie up, i.e. to deprive of freedom. Ex.: *Attacher un chien avec une chaîne.*

806.

Ligne, *n.f.* General term for "line". Ex.: *Ligne droite. Regiment de ligne.*
Line (steamship, railway, etc.), i.e. the company from the point of view of name or title. Ex.: *La ligne Cunard.*
Railway or tramway line considered as a means of transport between two places. Ex.: *Ligne principale.*
Family line, i.e. the descendants in line from a common progenitor. Lineage. Ex.: *Ligne directe, collatérale.*

Lignée, *n.f.* Lineage in the sense of descendants or issue generally. Ex.: *Une nombreuse lignée.*

Trait, *n.m.* A line made hastily without lifting the pen or pencil. Stroke or dash. Ex.: *Un trait de plume.*

Voie, *n.f.* Railway or tramway line, i.e. the actual track itself. Ex.: *Voie double.*

Réseau, *n.m.* Railway line, i.e. the company. The word denotes the whole system or network of lines comprising any particular company. Ex.: *Réseau du Nord.*

807.

Lever un plan, Faire un plan, *colloq.* *Lever un plan* means to get out a plan by working on site, in other words, "to survey". *Faire un plan* denotes the action of making a plan from information, measurements, etc., obtained beforehand.

808.

Liste, *n.f.*, **Rôle,** *n.m.* *Liste* is the general term for a "list". A *rôle* is a list of persons, or nominal roll, denoting in addition, rank or order. Ex.: *Rôle de contribuables.* (Note the expression *à tour de rôle,* meaning "in turn" or "in rotation".)

809.

Littéralement, *adv.* Literally, i.e. following the letter. Word for word. Ex.: *Traduction faite littéralement.*

À la lettre, Au pied de la lettre, *adv. exp.* To the letter, i.e. rigorously or within the strict meaning of the words. Ex.: *Appliquer la loi à la lettre.*

810.

Logement, *n.m.* The place where one lodges or lives. Lodgings. The word is used more from a personal point of view and may only refer to a part of any house or habitation. Ex. : *Avoir un logement au troisième. Logement garni.*

Logis, *n.m.* The place where one lives or dwells. Refers to any house or habitation as a whole. Ex. : *Changer de logis. Maître de logis.*

811.

Longtemps, *adv.* For a long time. Refers merely to the length of time. Ex. : *Je connais son frère depuis longtemps. Il a parlé pendant longtemps.*

Longuement, *adv.* Lengthily or at length. In detail. Refers more to the action than to the duration. Ex. : *Il a parlé longuement sur l'état des finances.*

812.

Maint, *adj.* Many. Many a. The word denotes a quantity, considered separately or apart. Ex. : *Je lui ai écrit maintes fois.*

Plusieurs, *adj.* Several. Merely indicates plurality. Ex. : *Plusieurs personnes ont quitté la séance avant la fin.*

813.

Lourd, Pesant, *adj.* *Lourd* means "heavy", taking into consideration the volume of any body. *Pesant* simply means "having weight". Figuratively speaking, *lourd* denotes greater heaviness than that expressed by *pesant.* Ex. : *Porter un lourd fardeau. Tous les corps sont pesants. Style pesant.*

814.

Maculer, *v.t.* To spot in the sense of dirtying. To maculate. Ex. : *Vêtement maculé de boue.*

Tacher, *v.t.* To dirty with individual stains. Ex. : *Tacher une nappe.* The word is also used figuratively. Ex. : *Une seule mauvaise action suffit pour tacher la plus belle vie.*

Tacheter, *v.t.* To put marks or spots on anything. Ex. : *La peau du léopard est tachetée.*

Entacher, *v.t.* To stain or injure morally. Ex. : *Entacher la mémoire de quelqu'un.*

Souiller, *v.t.* To dirty or soil completely. To sully. Ex. : *Souiller ses vêtements.* Also used in a figurative or moral sense. Ex. : *Souiller sa réputation, sa bouche.*

815.

Mail, Maillet, *n.m.*, **Maille, Mailloche,** *n.f.* *Maillet* is the general term for a mallet. *Mail* is the name given to the mallet used in the French game of *mail. Maille* is a long two-handed mallet. A *mailloche* is a large or heavy mallet.

816.

Mal, *n.m.*, **Maladie,** *n.f.* Mal means illness or disease in the sense of a complaint and merely denotes the absence of perfect health. Ex. : *De quel mal souffre-t-il ?* Maladie refers to the particular illness from which a person may be suffering. Ex. : *Elle souffre d'une maladie incurable.*

817.

Malaxer, *v.t.* To mix thoroughly. To work up. Ex. : *Malaxer du mortier, du beurre.*

Mélanger, *v.t.* To mix or blend. Implies a certain order or proportion of the substances mixed. Ex. : *Mélanger des couleurs.*

Mêler, *v.t.* To mix, generally in a haphazard fashion or without order. Ex. : *Mêler l'eau avec le vin.*
To mix in the sense of jumbling or confusing. Ex. : *Mes papiers sont mêlés.*

Se mêler, *v.t.* To mix or mingle when speaking of persons. Ex. : *Il se mêla à la foule de curieux.*

Mixtionner, *v.t.* Scientific term meaning "to mix". To compound. Ex. : *Mixtionner des drogues.*

818.

Mâle et femelle, Masculin et féminin. Contrary to English custom, it is highly incorrect to use the words *mâle* and *femelle* in connection with persons. The terms are reserved for animals, flowers, etc. Failing the exact term, so often forthcoming in French, for a female person (e.g. *employée, receveuse, mécanicienne, concurrente*, etc.) expressions such as "Female labour", "female guide" and "female witness" are rendered by *main d'œuvre féminine, guide du sexe féminin* (or *femme guide*) and *femme témoin* respectively. (In certain cases some words are both masculine and feminine according to the sex of the person referred to. For instance, "a male servant" is *un domestique* and "a female servant" *une domestique.*)

819.

Malfaisant, *adj.* Harmful or injurious. Denotes the action. Ex. : *Boisson malfaisante.*

Nuisible, *adj.* Injurious or detrimental more as the result of circumstances. Ex. : *Tout excès est nuisible.*

820.

Mauvais, *adj.* Bad in the sense of being unprincipled.

Méchant, *adj.* Bad or wicked. Denotes a hatred of all that is good or just.

Vilain, *adj.* Bad in the sense of being debased. Improper.

821.

Mallette, *n.f.* Small trunk or portmanteau.

Valise, *n.f.* Hand-bag for travelling.
Hand-bag of the "attaché" type. Portmanteau. Valise.

Sac, *n.m.* Lady's hand-bag.
A paper or cloth bag.
Sacoche, *n.f.* Large leather bag used for collecting money.
Réticule, *n.m.* A lady's cloth hand-bag usually closed by means of a cord, ribbon, etc.

822.

Manœuvre, Manouvrier, Ouvrier, Travailleur, *n.m.* A *manœuvre* is a workman who either does labouring temporarily or who, though working as a labourer, is capable of better-class work. A *manouvrier* is a professional labourer, incapable of anything better. *Ouvrier* is the general term for a workman. A *travailleur* is an industrious worker or a toiler. The word also denotes a member of the working class.

823.

Malcontent, *adj.* Discontented, i.e. not completely satisfied.
Mécontent, *adj.* Discontented in the sense of having received no satisfaction whatever.

824.

Manquer, *v.t.* To miss, i.e. to fail to hit. Ex. : *Manquer le but.*
To miss in the sense of neglecting to take advantage of. Ex. : *Manquer une occasion.*
To miss, i.e. to fail to meet or be present as arranged. Ex. : *Manquer un rendez-vous.*
To miss, i.e. to fail to catch. Ex. : *Il a manqué son train.* (See also *rater*.)
Manquer, *v.i.* To be missing or lacking. To be short of. Ex. : *La dernière page de ce livre manque. Il manque dix francs dans la caisse.*
Manquer à, *v.i.* To miss, i.e. to feel the absence of. Ex. : *Votre frère nous manque beaucoup.*
To be missing or absent. Ex. : *Manquer à une réunion.*
To fail in one's duty, etc. Ex. : *Ne pas manquer à son devoir.* (See also *faillir*.)
Manquer de, *v.i.* To lack totally or be without. Ex. : *Manquer d'argent, de patience.*
To miss in the sense of narrowly escaping. Ex. : *J'ai manqué de me faire écraser.* (See also *faillir*.)
To miss, i.e. to fail or neglect. Ex. : *Ne manquez pas de venir demain.*
Faillir, *v.i.* To miss narrowly, i.e. to have nearly. Ex. : *J'ai failli me noyer.* (*Faillir* is synonymous, in this sense, with *manquer de*; q.v.)
Faillir à, *v.i.* To fail in one's duty, etc. Ex. : *Faillir à sa parole.* (Synonymous with *manquer à*.)
Rater, *v.t.* To miss in the sense of not taking effect. Ex. : *Le fusil a raté.* Also used figuratively in this sense. Ex. : *Il a raté son coup.*
To miss, i.e. to fail to catch. Ex. : *Rater le train.* (Synonymous with *manquer* in this sense.)

825.

Maquette, *n.f.*, **Modèle,** *n.m.*   *Modèle* is the general term for "a model". A *maquette* is a sculptor's model, usually on a small scale, to indicate what the finished statue will be like.

826.

Marâtre, Belle-mère, *n.f.*   *Belle-mère* is the general term for "stepmother". *Marâtre* is the term employed in an ill sense and implies unkindness, cruelty, etc., towards the father's children.

827.

Masque, Loup, *n.m.*   *Masque* is the general term for "a mask". A *loup* is a small mask, usually made of velvet or satin and covering the eyes only.

828.

Marteau, *n.m.*, **Masse, Massette,** *n.f.*   A *marteau* is an ordinary hammer, a *masse* being a sledge hammer. A *massette* is a stone-breaker's hammer.

829.

Matelas, *n.m.*   A mattress stuffed with wool, hair, etc.
Sommier, *n.m.*   A spring mattress. The type containing spiral springs is known as a *sommier élastique*.

830.

Matin, *n.m.*   Morning, i.e. the early portion of the day, terminating at noon. Denotes time. Ex.: *Hier matin. Demain matin.*
Matinée, *n.f.*   Morning. Refers more to the occupation or events of the morning. Ex.: *Je dois sortir dans le courant de la matinée.*

831.

Médisance, *n.f.*   The saying of harmful, though true, things with intention to injure a person.
Calomnie, *n.f.*   Deliberate false accusation. Calumny.

832.

Matinal, *adj.*   Early (in the morning). Ex.: *Une promenade matinale. Matinal* in connection with persons means "to be up early". Ex.: *Vous êtes matinal aujourd'hui.*
Matineux, *adj.*   Said of persons who are in the habit of rising early. Ex.: *Ouvrier matineux.*
Matinier, *adj.*   Morning, i.e. early morning. Only used in the expression *L'Étoile matinière.*

833.

Mendier, *v.t.*   To beg, i.e. to ask for alms, charity, etc. Ex.: *Être réduit à mendier.*
Quémander, *v.t.*   To beg in the sense of soliciting with insistence. Ex.: *Quémander un emploi.*
Demander, *v.t.*   To beg, simply meaning "to ask". Ex.: *Je vous demande pardon.*

Supplier, *v.t.* To beg in the sense of entreating or beseeching. Ex.: *Je vous supplie de m'accorder cette faveur.*
(*N.B.*—The expression "I beg to . . .," etc., so often met with in commercial correspondence is translated *J'ai l'avantage de . . .,* or *J'ai l'honneur de . . .,* the latter being more formal.)

834.

Menétrier, *n.m.* An itinerant fiddler of the village-green variety.
Violoneux, *n.m.* General or popular term for "a fiddler".
Violoniste, *n.m.* A violinist or violin player. Denotes skill or the result of proper teaching.

835.

Mensonge, *n.m.* A deliberate lie intended to deceive.
Menterie, *n.f.* Familiar term for a lie, of a less serious nature than a *mensonge.* A fib.

836.

Se méprendre, *v.r.* To make a mistake in the sense of being under a misapprehension.
To understand wrongly. Ex.: *Vous vous méprenez sur ses intentions.*
Se tromper, *v.r.* To make a mistake. To be wrong. Ex.: *Je me suis trompé dans mon calcul.*
Se tromper de, *v.r.* To mistake, i.e. to take the wrong person or thing for the right. Ex.: *Se tromper de maison.*

837.

Mettre, *v.t.* To put or place generally, or in any manner. Ex.: *Mettre de l'argent dans son sac.*
Placer, *v.t.* To put or place in the proper position or where required. To arrange in order. Ex.: *Placer ses convives. Placer des meubles dans une pièce.*
Poser, *v.t.* To put or place suitably where intended. Ex.: *Poser un vase sur la table. Poser le pied par terre.*

838.

Meubles, *n.m.* Furniture, i.e. a collection of individual pieces of furniture. Ex.: *Les tables, les lits, les chaises sont des meubles courants.*
Mobilier, *n.m.* Furniture considered as a whole. A complete set of household furniture. Ex.: *Il a un mobilier superbe.*

839.

Mignard, Mignon, *adj. Mignard,* meaning "pretty", generally implies affectedness, whereas *mignon* does not. Ex.: *Un enfant mignon. Un parler mignard.*

840.

Millésime, *n.m.,* **Date,** *n.f.,* **Quantième,** *n.m. Date* is the general term for "date". *Millésime* is the date stamped on a coin or medal. *Quantième* is the date, i.e. the day of the month. Ex.: *Quel est le quantième aujourd'hui ?*

841.

Mirer, Viser, *v.i.* *Mirer* means "to take aim or direction with any instrument", whereas *viser* (to aim at) simply denotes a turning of the face in the direction aimed. Although *mirer* is therefore the correct term to employ in connection with rifles, guns, etc., *viser* is more often used as being the general expression.

842.

Mobile, *n.m.* Motive, the result of feeling and which incites to action. Incentive. Ex.: *L'intérêt est le mobile de beaucoup de nos actions.*

Motif, *n.m.* Motive. Denotes previous reflection or reasoning and may refer to inaction as well as action. Ex.: *Nous ne comprenons pas le motif de son refus.*

843.

Modeste, *adj.* Moderate. Not excessive. Ex.: *Des prétentions modestes.*

Modique, *adj.* Small or low in size, quantity, value, etc. Ex.: *Vendre à des prix modiques.*

844.

Moisson, *n.f.* Harvest (of wheat and other cereals).

Récolte, *n.f.* Harvest or crop. The word covers land products generally and refers either to the gathering in or to the crop itself.

845.

Monnaie, *n.f.* Money, i.e. gold, silver, nickel or copper coin. Ex.: *Monnaie d'or.*

Argent, *n.m.* Money in the sense of currency of any description. Ex.: *Verser une somme d'argent.* (*N.B.*—"Paper-money" is *papier-monnaie.*)

846.

Monte-charge, *n.m.* Lift for goods, merchandise, or materials, such as used in a factory, builder's yard, etc. Hoist. (Certain hoists for special use are known by the kind of goods conveyed, e.g. *monte-plats, monte-sac.*)

Ascenseur, *n.m.* Lift in a hotel, apartment house, etc., for the exclusive use of persons.

847.

Morceau, *n.m.* A small or detached piece of the whole. A morsel (of food). Ex.: *Morceau de pain, papier, bois, etc.*
A piece of music.

Pièce, *n.f.* Piece as a whole intended to be cut or otherwise divided into parts. Ex.: *Pièce de drap.*
The various parts or pieces, each complete in themselves, forming a whole when put together. Ex.: *Pièce de charpente. Les pièces d'une machine.*
A theatrical piece (comedy, tragedy, etc.).

Bout, *n.m.* A piece of anything capable of being divided up lengthwise. Ex.: *Bout de ficelle, bois, chandelle, etc.*
Éclats, *n.m.*, **Miettes,** *n.f.* The small parts or remains of anything smashed or broken. Ex.: *Voler en éclats. La statue s'est brisée en miettes.*

848.

Mot, *n.m.* Word, i.e. an arrangement or group of letters forming a part of speech. Ex.: *Les derniers mots de sa lettre sont illisibles.*
Word, in the sense of a very brief communication. Ex.: *J'ai un mot à vous dire. Envoyer un mot à quelqu'un.*
Parole, *n.f.* Word in the sense of a term employed for the expression of thought. Ex.: *Les paroles d'un opéra. Paroles distinctes.*
Word (of honour). Ex.: *Homme de parole. Tenir sa parole.*

849.

Moteur, *n.m.* Internal-combustion engine for any purpose. Ex.: *Moteur à essence, à gaz, à huile, etc. Moteur à quatre cylindres.*
Machine, *n.f.* Steam engine. Ex.: *Machine à vapeur.*
Railway engine or locomotive.

850.

Mou, *adj.* Soft, i.e. yielding easily to pressure. Ex.: *Terre molle. Mou comme du beurre.*
Doux, *adj.* Soft as opposed to hard, strong, loud, etc. Ex.: *Une lumière douce. Couleurs douces. Accent doux.*
Soft or smooth to the touch. Ex.: *Le velours est très doux.*
Tendre, *adj.* Soft with reference to substances capable of being worked easily. Ex.: *Pierre, bois tendre.*
Mollet, *adj.* Soft, i.e. yielding gently when in contact with the body. Downy. Ex.: *Lit mollet.*

851.

Moulinet, *n.m.* Turnstile such as found at the entrance to a field, footpath, etc.
Tourniquet, *n.m.* Turnstile placed at the entrance to a sports ground or place of amusement.

852.

Mourant, Moribond, *n.m.* A *mourant* is a person who is actually dying at the time. A *moribond* is only dying gradually; the end may not be immediate.

853.

Mur, *n.m.*, **Muraille, Paroi,** *n.f.* A *mur* is an ordinary wall surrounding property or forming part of a house. *Muraille,* implying size, strength and extent, is a wall for defence or fortification, such as that surrounding a town. A *paroi* is a small or partition wall other than in brickwork, separating the various rooms of a house.

854.

Nage, *n.f.* The act of swimming. Ex.: *Traverser une rivière à la nage.*
Natation, *n.f.* Swimming, considered in an abstract sense. The art of swimming. Natation. Ex.: *École de natation.*

855.

Nappe, *n.f.* The white linen table-cloth used for meals.
Tapis, *n.m.* Table-cloth or cover, usually coloured, for use at other than meal times.

856.

Narine, *n.f.* The nostril, with reference to human beings.
Naseau, *n.m.* The nostril of certain animals such as the horse, cow, ass, etc.

857.

Néant, *n.m.* Nothing, in the sense of non-existence or total absence. Nil. Ex.: *Nous rentrerons dans le néant d'où nous sortons.*
Rien, *n.m.* Nothing, as opposed to something or any quantity. Ex.: *Il a acheté cette propriété pour presque rien.*

858.

Négoce, *n.m.* The various operations, considered as a whole, necessary for any business or trade. The word especially denotes negotiation between producer or manufacturer and the consumer. Ex.: *Faire le négoce des vins.*
Commerce, *n.m.* Business or trade in general. Ex.: *Être dans le commerce.*

859.

Mouvoir, Remuer, *v.t.* To move (any object or article). Refers to the actual movement. Remuer is the commoner term.
Emouvoir, *v.i.* To move in the sense of affecting one's feelings. Ex.: *Il fut très ému par la nouvelle.*
Déplacer, *v.t.* To move from one place to another. Ex.: *Déplacer un meuble.*
Déranger, *v.t.* To move in the sense of disturbing. Ex.: *Ne dérangez pas mes papiers.*
Déménager, *v.i.* To move, i.e. to change one's place of residence.
Porter, *v.i.* To move in the sense of leading or inducing. Ex.: *Les circonstances l'ont porté à répondre ainsi.*
Bouger, *v.i.* To move without, however, changing place. To stir. Ex.: *Il bouge continuellement sur sa chaise.*
To move from one place to another, with reference to persons. To budge. Ex.: *Ne bougez pas de là!*
v.t. To move any article or object. (The word is only used familiarly in this sense.) Ex.: *Bouger une chaise.*

860.

Mule, *n.f.,* **Mulet,** *n.m.* A *mule* is a she-mule and a *mulet* a he-mule. The latter term is, however, that generally employed.

861.

Ne ... pas, Ne ... point. *Ne ... point* is a much stronger term than *ne ... pas* and denotes an absolute or irrevocable negation. Ex.: *Il ne viendra pas* implies that the person in question may come on some other occasion. *Il ne viendra point* means "he will never come at all".

862.

Net, Propre, *adj*. *Propre* means more than *net* and implies neatness or tidiness in addition to cleanliness. Ex.: *Des mains nettes. Un enfant propre.*

863.

Nom, Renom, *n.m.*, **Renommée,** *n.f.* These three words mean "renown" or "reputation" in varying degrees. *Nom* corresponds to "name" in this sense and denotes distinction by reason of quality, character, etc. Ex.: *Se faire un nom. Renom* means more than *nom* and indicates renown or reputation. Ex.: *Acquérir un grand renom. Renommée* denotes a still more extensive celebrity and corresponds to "fame" in English. Ex.: *Cette maison jouit d'une grande renommée.*

864.

Nombrer, *v.t.* To number, i.e. to determine the quantity of. To count or compute. The word does not necessarily imply an exact calculation. Ex.: *Nombrer les étoiles est une chose impossible.*

Dénombrer, *v.t.* To number, i.e. to determine the quantity of. Official term implying an exact and detailed calculation. Ex.: *Dénombrer une armée, une flotte.*

Numéroter, *v.t.* To number, i.e. to assign a number for the purpose of indicating the order or sequence. Ex.: *Numéroter les pages d'un livre.*

Recenser, *v.t.* To number or count. The word is generally reserved for use in connection with the inhabitants of a country. To take the census. Ex.: *Recenser la population.*

Chiffrer, *v.t.* To number, i.e. to express in, or calculate by means of, figures. Ex.: *Les frais se chiffrent par milliers.* Also used in the same sense as *numéroter* (q.v.).

865.

Nommer, *v.t.* To call a person by his or her proper name. Ex.: *Le nommé Pierre.*

Appeler, *v.t.* To call, i.e. to cry out for the purpose of attracting attention. Ex.: *Appeler son chien. Appeler au secours.*

To call, i.e. to designate or describe. Ex.: *On appelle une bicyclette un vélo.*

To call in the sense of appointing to a position, charge, etc. Ex.: *Être appelé au trône.*

To call, i.e. to summon or send for. Ex.: *Appeler le docteur.*

To call by name or any other appellation. Ex.: *On m'appelle Jean.*

Dénommer, *v.t.* To call or describe a person generally in any document or deed. Ex.: *Ci-après dénommé le vendeur.*

866.

Nombre, *n.m.* Number in the sense of a quantity. Ex.: *Un nombre de personnes.*
Any arithmetical number. Ex.: *Nombre pair, cardinal.*
Numéro, *n.m.* Number serving to indicate order, sequence, etc. *Quel est le numéro de sa maison?*
Chiffre, *n.m.* Number, i.e. the figure or figures used to express same. Ex.: *Chiffres romains.*

867.

Noce, *n.f.*, **Mariage,** *n.m.* *Mariage* has the same meaning as "marriage" and denotes the actual union. Ex.: *Mariage civil.* *Noce* (generally used in the plural) refers more to the circumstances or events surrounding a marriage and corresponds to "wedding" in English. Ex: *Noces d'or. Les Noces de Cana.*

868.

Noix, *n.f.* General term for the nut of certain trees. Ex.: *Noix de coco, du Brésil.*
Walnut, i.e. the fruit of the walnut tree.
Noisette, *n.f.* The fruit of the hazel. The hazel-nut.
Noyer, *n.m.* Walnut, i.e. the wood of the walnut tree.

869.

Nippes, Hardes, *n.f.*, **Habits, Vêtements, Habillement, Complet,** *n.m.*
Nippes refers, strictly speaking, to clothes of an ornamental nature, while *hardes* implies utility. However, the two words are, generally, only used in the plural to denote old or shabby clothes. *Habits* means "clothes" in the sense of outer garments. *Vêtements* covers all the various kinds of clothes worn at the same time, including linen, underclothing, etc. *Habillement* means "clothes" in the sense of dress and refers to style or appearance. *Complet* is the general term for a suit of clothes.

870.

Nobilité, *n.f.* Nobility, i.e. the corps or body of those who are of noble birth or rank.
Noblesse, *n.f.* Nobility, i.e. the state of being of noble birth or rank. Ex.: *Lettres de noblesse.*
Nobility or nobleness of mind, character, etc.

871.

Nourrir, Alimenter, Sustenter, Ravitailler, *v.t.* *Nourrir* and *alimenter* are synonymous except that the latter refers more to the actual food supplied and therefore means "to feed" in the sense of supplying with food, *nourrir* denoting, on the other hand, the consumption of same. Ex.: *Nourrir des bestiaux. Alimenter une garnison.* *Alimenter* also means "to feed" any machine, recipient, etc., which requires attention in this sense. Ex.: *Alimenter une chaudière, un réservoir.* *Sustenter* corresponds to "sustain" in English and implies the supply of sufficient food necessary for maintaining life. Ex. : *Sustenter un malade*. *Ravitailler* means "to replenish" or "to revictual" with reference to food, fuel, munitions, etc. Ex. : *Ravitailler une armée*.

872.

Numéral, *adj*. Serving to express a number. Numeral. Ex. : *Adjectif numéral*.
Numérique, *adj*. Relating to numbers. Numerical. Ex. : *Supériorité numérique d'une armée*.

873.

Nuit, *n.f.* Dark, i.e. after nightfall. Ex. : *Il fait nuit*.
Sombre, *adj*. Dark in the sense of lacking light. Obscure. Ex. : *L'intérieur de Notre Dame à Paris est sombre*.
Dark or dull as opposed to light or gay, with reference to colours. Ex. : *Elle porte toujours des couleurs sombres*.
Brun, *adj*. Dark as opposed to fair, with reference to persons. Ex. : *Elle est blonde mais son frère est brun*.
Foncé, *adj*. Dark with reference to the shade of any colour. Ex. : *Robe rouge foncé*.

874.

Nul, Aucun. Both these words are employed either as an adjective ("no", "not any") or as a pronoun ("none", "nobody"), *nul* excluding in a more absolute sense than *aucun*. As an adjective the former may be complete in itself whereas *aucun* requires an additional negative. The terms are generally used in the singular only. Ex. : *Il n'a aucune chance de réussir. Nul n'est prophète en son pays. Je crains qu'aucun de vous ne puisse le faire. L'erreur est insignifiante et de nulle conséquence*.

875.

Nourrissant, *adj*. Giving much nourishment. Nourishing. Denotes the effect. Ex. : *Certains légumes sont très nourrissants*.
Nutritif, *adj*. Capable of nourishing. Nutritive. Ex. : *Les parties nutritives d'un aliment*.
Nourricier, *adj*., **Nutricier**, *adj*. Actually nourishing. Denotes the act of nourishing. Ex. : *Sucs nourriciers*.

876.

À nouveau, *adv. exp*. Again. Implies an act of an entirely different nature. Ex. : *Il essaya à nouveau de les persuader*.
De nouveau, *adv*. Again. Denotes similarity of action. Ex. : *Il est parti de nouveau à Paris*.
Derechef, *adv*. Again, i.e. afresh or from the beginning. Ex. : *Il a fait derechef la même proposition*.
Encore, *adv*. Again. General term merely denoting repetition. Ex. : *Le train a encore du retard aujourd'hui*.

877.

Nuage, *n.m.*, **Nue, Nuée,** *n.f.* These words only differ as regards the point of view from which regarded. *Nuage* implies density or obscurity; *nue* indicates height, while *nuée* denotes quantity or extent. Ex.: *Un ciel sans nuage. L'avion disparut dans les nues. Sombre nuée qui annonce la tempête.* *Nuée* is also used figuratively to denote a cloud or large quantity. Ex.: *Le vent soulève des nuées de poussière.*

878.

Nuancer, *v.t.* To shade in the sense of arranging the various shades or tones in proper order. Ex.: *Un tableau bien nuancé.* Also used figuratively. Ex.: *Morceau de musique gracieusement nuancé.*

Nuer, *v.t.* To shade or blend, i.e. to form tones or shades with one or more colours. The word is generally used in connection with embroidery only, and never figuratively. Ex.: *Une broderie nuée est une broderie multicolore à teintes nuancées.*

879.

Neuf, *adj.* New, i.e. never having been used. Ex.: *Un complet neuf.*
Nouveau, *adj.* New, i.e. not previously seen or known. (In this sense *nouveau* is placed after the noun.) Ex.: *Un livre nouveau.*
New, meaning "fresh" or "another". (Placed before the noun when used in this sense.) Ex.: *Mettre une nouvelle robe.*
Tendre, *adj.* New with reference to bread.

880.

Odeur, *n.f.* Smell, pleasant or otherwise, as given off by any body. Odour. Ex.: *L'odeur du goudron est saine.*
Odorat, *n.m.* Smell, i.e. the sense of smell. Ex.: *Avoir l'odorat fin.*
Senteur, *n.f.* Smell (of a pleasant or agreeable nature only). Refers more to the effect on one's sense of smell. Ex.: *La senteur de la rose est très agréable.*

881.

Odorant, Odoriférant, *adj. Odorant* (odorous) denotes the emission of an odour, pleasant or otherwise. Ex.: *Fleur odorante. Quartier mal odorant. Odoriférant* (odoriferous) implies a strong or penetrating pleasant smell. Ex.: *L'encens est odoriférant.*

882.

Obédience, *n.f.* Obedience in the sense of submission to (papal) authority. Only used in connection with ecclesiastical matters. Ex.: *Ambassadeur d'obédience.*
Obéissance, *n.f.* General term for "obedience". Ex.: *L'enfant doit obéissance à ses parents.*

883.

Obligeant, *adj.* Obliging. Refers more to the manner of showing one's willingness to be helpful or render service. Ex.: *Manières obligeantes. Ton obligeant.*
Serviable, *adj.* Obliging, i.e. willing to render service or be helpful. Ex.: *Homme serviable.*

884.

Obliger à, Obliger de, Contraindre à, Contraindre de, Forcer à, Forcer de, *v.t.* The use of *à* with these verbs implies either strict necessity or a moral obligation, constraint, etc. *De* is only used when the action is considered from the point of view of its result. Ex.: *C'est une dette que mon honneur m'oblige à payer. Elle est obligée de se reposer par ces grandes chaleurs. Le respect me force à me taire, la reconnaissance m'y oblige, l'autorité m'y contraint. L'ennemi a été forcé de se retirer devant la supériorité de notre artillerie.*

885.

Observance, *n.f.* The result of keeping or complying faithfully with any rule, law, etc. Ex.: *L'observance de la loi.*
Observance as a rule or practice. Ex.: *L'observance d'une vie simple.*
Observation, *n.f.* The act of observing or complying with any rule or law. Ex.: *Manque d'observation d'un règlement.*

886.

Oiseux, *adj.* Idle, i.e. accustomed to doing nothing.
Oisif, *adj.* Idle in the sense of being unoccupied. Also used with reference to things. Ex.: *Laisser sa plume oisive.*

887.

Ombrager, *v.t.* To shade in the sense of covering or screening from light or heat. Ex.: *Un grand chapeau ombrageait son visage.*
Ombrer, *v.t.* To shade, i.e. to fill in the dark portions of any drawing, etc. Ex.: *Ombrer un dessin.*

888.

Ombrelle, *n.f.,* **Parasol,** *n.m.* An *ombrelle* is a small fancy sunshade for ladies. *Parasol* refers to the larger and plainer article.

889.

On, Ils, *pron.* *On* means "they" in an indefinite sense and refers to nobody in particular (only used in the singular). Ex.: *On dit qu'il ne se remettra plus. Ils* denotes certain specific persons or things. Ex.: *Je n'aime pas ses amis; ils ne m'inspirent aucune confiance.*

890.

Œillade, *n.f.* Furtive glance cast for the purpose of attracting attention or intimating. Ogle. Ex.: *Elle me fit une œillade significative.*
Coup d'œil, *n.m.* Hasty or rapid glance. Ex.: *Il jeta un coup d'œil sur le tableau.*
Regard, *n.m.* Glance or look, more sustained than a *coup d'œil.* Ex.: *Je rencontrai son regard furieux.*

891.

Occident, Ouest, Couchant, *n.m.* Occident, ouest, and couchant are the antonyms of orient, est and levant respectively. (See Group 803.)

892.

S'occuper à, *v.r.* To be occupied with or engaged in. Ex. : *Il s'occupe à instruire son fils.*
S'occuper de, *v.r.* To devote one's attention to. To concern oneself with. The term does not necessarily denote whole-time occupation and is generally followed by a noun or pronoun. Ex. : *Il s'occupe de l'instruction de son fils.*

893.

Ondée, *n.f.* Sudden shower of short duration.
Averse, *n.f.* Sudden and heavy shower. Downpour.
Giboulée, *n.f.* Sudden shower of short duration, often accompanied by hail or snow. *Les giboulées de Mars* is the French rendering of "April showers".

894.

On ne saurait, On ne peut, *colloq.* On ne saurait denotes the physical impossibility of doing anything. On ne peut refers to the impossibility of the thing itself. Ex. : *On ne saurait vous accorder l'autorisation demandée. On ne peut trouver aucune preuve de sa culpabilité.*

895.

Ordonner, *v.t.* To order, i.e. to give instructions or an order. To command. Ex. : *Il m'ordonna de revenir.*
Commander, *v.t.* To order goods, material, etc., for delivery. Ex. : *Commander ferme.*

896.

Organe, *n.m.* Organ, i.e. a part of any living body, intended for performing a special or vital operation. Ex. : *L'organe de l'ouïe.* Organ in the sense of a means or instrument by which anything is done. Ex. : *Ce journal est l'organe du parti socialiste.*
Orgue, *n.m.* Organ, i.e. the most harmonious and complicated of wind instruments. (*N.B.—Orgue* is feminine in the plural.)

897.

Orientation, *n.f.* The determining of a position with regard to the cardinal points. Ex. : *L'orientation peut se faire à l'aide des astres.*
Orientement, *n.m.* The position of any building with regard to the cardinal points. The word is generally reserved for use in connection with churches or cathedrals.

898.

Ondoiement, Baptême, *n.m.* Baptême is the general term for "baptism" or "christening". An *ondoiement* is a private christening devoid of any ceremony.

899.

Original, *adj.* Original, i.e. not a subsequent copy. First in order. Ex. : *Tableau original. Copie originale d'un document.*
Original in the sense of novel or out of the ordinary. Ex. : *Votre idée est très originale.*
Originel, *adj.* Original, i.e. going back to the source or origin. Ex. : *Péché originel.*

900.

Ordinairement, *adv.* Ordinarily. Denotes frequency whence a habit or custom. Ex. : *Il vient nous voir ordinairement toutes les semaines.*
D'ordinaire, *adv. exp.* Generally. Usually. Marks the particular habit or custom. Ex. : *On croit d'ordinaire que le vapeur a sombré.*
À l'ordinaire, Comme d'habitude, *adv. exp.* As usual. In the usual manner. Ex. : *Vous viendrez ce soir comme à l'ordinaire.*
Pour l'ordinaire, *adv. exp.* Ordinarily. Usually. Denotes a definitely established custom.

901.

Orthographier, *v.t.* To spell when writing.
Épeler, *v.t.* To spell aloud. To name the letters of a word.

902.

Orner, *v.t.* To decorate, i.e. to add that which ornaments or improves the appearance. To ornament. Ex. : *Ces tapisseries ornent bien votre salon.* Also used figuratively. Ex. : *Discours orné.*
Parer, *v.t.* To decorate for the purpose of display, ceremony, etc. To deck. Ex. : *Les jardins publics étaient parés pour la fête.* Also used figuratively. Ex. : *Parer son style.*
Décorer, *v.t.* To decorate suitably or in a fitting manner. Ex. : *Décorer un autel.*
Pavoiser, *v.t.* To decorate with flags. Ex. : *La ville était pavoisée à l'occasion de la visite du roi.*

903.

Os, Ossements, *n.m.* *Os* is used to indicate bones considered either as forming part of a body or from the point of view of their use. *Ossements* denotes a collection of loose bones devoid of any flesh. Ex. : *Le fémur est le plus grand de tous les os du corps humain. Le cercueil ne contenait que des ossements.*

904.

Oui, Si, *adv.* *Oui* is used after a question asked affirmatively, *si* in reply to a question containing a negative. Ex. : *Êtes vous sûr de l'avoir vu ? Oui. N'êtes-vous pas en retard ? Si, nous n'avions pas l'heure.*

905.

Ourdir, *v.t.* To commence preparing or arranging a plot.
Tramer, *v.t.* To complete all necessary arrangements for carrying out a plot.
Machiner, *v.t.* To plot. Denotes extreme treachery or perfidiousness.

Conspirer, *v.t.* To conspire, generally against public or government affairs.
Conjurer, *v.t.* To plot or conspire. Denotes that the conspirators are under oath not to betray their cause.
Comploter, *v.t.* General term meaning "to plot".

906.

Outrageant, Outrageux, *adj.* *Outrageant* means actually outraging. *Outrageux* denotes the character of being outrageous.

907.

Éclat, *n.m.* General term for a chip, fragment or splinter of wood stone, glass, etc.
Écharde, *n.m.* Splinter or small pointed piece of wood.
Esquille, *n.f.* Splinter or small broken piece of bone.

908.

Au moins, Du moins, *adv. exp.* *Au moins* denotes the least which should be done for the same purpose and corresponds to "At all events" or "At any rate". *Du moins* has practically the same meaning as "however", "nevertheless", and marks an equivalent. Ex. : *Au moins donnez-nous de vos nouvelles. Il est tard, du moins pourrons-nous faire acte de présence à la réunion.*

909.

Moins de, Moins que, *adv.* *Moins de* is used to denote an inferiority expressed by a number. *Moins que* indicates the result of a comparison. Ex. : *Il a cultivé moins de cinquante hectares cette année et c'est encore moins que l'année dernière.*

910.

Pacage, *n.m.* Natural pasture land, reserved as such, to which cattle are brought to graze. Ex. : *Droit de pacage.*
Pâtis, *n.m.* A piece of uncultivated land, such as a common, capable of being used for grazing purposes.
Pâturage, *n.m.* Field or piece of land specially prepared and maintained for grazing. Pasturage.
Pâture, *n.f.* Any piece of land affording limited facilities for grazing. Pasture.

911.

Palan, *n.m.* Lifting tackle consisting of two or more separate blocks each having all its pulleys on the same axis.
Moufle, *n.f.* Block and fall or pair of pulley blocks.

912.

Paletot, *n.m.* A light loose overcoat. Paletot.
Pardessus, *n.m.* General term for the civil overcoat.
Capote, *n.f.* Military great-coat or overcoat.
Surtout, *n.m.* Close-fitting frock-coat or overcoat. Surtout.
Pélisse, *n.f.* Gentleman's fur or fur-lined overcoat.

913.

Palier, Coussinet, Roulement, *n.m.* A *palier* is a bearing as a whole comprising a *coussinet* which is the part in contact with the revolving shaft, or a *roulement*, i.e. a ball or roller bearing.

914.

Se pâmer, *v.r.* To be overcome or ready to faint as a result of emotion, etc. Ex. : *Se pâmer de peur, de joie.*

S'évanouir, *v.r.* To faint, swoon or lose consciousness. Ex. : *Il s'est évanoui à la vue de son père écrasé.*

915.

Plume, *n.f.*, **Panache,** *n.m.* *Plume* is the general term for "feather." A *panache* is a plume or bunch of feathers either worn as a head-dress or employed for decorative purposes.

916.

Par, De, *prep.* "By" after a past participle is generally translated by *par* when denoting action, and by *de* to indicate feeling or sentiment. Ex. : *Il a tout fait par ses propres moyens. Ce vieux curé est très aimé de tous ses paroissiens.*

917.

Par, Pour, *prep.* *Par*, meaning "for", is used after such words as *connu, renommé, célèbre*, etc., instead of *pour* which is the general term. Ex. : *Cet homme est connu par son intransigeance. Voici une lettre pour vous.* (N.B.—An expression such as "France is renowned for its wines" is, however, translated *La France est renommée pour ses vins.*)

918.

Paravent, *n.m.* Portable screen, generally folded, for protection against draughts.

Écran, *n.m.* Portable screen placed before a fire as a protection against excessive heat.

Screen such as used for cinematographic or similar purposes.

Pare-étincelles, *n.m.* Portable screen placed before a fire for arresting sparks.

Pare-brise, *n.m.* Wind screen of a motor-car.

919.

Parcourir, Compulser, *v.t.* *Parcourir* means "to read hurriedly" or "glance through". *Compulser* denotes a more thorough or attentive examination of any document, book, etc. Ex. : *Il s'arrêta un moment pour parcourir la proclamation. Laissez-moi le temps de compulser tous ces documents.*

920.

Parcourir, Visiter, *v.t.* *Visiter* is the general term meaning "to visit". Ex.: *Visiter un pays, un ami.* *Parcourir* means "to visit" in the sense of going all over. Ex. : *De nombreux touristes s'efforcent de parcourir Paris en quelques jours.*

921.

Parcours, *n.m.* The course followed by any river, stream, etc. Ex.: *Le parcours de la Loire est plus long que celui de la Seine.*
Cours, *n.m.* The course of any river, stream, etc., with reference to its flow or direction. Ex.: *Le cours du Rhône est très rapide par endroits.*

922.

Parfois, Quelquefois, *adv.* These two words are used indifferently for "sometimes". *Parfois*, however, denotes greater frequency and corresponds more strictly to "at times" or "on occasions". Ex.: *Elle vient nous voir quelquefois. Il nous ennuie parfois avec ses histoires.*

923.

Parmi, Entre, *prep.* Among or amongst. *Parmi* marks a distinction within any group or collection whereas *entre* does not. Ex.: *Laissez-moi prendre place parmi vous. Lequel d'entre vous veut m'aider ?*

924.

Parquet, Plancher, Étage, Carrelage, Dallage, *n.m.* A *parquet* is a floor in oak or some other hard wood usually laid to form a special design. Ex.: *Parquet en chêne ciré.* A *plancher* is an ordinary plank floor in deal or similar wood and without any artistic element. Ex.: *Le plancher d'un baraquement.* The word also denotes the timber on which a floor is laid. An *étage* is a floor in the sense of a storey. Ex.: *Maison de quatre étages. Carrelage* and *dallage* refer exclusively to tiled floors, the tiles of a *dallage* being much larger than those of a *carrelage*.

925.

Part, *n.f.* Part in the sense of "share". Denotes what is due. Ex.: *Il n'a pas encore reçu sa part.* Also used figuratively. Ex.: *Pour ma part.*
Partie, *n.f.* A part of anything with respect to, and detached from, the whole. Ex.: *Ils se sont chargés d'une partie des frais.*
Portion, *n.f.* Part or portion. Calls to mind the quantity or amount received. Ex.: *Les portions d'un héritage.*

926.

Parti, *n.m.* Party, i.e. a group or association of persons united for political or other purposes. Ex.: *Le parti socialiste.*
Partie, *n.f.* Party in the sense of a gathering for the purpose of pleasure, recreation, etc. Ex.: *Partie de plaisir, de chasse.*
Each of the contending parties in a lawsuit. Ex.: *Partie plaignante.*
Each of the parties to any agreement, contract, etc. Ex.: *Les parties contractantes.*

927.

Parvenir, *v.i.* To succeed in the sense of managing. Implies an effort. Ex. : *Il est parvenu à décrocher le tableau.*
Arriver, *v.i.* To succeed, i.e. to reach or attain. Ex. : *Avec de la patience on arrive à tout.*
Réussir, *v.i.* To succeed or accomplish what is attempted. Ex. : *L'expérience ne réussit pas.*
Succéder, *v.i.* To succeed in the sense of following in order or taking the place of. Ex. : *Le Roi Edouard VII succéda à sa mère la Reine Victoria. La nuit succède au jour.*

928.

Passer, *v.i.* To pass in the sense of elapsing or going by. Merely denotes relative short duration. Ex. : *Le temps passe.*
Se passer, *v.r.* To pass away or draw to an end. Implies a decline, decrease, etc. Ex. : *La belle saison se passe.*

929.

Être passé, Avoir passé, *v.i.* *Passer* is conjugated with *avoir* to denote the act of passing, and with *être* to express the state. Ex. : *Le facteur n'est pas encore passé ; hier il a passé sans rien nous apporter.*

930.

Passereau, *n.m.* A bird of the sparrow family.
Moineau, *n.m.* The common sparrow.

931.

Pasteur, *n.m.* Shepherd. The word is rarely employed nowadays in its proper sense except with reference to ancient races. Used in a figurative sense *pasteur* often denotes a person having the cure of souls. Ex. : *Le Bon Pasteur.*
Pâtre, *n.m.* Shepherd or herdsman. Applies to a person in charge of domestic animals of any description (cows, oxen, sheep, etc.).
Berger, *n.m.* Only refers, strictly speaking, to those in charge of sheep or goats.

932.

Patelin, Patelineur, Papelard, *n.m.* A *patelin* is a wheedler by nature. A *patelineur* is a person who wheedles on occasions. A *papelard* is a hypocrite who wheedles beneath a sanctimonious air.

933.

Pâtir, *v.i.*, **Souffrir, Subir,** *v.t.* *Souffrir* is the general term meaning "to suffer" either physically or morally. *Pâtir* is usually employed in an absolute sense and implies want, privation, etc., on the part of the sufferer. Ex. : *Souffrir la faim. Les pauvres pâtissent en hiver.* *Subir* means "to suffer" in the sense of enduring or undergoing. Ex. : *Subir la mort.*

934.

Pavillon, Drapeau, *n.m.* *Drapeau* is the general term for a flag. Ex. : *Drapeau national. Drapeau rouge.* A *pavillon* is a naval flag used either for signalling or to indicate the nationality of the ship on which flown. Ex. : *Pavillon de commandement. Hisser un pavillon.*

935.

Paye, *n.f.* Payment made regularly, especially in the army or navy. Paying out. Ex. : *Jour de paye.*
Paiement, *n.m.* Any individual or incidental payment. Ex. : *Le paiement d'une dette.*
Solde, *n.f.* Pay, i.e. payment received for services rendered. The term is especially used in connection with military pay. Ex. : *Officier à la demi-solde.*
Pay in the sense of service. Ex. : *Être à la solde de quelqu'un.*

936.

Peigne, Démêloir, *n.m.* A *peigne* is a comb worn as an ornament. A *démêloir* is the article actually used for combing or arranging the hair.

937.

Pédant, *adj.* Pedantic with reference to persons. Ex. : *Un air pédant.*
Pédantesque, *adj.* Pedantic concerning language or style. Ex. : *Citations pédantesques.*

938.

Peindre, *v.t.* To paint generally, either as an artist or a painter. Ex. : *Peindre un tableau, une maison.*
Peinturer, *v.t.* To colour-paint any surface. Ex. : *Peinturer un mur.*
Peinturlurer, *v.t.* To paint badly, i.e. with unsuitable or vivid colours. To daub. Ex. : *Maison peinturlurée.*

939.

Penser à, *v.i.* To think of or about in the sense of calling to mind or memory. Ex. : *Je pense à mon frère qui est parti à la guerre. A quoi pensez-vous ?*
Penser de, *v.i.* To think of or about, i.e. to have an idea or opinion about anything or anybody. Ex. : *Que pensez-vous de son projet ?*

940.

Penser, *v.i.* and *v.t.* General term meaning "to think". (See Group 939.)
Rêver à, *v.i.* To think idly or abstractedly. To muse. Ex. : *Elle rêvait au temps heureux des vacances.* (*Rêver de* means "to dream".)
Songer, *v.i.* To think of or about in the sense of bearing in mind or devoting one's attention to. Ex. : *Songez au danger qui vous menace.*

941.

Pendant que, *conj. exp.* Whilst or while, i.e. during the time that. Denotes simultaneity of two events. Ex.: *Il écoutait attentivement pendant qu'on lisait le rapport.*
Tandis que, *conj. exp.* Whilst, meaning "whereas". Ex.: *Les uns réclamaient sa mort tandis que les autres étaient enclins à la clémence.*

942.

Pensée, *n.f.* Any individual thought. Denotes the result of thinking. Ex.: *N'avoir que de bonnes pensées.*
Penser, *n.m.* The way or faculty of thinking. Also used as a poetic form of *pensée.*

943.

Périr, *v.i.* To perish, i.e. to come to a violent or unnatural end. To be destroyed. Ex.: *Périr par le feu.*
Dépérir, *v.i.* To perish in the sense of decaying or wasting away. Denotes gradual loss or destruction. Ex.: *Plante qui dépérit.*

944.

Persan, Persique, Perse, *adj.* *Persan* refers to modern Persia. *Persique* is only used in connection with ancient Persia. Ex.: *La langue persane. L'architecture persique.* *Perse* refers to the ancient Persians. Ex.: *Dynastie perse.* (N.B.—"The Persian Gulf" is translated *Le Golfe Persique.*)

945.

Pesage, *n.m.* The act of weighing. Ex.: *Appareil de pesage.*
Pesée, *n.f.* Weighing. Refers either to the act of weighing or to its result. Ex.: *Faire la pesée d'une marchandise. Une pesée de dix tonnes.*

946.

Picoter, *v.t.* To cause a smarting or tingling sensation. Ex.: *Cette fumée me picote les yeux.*
Piquer, *v.t.* To be piquant, burning or sharp to the taste. Ex.: *Cette sauce pique fort.*
To prick or penetrate slightly. Ex.: *Elle s'est piquée en cueillant des fleurs.*
To sting or bite with reference to animals, insects, etc. Ex.: *Une guêpe l'a piquée au bras.*

947.

Pieuvre, *n.f.*, **Poulpe,** *n.m.* *Pieuvre* is the name by which certain varieties of octopus are commonly known. *Poulpe* is the generic term.

948.

Pinceau, Blaireau, *n.m.*, **Brosse,** *n.f.* *Brosse* is the general term for a brush. A *pinceau* is a brush with a long handle such as used by painters. A *blaireau* is a shaving brush, the better-class article being made from the hair of the *blaireau* or badger.

949.

Plaisir, *n.m.* Pleasure. Gratification of the mind or of the senses. Ex.: *Quel plaisir de vous revoir !*

Plaisance, *n.f.* Pleasure, i.e. for the purpose of affording pleasure. Only used nowadays in the expression *de plaisance*. Ex.: *Bateau de plaisance.*

950.

Plant, *n.m.*, **Plante,** *n.f.* *Plante* is the general term for a plant. A *plant* is a young plant before being definitely planted anywhere.

951.

Plaque, *n.f.* Small plate of iron or other metal, marble, etc., for any purpose. Ex.: *Une plaque commemorative. Plaque indicatrice.* Photographic plate (unexposed).

Assiette, *n.f.* The plate used for meals.

Argenterie, *n.f.* Silver plate.

Tôle, *n.f.* Plate- or sheet-iron. Ex.: *Tôle galvanisée.*

Cliché, *n.m.* Photographic plate (developed) or negative.

Planche, *n.f.* An engraved plate used for printing. Also the print or engraving obtained therefrom.

952.

Plein, *adj.* Full. Merely denotes the state. Ex.: *Un panier plein de fruits.*
Full, i.e. containing a great quantity. Ex.: *Musée plein de visiteurs.*

Rempli, *adj.* Full. Filled. Refers more to the action of filling. Ex.: *Votre version est remplie de fautes.*

Complet, *adj.* Full, i.e. filled to its proper capacity. Ex.: *Tramway complet.*

Comble, *adj.* Full, i.e. incapable of holding any more. Ex.: *Salle comble.*

953.

Poêle, *n.m.* Closed ornamental stove for heating purposes only.

Foyer, *n.m.* Open fireplace.

Fourneau, *n.m.* Small stove for cooking purposes. Ex.: *Fourneau de cuisine.*

Cuisinière, *n.f.* Large kitchen stove or range.

954.

Point du jour, *n.m.* The beginning or break of day. Daybreak.

Pointe du jour, *n.f.* The first glimmer of dawn visible in the heavens. Peep of day.

955.

Poitrail, *n.m.* The chest of a horse.

Poitrine, *n.f.* The human chest or breast.

Gorge, *n.f.* The breast (i.e. the bosom) of a woman.

956.

Police, *n.f.* Policy or contract of, e.g., insurance. Ex. : *Police d'assurance.*
Politique, *n.f.* Policy, i.e. the manner of regulating or guiding public or private affairs. Ex. : *La politique du gouvernement a été sévèrement critiquée.*

957.

Pont levant, *n.m.* Lifting bridge over a canal or river.
Pont-levis, *n.m.* Drawbridge such as that built over a moat at the entrance to a fort, etc.

958.

Porte, Portière, *n.f.* *Porte* is the general term. A *portière* is a railway or other carriage door.

959.

Poster, *v.t.* To post or place for observation, defence, etc. Ex. : *Poster une sentinelle.*
Aposter, *v.t.* To post or place for a criminal or discreditable purpose. Ex. : *Aposter un assassin, un espion.*

960.

Potelé, *adj.* Plump. Only used in connection with human beings, especially children. Ex. : *Bras potelé.*
Dodu, *adj.* Plump. Refers, strictly speaking, to animals, but also used in connection with persons. Ex. : *Une dinde dodue. Des joues dodues.*

961.

Potiron, *n.m.* The large pumpkin, shaped like an apple, used for making soup.
Citrouille, *n.f.* Elongated edible pumpkin.

962.

Pour, *prep.*, **Pour que, Afin de, Afin que,** *conj.* *Pour* and *pour que* denote a more general or less precise purpose than that implied by *afin de* and *afin que.* Ex. : *Elle a dit cela pour rire. J'ai fait cela afin que vous soyez tranquille.* (N.B.—*Pour* and *afin de* are invariably followed by an infinitive ; after *afin que* and *pour que* the subjunctive mood is required.)

963.

Poussière, *n.f.*, **Poussier,** *n.m.* *Poussière* is the general term for "dust". Ex. : *Couvert de poussière.* *Poussier* is used with reference to matter which has been reduced to dust. Ex. : *Poussier de charbon, de thé.*

964.

Proche, Prochain, *adj.* *Proche* and *prochain* may both refer either to time or place. The latter, however, denotes a greater proximity. Ex. : *C'est un très proche parent. Je vous écrirai par un prochain courrier.*

965.

Peuplade, Tribu, *n.f.* A *peuplade* is a tribe or horde lacking organization or civilization. Ex. : *Les peuplades de l'Afrique.* *Tribu* refers to a distinct class or division of people under one chief and having the same origin. Ex. : *Les douze Tribus d'Israël.*

966.

Pilotage, Lamanage, *n.m.* *Pilotage* is the general term for "piloting", irrespective of locality. *Lamanage* refers only to coast, harbour or port piloting by local experts (*lamaneurs*).

967.

Prétendre, *v.i.* To pretend in the sense of laying claim to. Ex. : *Prétendre à un héritage.*
Prétexter, *v.t.* To pretend, i.e. to give as a pretext. Ex. : *Pour partir il pretexta une affaire urgente.*

968.

Procès, *n.m.* Case in the sense of a trial or lawsuit. Refers to the actual proceedings themselves. Ex. : *Procès civil, criminel.*
Cause, *n.f.* Legal case or trial, considered as a whole. Ex. : *Remettre une cause à quinzaine.*
Cas, *n.m.* Case in the sense of event, circumstance or happening. Ex. : *En cas de besoin.*
Affaire, *n.m.* Familiar term for a case of a legal or other nature. Affair. Ex. : *L'affaire Dreyfus.*

969.

Prône, Sermon, *n.m.* *Sermon* is the general term for "sermon". *Prône* refers to the parochial sermon preached on Sundays at the chief service, usually in the form of a lecture or instruction. Homily.

970.

Promenade, *n.f.*, **Promenoir,** *n.m.* *Promenade* refers either to a walk for recreative purposes or to the place where such exercise is taken. A *promenoir* is a space reserved for walking at a concert, etc.

971.

Propre à, Propre pour, *adj.* *Propre à,* meaning "fit for", denotes what is necessary for any general purpose. *Propre pour* marks the quality or conditions required for a special purpose. Ex. : *C'est un propre à rien. Cette machine n'est guère propre pour l'usage auquel vous la destinez.*

972.

Provisoire, Provisionnel, *adj.,* **Par provision,** *adv. exp.* *Provisoire* is the general term meaning "provisional" or "temporary". Ex. : *Arrangement provisoire.* *Provisionnel* is used in connection with matters of an official nature. Ex. : *Règlement provisionnel. Par provision* is employed in legal phraseology. Ex. : *Jugement par provision.*

973.

Pucelle, *n.f.* A virgin. Ex. : *La Pucelle de France.*
Demoiselle, *n.f.* A young unmarried lady.
Mademoiselle, *n.f.* The term employed when addressing a young lady as "Miss" (*Mlle* is the abbreviated form). Ex. : *Mademoiselle une telle.*

974.

Puisque, *conj.* Since, in the sense of "seeing that". Ex. : *Partez donc, puisque vous le voulez.*
Depuis, *adv.* Since, i.e. from the time that. Ex. : *Il est toujours malade depuis qu'il est parti à Paris.*

975.

Puits, *n.m.*, **Mine, Fosse,** *n.f. Mine* corresponds to "mine" in English and denotes the position, in the earth, of any mineral deposit. A *puits* is the pit or excavation made for working such deposit. *Fosse* is the term employed in the north of France for a *puits*.

976.

Quand, *adv.* When. Denotes the time or moment. Ex. : *Venez quand vous voudrez. Quand est-il parti ?*
Lorsque, *conj.* When. Refers more to the occasion or circumstance. (*N.B.*—Unlike *quand*, *lorsque* cannot be used interrogatively.) Ex. : *Lorsque nous serons seuls je vous apprendrai une grande nouvelle.*
Que, *conj.* When. Recalls some specific event or circumstance previously referred to. Ex. : *Elle était à peine sortie que la pluie tomba.*
Où, *conj.* When. Denotes the time or occasion and is preceded by a noun. Ex. : *Je me souviens du temps où elle aimait nous rendre visite.*
Lors de, *prep. exp.* When, meaning "at the time of". The expression is invariably followed by a noun. Ex. : *Il n'avait que trente ans lors de sa mort.*

977.

Quant à, *prep. exp.* As for. As to. As far as concerns. Ex. *Quant à lui il n'a pas de choix. Quant à cela.*
Pour, *prep.* In the opinion of. Ex. : *Pour moi, il ne réussira pas.*

978.

Quarante, *adj.* Forty (exactly).
Quarantaine, *n.f.* About or approximately forty. Ex. : *Envoyer une quarantaine de faire-part.*
The age of forty. Ex. : *Friser la quarantaine.*

979.

Quinte, Toux, *n.f. Toux* is the general term for a cough. A *quinte* is a fit of coughing.

980.

Quinze, *adj.* Fifteen (exactly).
Quinzaine, *n.f.* About or approximately fifteen. (The expression *quinzaine de jours* is commonly used to denote a fortnight.) Ex. : *Remettre une affaire à quinzaine.*

981.

Quoique, Bien que, *conj.* *Quoique* and *bien que* are synonymous and differ only from a grammatical point of view. *Bien que* is invariably followed by a verb used in the subjunctive mood, whereas *quoique* may precede a verb (subjunctive mood), adverb or adjective. Ex. : *Nous partirons, bien que le temps ne soit pas propice. Quoique agé, il est encore agile.*

982.

Radiant, *adj.* Radiant, i.e. emitting rays of light or heat. Ex. : *Chaleur radiante.*
Radieux, *adj.* Radiant in the sense of being brilliant with light. Ex. : *Soleil radieux.*
Radiant in a figurative sense, i.e. beaming. Ex. : *Visage radieux.*
Rayonnant, *adj.* Radiating with light or brilliance. Ex. : *Rayonnant de lumière.*
Beaming, with reference to persons. Ex. : *Être rayonnant de joie.*

983.

Raffiner, *v.t.* To refine (sugar, oil, etc.).
Affiner, *v.t.* To refine metals.

984.

Raison, *n.f.* Right, in the sense of being correct. Ex. : *Vous avez raison.*
Droit, *n.m.* Right, i.e. that to which one has a just claim. Ex. : *Jouir de ses droits. Droits civils.*
Droite, *n.f.* The right-hand side of a road, etc. Ex. : *Tenir la droite.*

985.

Râle, Râlement, *n.m.* A *râle* is the actual noise caused by the spasmodic breathing of a person about to die. Ex. : *Le râle de la mort. Râlement* denotes the fit or attack which occasions a *râle*.

986.

Ramoner, Balayer, *v.t.* *Balayer* is the general term meaning "to sweep", *Ramoner* only being used with reference to chimneys.

987.

Rancidité, *n.f.* The quality of being rank or rancid. Rancidity.
Rancissure, *n.f.* The actual rankness existing in any matter.
Rancissement, *n.m.* The act of becoming rank or rancid.

[146]

988.

Rang, *n.m.* Rank, i.e. grade, degree or class, social or otherwise. Ex.: *Les rangs de la société. Son père a rang* (or *a le grade*) *de colonel.*
Row or line, considered in itself, of persons or things. Ex.: *Sortir des rangs. Réserver une place au premier rang.*
Rank, in the sense of class or category. Ex.: *Pasteur est mis au rang des bienfaiteurs de l'humanité.*
Rangée, *n.f.* Row or line. *Rangée* calls to mind the things composing a row and is used with a *complément.* Ex.: *Rangée de maisons, d'arbres.* (N.B.—*Rang* is the word used, in this sense, to denote a row of persons. Ex.: *Un rang de soldats.*)

989.

Raccommoder, *v.t.* General term meaning "to mend" Ex.: *Raccommoder une chaise, un vêtement, des bas.*
Rapiécer, *v.t.* To mend clothing by adding a piece or pieces. Ex.: *Rapiécer un pantalon.*
Rapetasser, *v.t.* To mend clothing roughly or clumsily.
Rapiéceter, *v.t.* To mend clothing by means of numerous small pieces.
Ravauder, *v.t.* To mend clothing roughly by pulling together with a needle. To botch.

990.

Se rappeler, Se souvenir, *v.r.* These terms have precisely the same meaning. *Se rappeler* takes a *complément direct* or is followed by *que,* whereas *se souvenir* can only be used with *de.* Ex.: *Autant que je puis me le rappeler. Je me rappelle qu'il a fait mauvais temps ce jour-là. Je ne me souviens pas de son nom. Je m'en souviens.*

991.

Rassasier, *v.t.* To completely satisfy the senses or the appetites. To satiate. Ex.: *Rassasier sa faim.*
Assouvir, *v.t.* To gratify any abnormal or excessive appetite, etc. To glut. Ex.: *Assouvir sa haine, sa cupidité.*

992.

Redevable, Débiteur, *adj.* *Redevable,* meaning "debtor" or "owing", refers to the debtor; *débiteur* refers to the debt and is generally confined to accountancy. Ex.: *Il m'est redevable d'une assez forte somme. Compte débiteur.*

993.

Rêche, *adj.* Rough to the taste or touch. Ex.: *Étoffe, vin rêche.*
Rude, *adj.* Rough in the sense of being hard. Ex.: *Un rude travail.*
Raboteux, *adj.* Rough, i.e. uneven with reference to surfaces. Ex.: *Chemin raboteux.*
Âpre, *adj.* Rough or sharp to the taste. Ex.: *Certains fruits sont âpres au goût.*

Brut, *adj.* Rough in the sense of being unfinished. Ex.: *Diamant brut.*

Brusque, *adj.* Rough or abrupt with reference to a person's manners. Ex.: *Caractère brusque.*

994.

Rechute, *n.f.* Relapse with reference to illness or from a moral point of view.

Récidive, *n.f.* Legal term for a repetition of the same offence, crime, etc. Second offence. Ex.: *En cas de récidive.*

995.

Réclamer, *v.t.* To claim or lay claim to, from any motive. Ex.: *Réclamer des dommages-intérêts.*

Revendiquer, *v.t.* To claim that to which one has a right. Generally implies legal action. Ex.: *Auteur qui revendique ses droits.*

996.

Renouvellement, *n.m.*, **Reconduction,** *n.f. Renouvellement* is the general term for "renewal". Ex.: *Renouvellement d'un abonnement.* *Reconduction* refers to the renewal of a lease and is only employed in the expressions *reconduction expresse, tacite reconduction.*

997.

Recouvrer, *v.t.* To recover in the sense of regaining. Ex.: *Recouvrer la santé. Recouvrer le montant d'une dette.*

Recouvrir, *v.t.* To recover, i.e. to cover again. Ex.: *Recouvrir un livre.*

Se remettre, Se rétablir, *v.r.* To recover from the effects of illness, an accident, etc. Ex.: *On dit qu'il ne s'en remettra pas.*

Revenir, Revenir à soi, *v.i.* To recover (one's senses). To come to.

998.

Se produire, *v. imp.* To happen. Marks the manner or circumstances of any event. Ex.: *Il s'est produit un évènement qui a changé toute sa vie.*

Se passer, *v. imp.* To happen. Indicates the accomplishment. Ex.: *Il s'est passé bien des choses à mon insu.*

Arriver, *v. imp.* To happen.. Merely denotes the happening or taking place of any event. Ex.: *Il lui est arrivé un grave accident.*

Advenir, *v. imp.* To happen or befall. Implies that the event in question is subsequent to another. The term is not generally met with in everyday conversation, being more suited to an elevated style of expression. Ex.: *Fais ce que dois ; advienne que pourra.*

Venir à, *v.i.* To happen (by chance). Ex.: *S'il venait à tomber malade, il n'aurait personne pour le soigner.* (*N.B.*—Expressions such as "Do you happen to . . ." are rendered in French by simply using the verb which follows in the conditional. Ex.: *Auriez-vous du feu s'il vous plaît ?*)

FRENCH SYNONYMS 999-1005

999.

Recueil, *n.m.,* **Collection,** *n.f.* A *recueil* is a collection of, e.g., laws, poems, music, prints, etc., bound together, each piece having some connection or relationship with the others. Ex.: *Recueil de lois, de discours.* *Collection* merely denotes an assembled quantity of things of a like nature. Ex.: *Collection de tableaux, de timbres-poste.*

1000.

Réfléchir, Refléter. *Réfléchir* means "to reflect" with reference to heat, light, etc., also "to reflect" in the sense of pondering or thinking over. *Refléter* means to reflect by throwing back or reproducing either physically or figuratively. Ex.: *Les miroirs réfléchissent la lumière et reflètent les images. Agir sans réfléchir. Le visage reflète souvent les pensées.*

1001.

Règne, *n.m.* Kingdom from the point of view of Natural History. Ex.: *Le règne animal.*
Royaume, *n.m.* Kingdom, i.e. the territory governed by a king or queen. Ex.: *Le royaume d'Angleterre.*

1002.

Rein, *n.m.* The human kidney.
Rognon, *n.m.* An animal's kidney, especially any variety considered as eatable. Ex.: *Rognons de bœuf, de mouton.*

1003.

Réformateur, *adj.* Reforming or tending to reform. Ex.: *Esprit réformateur.*
Réformatoire, *adj.* Concerning the reformation of morals, habits, discipline, etc. Ex.: *Commission réformatoire.*

1004.

Refuser, *v.t.* To refuse in the sense of not accepting. Ex.: *Refuser une offre.*
To refuse, i.e. not to grant, give, authorize, etc. Ex.: *Refuser son consentement.*
(*N.B.—Refuser* takes *de* when followed by a verb. Ex.: *Il refuse de nous écouter.*)
Se refuser à, *v.r.* To refuse, in the sense of resisting or objecting to. Ex.: *Il se refuse à livrer son secret.*

1005.

Recto, Verso, Endroit, Envers, Avers, Revers, *n.m.* *Recto* and *verso* denote the front and back respectively of a document or sheet of paper; *endroit* and *envers* the right and wrong sides of a piece of cloth, and *avers* and *revers* the front and back of a coin or medal.

[149]

1006.

Relâche, *n.f.* Respite or suspension. Merely denotes the state. **Ex.:** *Travailler sans relâche.*

Relâchement, *n.m.* The act of relaxing. **Ex.:** *Le relâchement de l'esprit.*

1007.

Reliquat, *n.m.* Balance of an account, i.e. what is still owing after same has been made up.

Solde, *n.m.* Balance, i.e. the amount needed, either way, to balance an account. **Ex.:** *Solde débiteur, créditeur.*

Balance, *n.f.* Balance, i.e. the result obtained by balancing the debit and credit sides of an account. **Ex.:** *Faire la balance d'un compte.*

1008.

Remarquer, *v.t.* To remark or note that which has merely attracted attention. To notice. **Ex.:** *Il est à remarquer que . . .*

Observer, *v.t.* To remark or note as a result of study or examination, and for the purpose of giving information, passing an opinion, etc. **Ex.:** *Buffon observait les animaux.* (N.B.—A "remarks" column would therefore be headed *observations*.)

1009.

Renseigner, *v.t.* To give information regarding any matter, subject, etc. Implies that the recipient is already *au courant* to a certain extent. **Ex.:** *Je vous renseignerai demain sur cette affaire.*

Informer, *v.t.* To inform, i.e. to give a general account as a whole. **Ex.:** *Informer quelqu'un de ce qui se passe.*

1010.

Rente, *n.f.*, **Revenu,** *n.m.* *Rente* refers to income produced by capital and received periodically as a fixed sum. **Ex.:** *Vivre de ses rentes. Avoir cent mille francs de rente. Revenu* has a wider meaning and covers income or revenue derived from any source. **Ex.:** *Impôt sur le revenu.*

1011.

Répondre, Repartir, Répliquer, Riposter, *v.t.* and *i.* *Répondre* is the general term meaning "to reply". **Ex.:** *Répondre à une question. Repartir* marks a reply in the sense of a retort or rejoinder. *Répliquer* means "to reply" in the sense of answering back or replying to a previous answer. **Ex.:** *Répliquer par une impertinence. Riposter* denotes a ready or quick answer to a gibe or taunt.

1012.

Résilier, Annuler, *v.t.* *Annuler* is the general term meaning "to annul" or "to cancel", *résilier* being reserved for use in connection with agreements such as a lease, contract, etc. **Ex.:** *Annuler une commande. Résilier un bail.*

1013.

Repentance, *n.f.* Repentance, i.e. contrition for having done wrong, committed sin, etc.

Repentir, *n.m.* Repentance in the sense of regret for having or not having done a certain thing.

1014.

Résoudre de, Résoudre à, *v.t.,* **Résolu, Résous,** *pa.p.* Résoudre takes *de* when the infinitive which follows is the direct object. Ex. : *Il résolut de partir immédiatement.* When the infinitive following is used as an indirect object *résoudre* takes *à*. Ex. : *J'ai résolu mon frère à rester ce soir.* (*N.B.—Résolu* has two forms of past participle, *résolu* meaning "resolved", i.e. "decided", and *résous* used to denote a physical change or decomposition.)

1015.

Se rendre, Aller, *v.i.* *Aller* refers more to the actual transfer from one place to another, *se rendre* calling to mind the arrival at destination. For all practical purposes, however, the two expressions have the same meaning, *aller* being more commonly employed. Ex. : *Aller en Angleterre. Se rendre à une réunion.*

1016.

Reste, *n.m.* Remainder or residue of that which has been wasted, destroyed, consumed, etc. Ex. : *Il vit modestement avec les restes de sa fortune. Le reste d'une armée.*
That which remains to complete. Ex. : *Je saisis la moitié de ce que vous dites et je devine le reste.*

Restant, *n.m.* That which remains over. Ex. : *Il a acheté sa maison et placé en rentes viagères le restant de l'argent qu'il avait.*

1017.

Au reste, *adv. exp.* Also. Besides. Indicates a note or remark of a similar nature added to what has already been said. Ex. : *Ne lui donnez pas cet argent ; au reste il ne saurait qu'en faire.*

Du reste, *adv. exp.* However. Nevertheless. Denotes an addition, not necessarily of the same kind, and often in opposition. Ex. : *Si vous jugez, offrez-lui un secours ; du reste il ne l'acceptera pas.*

Au demeurant, *adv. exp.* After all. However. Marks a conclusion or end intended to complete. Ex. : *Il est d'un caractère ombrageux mais, au demeurant très serviable.*

Au surplus, *adv. exp.* Besides. Withal. Indicates an addition to, or advance on, what is already sufficient. Ex. : *C'est un excellent domestique au surplus très dévoué.*

1018.

Retardataire, *adj.* Having the character of being late, behind time, in arrears, etc., with reference to persons. Ex. : *Un conférencier retardataire.*

Tardif, *adj.* That which comes or arrives late. Tardy. Ex. : *Une réponse tardive.*

1019.

Rideau, *n.m.*, **Portière,** *n.f.* Rideau is the general term for "curtain". A *portière* is a curtain hung in a doorway.

1020.

Roc, *n.m.*, **Roche,** *n.f.*, **Rocher,** *n.m.* A *roc* is a solid mass of hard stone rising above the surface of the ground. A *roche* is an isolated rock of considerable size and not usually so hard as a *roc*. *Rocher* denotes a high pointed rock, difficult of access.

1021.

Romanesque, *adj.* Romantic in the sense of being extravagant or fantastic. Ex. : *Une jeune fille aux idées romanesques.*
Romantique, *adj.* Romantic, i.e. above prosaic reality. Sentimental. Poetic. Ex. : *Site romantique.*

1022.

Rôt, *n.m.* Roast meat considered as a part of the meal at which served. Ex. : *Servir le rôt.*
Rôti, *n.m.* The actual roast meat served. Ex. : *Un rôti de bœuf.*

1023.

Rustaud, *adj.* Having the character of a peasant devoid of manners or education. Uncouth.
Rustique, *adj.* Rustic. Denotes a preference for things pertaining to the country, rather than a lack of refinement.
Rustre, *adj.* Surly or loutish to an extreme degree.

1024.

Sacre, Couronnement, *n.m.* *Couronnement* denotes the actual crowning of a king, queen, etc., *sacre*, the religious ceremony by which the act is consecrated.

1025.

Sage, Bon, *adj.* *Bon* is the general term meaning "good". Ex. : *Je vous remercie de vos bons conseils. Elle est bonne pour sa vieille mère.* *Sage* is used with reference to children who are good in the sense of being well behaved. Ex. : *Les enfants sages obéissent toujours à leurs parents.*

1026.

Sale, *adj.* Dirty, i.e. covered with dirt of some description or other. Filthy. Ex. : *Une rue sale.* The word is also used figuratively. Ex. : *Une sale affaire.*
Malpropre, *adj.* Dirty or unclean. *Malpropre* denotes the absence of cleanness rather than the presence of dirt. Hands which merely needed washing would therefore be described as *des mains malpropres*, whereas dirty hands (i.e. covered with mud) would be rendered as *des mains sales.*
Dirty in the sense of being untidy, slovenly or squalid. Ex. : *Une chambre malpropre.*

1027.

Salut, *n.m.* A demonstration of civility, respect or friendliness such as a greeting, bow, kiss, raising one's hat, etc.
Salutation, *n.f.* A *salut* of a very respectful or assiduous nature. The action or manner of making a *salut*.
Révérence, *n.f.* A ceremonious bow or courtesy. Reverence.

1028.

Sardonique, Sardonien, *adj.* *Sardonien* is used only from a medical or physiological point of view to express a laugh of a convulsive nature. *Sardonique* is the general term and refers to the feeling which occasions a laugh or grin.

1029.

Satané, *adj.* Worthy of Satan. Devilish. Damned. Ex. : *Quel satané temps !*
Satanique, *adj.* Having the character of Satan. Diabolical. Satanical. Ex. : *Cruauté satanique.*
Satanesque, *adj.* Resembling Satan in appearance. Ex. : *Cet acteur a un jeu vraiment satanesque.*

1030.

Secousse, *n.f.* Shock or shaking. Refers to the actual concussion. Ex. : *Secousse sismique.*
Choc, *n.m.* Shock from the point of view of its result or effect. Ex. : *Le choc brisa toute la vaisselle. Soutenir le choc.*

1031.

Seing, *n.m.,* **Signature,** *n.f.* A *seing* is the name signed at the foot of a document, the *signature* being, strictly speaking, the signing or characteristic way of writing a *seing.* The latter is, however, now only used in the expressions *blanc-seing* and *sous seing privé, signature* denoting either the name or the signing thereof. Ex. : *Apposer sa signature. La signature d'un contrat.*

1032.

Selon, Suivant, *prep.* *Selon,* meaning "according to", denotes conformity, *suivant* implying a result or consequence. The distinction is not, however, always observed, the two words being, for practical purposes, synonymous. Ex. : *Vivre selon ses moyens. Orthographier suivant l'Académie.*

1033.

Semer, Ensemencer, *v.t.* *Semer* refers to the seed sown ; *ensemencer* to the ground in which sown. Ex. : *Semer du blé. Ensemencer un champ.*

1034.

Sens, *n.m.* Way with regard to any established motion or movement. Ex. : *Tourner dans le sens des aiguilles d'une montre. Sens unique.*
Direction, *n.f.* Way, i.e. the right direction. Ex. : *Changer de direction. La direction de Paris.*

1035.

Sentir, *v.t.* To feel, i.e. to perceive by means of the organs of the body. Ex. : *Sentir la faim, le froid.*
To feel in the sense of experiencing morally or figuratively. Ex. : *Sentir l'ironie d'un propos.*

Éprouver, *v.t.* To feel, i.e. to be affected by, generally in a physical sense. To suffer. Ex. : *Éprouver une douleur à l'épaule.*

Ressentir, *v.t.* To feel or experience through the mind. Ex. : *Ressentir un malaise, du bien-être.*
To feel strongly, i.e. to resent. Ex. : *Ressentir une injure.*

Se ressentir de, *v.r.* To feel the influence or effects of. Ex. : *Il se ressent toujours de son accident.*

Pressentir, *v.t.* To feel in the sense of having a presentiment. To foresee. Ex. : *Pressentir sa fin.*

Tâter, *v.t.* To feel, i.e. to press lightly or handle gently. Ex. : *Tâter le pouls à quelqu'un.* Also used figuratively. *Tâter le terrain.*

Palper, *v.t.* To feel for the purpose of judging or appreciating any quality, condition, etc. Ex. : *Palpez ce drap ; sa qualité est incontestable.*

Tâtonner, *v.i.* To feel one's way, either in a physical or figurative sense. Ex. : *Tâtonner dans l'obscurité. Toute science commence par tâtonner.*

1036.

Injure, *n.f.*, **Mal,** *n.m.*, **Blessure,** *n.f.* An *injure* is an injury in the sense of an affront. *Mal* means "injury", i.e. damage or hurt. Ex. : *Il s'est fait mal en tombant. Blessure* denotes a physical injury or wound.

1037.

Altesse, *n.f.* Highness, i.e. the title of honour given to princes.
Hautesse, *n.f.* Highness, a title of honour applied only to the sultan.

1038.

Ôter, Enlever, *v.t. Ôter,* meaning "to remove", refers rather to the state of being without what is removed. *Enlever* marks the action of removing. Ex. : *Ôter la nappe. Enlever une porte de ses gonds.*

1039.

Service, *n.m.*, **Faction,** *n.f.* The expression *être de service* refers to duty of any description. *Être de faction* only applies to guard duty.

1040.

Séculier, *adj.* Secular, i.e. not regular or bound by monastic vows. Ex. : *Prêtre séculier.*
Secular or temporary as opposed to spiritual. Ex. : *Tribunal séculier.*

Séculaire, *adj.* Secular, i.e. referring to or happening once in a century. Ex. : *Arbre, année séculaire.*

1041.

Signalement, *n.m.* Description of a person or animal for identification purposes.
Description, *n.f.* Description in a general sense. Ex.: *La description d'un voyage.*
Désignation, *n.f.* Detailed description for the purpose of indicating any article, property, etc. Ex.: *La désignation d'une marchandise.*
Sorte, *n.f.* Description, meaning "kind" or "sort". Ex.: *Des gens de toutes sortes.*

1042.

Société, Compagnie, *n.f.* *Société,* meaning a commercial or industrial company, denotes the legal or official aspect ; *compagnie* refers more to the members composing the company. Ex.: *La Compagnie du chemin de fer du Nord est une société anonyme.*

1043.

Soixante, *adj.* Sixty (exactly).
Soixantaine, *n.f.* About or approximately sixty.

1044.

Soin, *n.m.* Care, meaning "pains" or "application". Ex.: *Travailler avec soin.*
Souci, *n.m.* Care in the sense of anxiety. Ex.: *Vivre sans souci.*
Attention, *n.f.* Care, i.e. heed or attention. Ex.: *Faire attention à sa santé.*
Garde, *n.f.* Care. Means "to mind" or "to beware" when used with *prendre.* Ex.: *Prenez garde de tomber.* (*N.B.—Prendre garde* strictly means "to guard against" and is not therefore used negatively. "Mind you do not fall" is, however, also translated *Ayez soin de ne pas tomber.*)

1045.

Soir, *n.m.* Evening, i.e. the close of day. Denotes time. Ex.: *Ce soir. Demain soir.*
Soirée, *n.f.* Evening. Refers to the occupation or events of the evening. Ex.: *Nous avons passé une bonne soirée hier au théâtre.*
Veillée, *n.f.* Evening, i.e. the period between the evening meal and bedtime. Ex.: *En hiver ils passent leurs veillées à lire.*

1046.

Songe, Rêve, *n.m.* A *songe* is less vague or incoherent than a *rêve* and generally leaves a more lasting impression. Ex.: *Dans l'antiquité on attribuait une signification aux songes.*

1047.

Sonner, *v.i.* To ring, with reference to the bell itself. Ex.: *Les cloches sonnent. Sonner à la porte de quelqu'un.*
  v.t. To ring, i.e. to cause to ring. Ex.: *Sonner l'alarme.*
  v.t. To ring for. Ex.: *Sonner l'office, un domestique.*

Tinter, *v.i.* To ring in a slow or measured manner. Refers to the bell. Ex. : *La cloche tinta trois fois.*
To ring, giving a rapid high-pitched note. To tinkle. Ex. : *Les grelots tintent.*
To ring in the sense of emitting a ringing sound. Ex. : *Faire tinter un verre, une pièce d'argent.*

1048.

Séducteur, *adj.* Seductive, i.e. capable of alluring or leading into error. Ex. : *L'or séducteur.*
Séduisant, *adj.* Tempting or enticing. Denotes the state or quality. Ex. : *Une offre séduisante.*

1049.

Soudain, Subit, *adj.* *Soudain* means sudden in the sense of being quick or rapid. *Subit* denotes something unexpected or unlooked for. Ex. : *Fuite soudaine. Un changement subit.*

1050.

Sot, *adj.* Stupid. Destitute of sense or judgment.
Idiot, *adj.* Idiotic. Deprived of intelligence.
Fou, *adj.* Mad. Insane. Deprived of reason.
Imbécile, *adj.* Stupid. Weak-minded.
Lunatique, *adj.* Of peculiar behaviour. Mentally deranged.
Maniaque, *adj.* Having a mania or fad. Eccentric.

1051.

Soupçon, *n.m.*, **Suspicion**, *n.f.* *Soupçon* means "suspicion" in a general sense. *Suspicion* is a legal term denoting doubt as to the perfect impartiality of a court. Ex. : *Le soupçon pèse sur lui. Suspicion légitime.*

1052.

Soupçonner, *v.t.* To suspect, i.e. to mistrust or imagine to be guilty. (Synonymous, in this sense, with *suspecter*.) Ex. : *Soupçonner quelqu'un d'un crime.*
To suspect in the sense of surmising or imagining. Ex. : *Je le soupçonne d'être l'auteur de cette farce.*
Suspecter, *v.t.* To suspect, i.e. to mistrust or imagine to be guilty. Ex. : *Suspecter l'honnêteté d'un domestique.*

1053.

Sourire, Souris, *n.m.* *Sourire* denotes the act of smiling; *souris* the result or effect. *Sourire* is, however, the term invariably employed for a "smile".

1054.

Souscription, *n.f.* Subscription, i.e. the act of subscribing or promising to pay a certain sum of money. Also any sum so subscribed. Ex. : *Souscription à un emprunt. Une souscription de cent mille francs.*

Abonnement, *n.m.* Subscription to any newspaper, book, periodical, etc.
Cotisation, *n.f.* Subscription in the sense of a voluntary contribution to a common fund.

1055.

Spectacle, *n.m.* Theatrical performance from the point of view of show or effect. Ex. : *Aimer le spectacle.*
Représentation, *n.f.* Theatrical performance, i.e. the act of giving same Ex. : *Représentation à bénéfice.*

1056.

Spiritisme, Spiritualisme, *n.m.* Since being definitely established in France, Spiritualism, i.e. the belief that communication with departed spirits is obtained by means of certain phenomena, has come to be known as *le spiritisme*, the word *spiritualisme* being only used to denote spiritualism or the philosophical doctrine opposed to materialism.

1057.

Station, Gare, *n.f.* Gare is the general term for a railway station, *station* denoting a station of secondary importance. All stations on the Paris underground are called *stations*.

1058.

Succursale, *n.f.* Branch of a bank, commercial house, etc.
Branche, *n.f.* Branch of a tree, river, family line, art, science, etc.
Embranchement, *n.m.* Branch (road, railway line, etc.). Ex. : *Voie, chemin d'embranchement.*

1059.

Sud, *n.m.* South, from the point of view of direction. Ex. : *Le vent du sud. Bourges est au sud de Paris.*
Midi, *n.m.* South. Denotes a district or region, with special reference to the south of France. (In the latter case the word is written with a capital M.) Ex. : *Nice est dans le Midi.*
South, with regard to the sun's position in the heavens. Ex. *Appartement exposé au midi.*

1060.

Suer, *v.i.* To sweat, with reference to human beings.
Suinter, *v.i.* To sweat in the sense of giving off moisture. Ex. : *Mur qui suinte.*

1061.

Superficie, Aire, *n.f.* Superficie means "area" in a general sense. Aire is used in connection with geometry. Ex. : *La superficie d'un terrain. L'aire d'un triangle.*

1062.

Signalé, *adj.* Signal or remarkable. Denotes the success or manner in which any quality, etc., has manifested itself. Ex. : *Victoire signalée.*
Insigne, *adj.* Signal. Noteworthy or notorious. Refers to the merit or actual quality itself. Ex. : *Un fripon insigne.*

1063.

Suppléer, *v.t.* To supply or make up what is deficient. Ex. : *Suppléer la somme nécessaire pour compléter 1,000 francs.* To make up for as a substitute. To take the place of as an equivalent. Ex. : *Le bonheur supplée les richesses.*

Suppléer à, *v.i.* To supply or make up for, in some form or other, that which is deficient. Ex. : *Suppléer en travaillant à l'insuffisance de son revenu.*

1064.

Saucisse, *n.f.* The small sausage made of fresh meat. Ex. : *Chair de saucisse.*

Saucisson, *n.m.* The large dried or smoked sausage of the German variety.

1065.

Tabouret, Escabeau, *n.m.* *Tabouret* implies something more elaborate than an *escabeau*. Ex. : *Tabouret de musique, de dessinateur. Escabeau de cuisine.*

1066.

Servante, Bonne, *n.f.*, **Serviteur, Domestique**, *n.m.* *Servante* applies more to servants in farmhouses. *Serviteur* is the term employed, when writing or speaking, to denote respect or civility. Ex. : *Votre humble serviteur.* A *domestique* is one of a number of servants in a house, a *bonne* being generally the only person employed as such.

1067.

Copie, Ampliation, *n.f.*, **Exemplaire, Double**, *n.m.* *Copie* is the general term and denotes a reproduction. Ex. : *Copie d'un tableau, d'une lettre. Pour copie conforme.* An *exemplaire* is a copy of any standard or original used for reproducing such copies. Ex. : *Exemplaire d'un livre, d'une photographie. Facture en triple exemplaire.* *Ampliation* is a legal or official term denoting a copy of any document, etc., having the same value or answering the same purpose as the original. Ex. : *Pour ampliation.* A *double* is the duplicate or only copy of any document, etc.

1068.

Tapis, *n.m.* General term for a large-sized carpet such as used in dining- or drawing-rooms.

Carpette, *n.f.* Rug or small carpet usually placed in the centre of a room.

Moquette, *n.f.* Carpet of the velvet-pile variety. Ex. : *Tapis en moquette.*

1069.

Tard, *adv.*, **Retard**, *n.m.* *Tard* means "late" simply with regard to the time of day. Ex. : *Il est arrivé tard le soir.* *Retard* denotes a comparison with the correct time at which the event, etc., should have taken place. Ex. : *Il est arrivé en retard pour la séance.*

1070.

Terre, *n.f.* General term for "land" as denoting one of the elements. Ex.: *La Terre Sainte. Descendre à terre.*
Terrain, *n.m.* Land with reference to the kind or quality, or purpose for which intended. Ex.: *Terrain sablonneux, fertile. Terrain à vendre.*
Terroir, *n.m.* Land. Refers to the proved quality for producing agriculturally. Land or soil. Indicates any taste, flavour, etc., imparted to what is produced thereon (especially wine). Ex.: *Vin qui a un goût de terroir.*

1071.

Théologique, *adj.* Theological. Pertaining to theology. Ex.: *Dissertation théologique.*
Théologal, *adj.* Theological, i.e. as taught or defined by theology. Ex.: *Les trois vertues théologales.*

1072.

Tiers, *adj.* Third. Denotes an addition to two others. Ex.: *Tiers ordre, état. Tierce personne, opposition.*
Troisième, *adj.* Third. Marks the order or number. Ex.: *Troisième classe.*

1073.

Timbre, *n.m.* A stamp for affixing to letters, documents, etc. Ex.: *Timbre-poste. Timbre de quittance, de chaudière.*
Cachet, *n.m.* A stamp, made of rubber, metal, etc., for marking. Ex.: *Cachet en caoutchouc.* (*Timbre* is also used in this sense.)

1074.

Tirer, *v.t.* To shoot a fire-arm. To fire. Ex.: *Tirer un coup de fusil. Tirer le canon.*
v.t. To aim or shoot at. Ex.: *Tirer un lièvre, du gibier.*
Fusiller, *v.t.* To shoot, i.e. to kill by shooting. Ex.: *Fusiller un espion, un chien.*

1075.

Tombe, *n.f.*, **Tombeau**, *n.m.*, **Fosse**, *n.f.* A *tombe* is the tombstone placed over a grave, a *tombeau* being a large tomb or tombstone erected in the form of a monument. Used in a figurative sense *tombe* means "the grave", i.e. "death", and *tombeau* a burial-place. Ex.: *Être au bord de la tombe. Les marins n'ont souvent que la mer pour tombeau.* A *fosse* is the grave or hole in which a body is buried.

1076.

Tomber par terre, Tomber à terre, *v.i.* *Tomber par terre* is said of anything which is already on the ground and which therefore merely falls from an upright position. *Tomber à terre* refers to something which is off the ground or in the air. Ex.: *Un arbre tombe par terre, mais son fruit tombe à terre.*

1077.

Tome, Volume, *n.m.* A *tome* is a volume or division of any work made by the author himself, a *volume* being the physical division, dependent on printing, binding, etc., made for the purpose of publication.

1078.

Tordu, *adj.* Twisted, i.e. not having its natural shape. Ex. : *Arbre tordu.*
Tors, *adj.* Twisted naturally or intentionally in spiral form. Ex. : *Colonne torse. Du fils tors.*
Retors, *adj.* Twisted, with reference to wool, cotton, silk, etc., thread.
Tortillé, *adj.* Twisted round itself several times. Ex. : *Des cheveux tortillés. Mouchoir tortillé.*

1079.

Tortu, *adj.* Crooked. Denotes the state. Ex. : *Un nez tortu.*
Tortué, *adj.* Made crooked. Denotes the action. Ex. : *Bâton tortué.*
Tortueux, *adj.* Crooked, i.e. winding or deviating. Tortuous. Ex. : *Chemin tortueux.*

1080.

Plutôt, *adv.* Sooner, i.e. rather or preferable. Ex. : *Mourir plutôt que de se rendre.*
Plus tôt, *adv. exp.* Sooner as regards time. Before. Ex. : *Elle n'a pu partir plus tôt.*

1081.

Tour, *n.m.*, **Tournure,** *n.f.* *Tour* denotes the ordinary or customary manner of arranging the words in a sentence. *Tournure* implies something unusual or out of the way. Ex. : *Sa lettre a un tour franc. Tournure lourde.*

1082.

Train, Équipage, *n.m.* *Train,* meaning a train or retinue, refers to the number comprising same; *équipage* to the quality or brilliance.

1083.

Trajet, *n.m.* Journey, i.e. the distance covered from start to finish. Ex. : *Le trajet de Londres à Paris peut s'effectuer en avion.*
Traite, *n.f.* Journey or distance accomplished without a break. Ex. : *Faire mille kilomètres d'une traite.*
Voyage, *n.m.* Journey or voyage in a general sense. Ex. : *Faire un voyage en chemin de fer.*

1084.

Travailleur, Travailliste, Ouvrier, *n.m.* *Travailleur* indicates actual labour and implies that a person is a hard worker, *travailliste* merely referring to work as a class or division of humanity Ex. : *Son père est travailleur. Le parti travailliste. Ouvrier* means " working " as opposed to wealthy or independent, and refers generally to manual labour. Ex. : *La classe ouvrière.*

1085.

À travers, Au travers, *prep.* *À travers,* meaning "through" or "across", implies that the movement is free or unhindered, and requires a direct object. *Au travers,* on the other hand, denotes obstruction, danger, etc., and is followed by *de.* Ex.: *Courir à travers champs. Passer au travers des rangs ennemis.*

1086.

Trembler, Trembloter, *v.i.* *Trembler* is the general term. *Trembloter* means "to tremble slightly" (but with a rapid movement).

1087.

Trente, *adj.* Exactly thirty.
Trentaine, *n.f.* About or approximately thirty.

1088.

Ondé, *adj.* Marked with a wave-like design. Ex.: *Tissu ondé.* Arranged in waves. Wavy. Ex.: *Des cheveux ondés naturellement.*
Ondulé, *adj.* Folded or bent in the form of waves. Corrugated. Ex.: *Tôle ondulée.*

1089.

Trou, *n.m.* Hole in the sense of an excavation or an opening right through a solid body. Ex.: *Trou de souris. Percer un trou dans un mur.*
Trouée, *n.f.* An opening right through, e.g., a hedge, fence, etc. A gap.

1090.

Se trouver, *v.r.,* **Être,** *v.i.* It is difficult to give any definite rule with regard to the use of *se trouver* meaning "to be". When indicating, with regard to persons, existence in any place, the term may be taken as signifying "to happen to be", and, when employed to denote a state or condition, may be translated by "to feel". Ex.: *Elle se trouve à Londres en ce moment. Se trouver fort embarrassé. Être* has a more general meaning and implies either a state or an existence in any place. Ex.: *Être heureux. La gare est à deux kilomètres d'ici.* However, the two verbs are, practically speaking, synonymous, their correct use being a matter of practice.

1091.

Unanimement, À l'unanimité, *adv.* *Unanimement* refers to the opinion; *à l'unanimité* to the manner of expressing same. Ex.: *Ils sont unanimement de cet avis. Le projet fut voté à l'unanimité.*

1092.

Uni, *adj.* Smooth, i.e. devoid of any irregularity. Ex.: *Une surface unie.*
Égal, *adj.* Smooth in the sense of being even. Ex.: *Une route égale.*
Lisse, *adj.* Smooth to the touch. Ex.: *Cheveux lisses.*

1093.

Usé, *adj.* Completely worn out. Ex. : *Vêtement usé.*
Usagé, *adj.* Having been used. Part-worn.
D'occasion, *adv. exp.* Second-hand. Denotes the " occasion " whereby an article, not being new, is offered for sale at a reduced price. Ex. : *Acheter une bicyclette d'occasion.*

1094.

Utiliser, *v.t.* To use in the sense of employing usefully. To utilize. Ex. : *Utiliser une découverte scientifique.*
User, *v.i.* To use or make use of that to which one is at liberty or has the right. Ex. : *User de son pouvoir, de violence.*
Être usité, *v.i.* To be used or in use as a custom. Ex. : *Locution peu usitée aujourd'hui.*
Se servir de, *v.r.* To use or make use of according to one's means or capability. Ex. : *Pour bien travailler il faut se servir de bons outils.*

1095.

Palier, *n.m.* The level, as opposed to an incline or gradient. Ex. : *Cette auto peut faire cent kilomètres à l'heure en palier.*
Niveau, *n.m.* Level in the sense of equal height or elevation. Ex. : *Passage à niveau. Cette route est au niveau de la mer.*

1096.

Valable, Valide, *adj.* Besides corresponding to " good " or " available " in English, *valable* means " valid " in the sense of holding good or being acceptable from a legal point of view. Ex. : *Quittance valable.* *Valide* means " valid ", i.e. carried out with the proper legal formalities. Ex. : *Mariage valide.*

1097.

Vallée, *n.f.*, **Vallon,** *n.m.* *Vallée* is the general term for " valley " or " vale ". A *vallon* is a small valley between two hills.

1098.

Végétal, *adj.* Vegetable, i.e. referring or belonging to plants. Ex. : *La vie végétale.*
  Vegetable, i.e. derived or obtained from plants. Ex. : *Huile végétale.*
Végétable, *adj.* Vegetable, i.e. consisting of or having the nature of plants. Ex. : *Corps végétable.*
Légumier, *adj.* Vegetable, i.e. having the nature of a vegetable. Ex. : *Le melon est un fruit légumier.*
Potager, *adj.* Concerning vegetables. Ex. : *Jardin potager.*

1099.

Vénimeux, *adj.* Venomous or transmitting poison, with reference to animals. Ex.: *Certains serpents sont vénimeux.* Also used figuratively. Ex.: *Langue vénimeuse.*
Vénéneux, *adj.* Containing poison, with reference to plants, etc. Ex.: *Champignons vénéneux.*

1100.

Ventilateur, *n.m.* A mechanical fan, generally driven by electricity. The enclosed fan employed in factories, etc., and sometimes known as a blower.
Éventail, *n.m.* The fan held by ladies for cooling themselves.
Van, *n.m.* The fan used for winnowing grain.

1101.

Veuvage, *n.m.* Widowhood. Refers to the duration. Ex.: *Se remarier après deux ans de veuvage.*
Viduité, *n.m.* The state of being a widow. Viduity. Ex.: *L'état de viduité.*

1102.

Vainement, En vain, *adv.* *Vainement* denotes the uselessness of any trouble taken; *en vain* refers to the failure to achieve the desired result. Ex.: *Parler sans être entendu, c'est parler vainement; parler sans persuader, c'est parler en vain.*

1103.

Vingt, *adj.* Exactly twenty.
Vingtaine, *n.f.* About or approximately twenty. Ex.: *Dépenser une vingtaine de francs.*

1104.

Violenter, *v.t.* To violate in the sense of doing violence to. To force or compel. Ex.: *Violenter la conscience, la nature.*
Violer, *v.t.* To violate, i.e. to profane or desecrate. Ex.: *Violer un tombeau, un temple.*
To violate in the sense of breaking or transgressing. Ex.: *Violer la loi, sa parole.*
To violate, i.e. to ravish or commit rape.

1105.

Virer, *v.i.,* **Tourner,** *v.t.* *Tourner* is the general term. *Virer* calls to mind the change brought about as a result of turning. Ex.: *Tourner une roue, la tête. Tourner à droite. Le vent vire au nord. Le tournesol vire au rouge au contact des acides. Virer de bord.*

1106.

Vieux, *adj.* Old as opposed to young. Ex.: *Un vieil homme.*
Old as opposed to recent or up to date. Ex.: *Une vieille coutume. Le bon vieux temps.*
Old in the sense of having a long existence. Ex.: *Une vieille maison.*

Ancien, *adj.* Old as opposed to new or modern. Ancient. Ex.: *Un ancien château. L'Ancien Testament.*
Antique, *adj.* Very old. Antique. Ex.: *Des meubles antiques.*

1107.

Vif, *adj.* Living, in a figurative sense. Ex.: *Une force vive. Eau vive.*
Vivant, *adj.* Living. Marks the manner of condition. *Nature vivante.* (*N.B.*—" To skin alive" is, however, translated *écorcher vif.*)
En vie, *adv. exp.* Alive. Merely denotes the existence of life.

1108.

Vite, *adv.* Quickly. Denotes the rapidity of any movement. Ex: *Parler, courir vite.*
Vivement, *adv.* Quickly, i.e. promptly, hastily, sharply, etc. Refers to the manner in which anything is done. Ex.: *Répliquer vivement. Se lever vivement.*

1109.

Vogue, *n.f.* Vogue, i.e. fashion which is the result of reputation, esteem, etc. Ex.: *Cet auteur est très en vogue.*
Mode, *n.f.* Fashion created by taste, whim, fancy, etc. Ex.: *Etre à la mode.*

1110.

Bon vivant, *n.m.* A gay or good-humoured person who takes life easily.
Bon viveur, *n.m.* A person who lives a life of pleasure or sensuality.

1111.

Vol, *n.m.* Flight, i.e. the action of flying. Ex.: *Tuer un oiseau au vol.* Flight, i.e. the distance covered. Ex.: *Le vol d'un pigeon peut être très long.*
Volée, *n.f.* A prolonged or sustained flight. Ex.: *Couvrir cent kilomètres d'une volée.*
Essor, *n.m.* The soar or soaring at the commencement of a flight. Ex.: *Prendre l'essor.*
Raid, *n.m.* Endurance flight made or attempted by an aeroplane, airship, etc. Ex.: *Le raid New York–Paris.*

1112.

Voler, *v.i.* General term meaning "to fly".
Voltiger, *v.i.* To fly short distances here and there. To flutter.
Voleter, *v.i.* To attempt to fly. To flutter.

1113.

Vouloir, *v.t.* To wish. To want. Implies reflection and a certainty that the object desired is suitable. Ex.: *Il voulait nous tromper. Je voudrais vous voir.* (*N.B.*—When used in the present indicative *vouloir* denotes insistence or determination. *Je veux qu'il vienne* and *il veut le tuer* mean respectively "I insist on his coming" and "he means to kill him". The correct translation of "I wish to see him" would be *Je voudrais le voir* or *je désire le voir.*)

Désirer, *v.t.* To wish for the possession or realization of. To desire. Implies earnestness or eagerness. Ex.: *Désirer la santé.*
Avoir besoin, *v.i.* To want in the sense of being in need of. To require. Ex.: *Il a besoin de repos.*
Avoir envie, *v.i.* To have a fancy or inclination. Denotes taste, an idea or whim. Ex.: *Elle a envie de passer quelques jours à la mer.*
Souhaiter, *v.t.* To wish or hope for. The term denotes a certain vagueness. Ex.: *Je souhaite qu'il ne vienne personne.* To wish, i.e. to express in the form of a hope, compliment, etc. Ex.: *Souhaiter la bonne année. Je vous souhaite tout le bonheur que vous méritez.*
Envier, *v.t.* To envy or be envious of what one does not possess. Ex.: *Envier le bonheur d'autrui.*

1114.

Condensateur, *n.m.* Condenser for electricity.
Condenseur, *n.m.* Condenser for steam.

1115.

Prévenir, *v.t.* To prevent in the sense of avoiding or rendering impossible. The word is only used in an absolute sense. Ex.. *Prévenir une maladie. Mieux vaut prévenir que guérir.*
Empêcher, *v.t.* To prevent by hindrance, obstruction or opposition. To stop. Ex.: *Empêcher un mariage. Le mauvais temps nous empêche de sortir.*

1116.

Histoire, *n.f.*, **Historique**, *n.m.* *Histoire* is the general term for "history". Ex.: *Histoire politique, naturelle.* *Historique* means "history" in the sense of an account regarding some individual event, circumstance, incident, etc. "The history of an invention" would therefore be *l'historique d'une invention* and not *l'histoire d'une invention* which means "the story of an invention".

1117.

Watergang, *n.m.*, **Wateringue**, *n.f.* *Watergang* is the term applied to small watercourses in the north of France and the Netherlands for draining low-lying land in the vicinity of the sea. From an administrative point of view such watercourses are known collectively as *wateringues*. Ex.: *Le curage des watergangs. L'administration des wateringues.*

1118.

Donc, *conj.* Then, meaning "therefore". Implies a conclusion. Ex.: *Partez donc, si vous y tenez.*
Alors, *adv.* Then, corresponding more to "in that case". Denotes a casual element. Ex.: *Alors la conférence ne vous intéressera pas.*

1119.

Amaigrir, *v.i.* To become thin gradually. Ex. : *Les privations amaigrissent.*

Maigrir, *v.i.* To grow or become thin. Denotes a more rapid change. Ex. : *Elle a maigri à la suite de sa maladie.*

1120.

Avec, De, *prep.* "With" is translated by *avec* when indicating company or the means, and by *de* when referring to the manner. Ex. : *Nous l'avons rencontré avec son frère. Couper avec un couteau. Crier de douleur.* "With it" and "with them" (except when referring to persons) are translated by *avec*. Ex. : *Le caissier a pris l'argent et est parti avec. Il a deux chiens mais ne sort jamais avec.*

1121.

Grandir, *v.i.* To grow (in height) with reference to persons or things. Ex. : *Cet enfant grandit à vue d'œil.*

Pousser, *v.i.* To grow, generally with reference to flowers, vegetables, etc. Ex. : *L'herbe pousse déjà.*

1122.

Reconnaissance, Gratitude, *n.f.* *Reconnaissance* means the acknowledgment of any service, favour, etc., and corresponds to "thankfulness"; *gratitude* denotes the feeling of affection inspired as a result. Ex. : *La gratitude est une reconnaissance affectueuse.*

1123.

Pied, *n.m.,* **Patte,** *n.f.* *Pied* is used to denote the foot of human beings, also animals such as the horse, elephant, pig, etc. *Patte* applies to animals having paws or claws, also to birds.

1124.

Mille, Mil. *Mille* as an adjective is invariable. Ex. : *Cinq mille hommes.* When indicating a date belonging to the Christian era *mil* is used instead of *mille*. Ex. : *La grande guerre de mil neuf cent quatorze.* (*N.B.*—"The year one thousand" is, however, translated *l'an mille.*) For dates other than those of the Christian era *mille* is employed. Ex. : *L'an quatre mille avant J.-C.*

1125.

Approcher, Rapprocher, *v.t.* *Approcher*, meaning "to place near", refers to the result; *rapprocher* marks the action of bringing or placing nearer. Ex. : *Approchez-vous, j'ai à vous parler. Il rapprocha son fauteuil du feu.*

1126.

Jouir, *v.i.* To enjoy, i.e. to take pleasure in having the use of. Ex. : *Jouir d'une bonne santé.*

Se réjouir, *v.r.* To experience joy or satisfaction. To enjoy oneself. Ex. : *Elle se réjouit au bord de la mer.*

1127.

Seul, *adj.* Single. Solitary. Refers to a person or object unaccompanied by any other. Ex. : *Un seul homme. C'est la seule chose à craindre.*
Unique, *adj.* Only, i.e. without another of its kind. Ex. : *Un fils unique.*

1128.

Si, Tant, Tellement, *adv.* *Si,* meaning "so", marks the manner, degree or extent. Ex. : *Elle est toujours si heureuse de nous voir. Tant* denotes rather the quantity, *tellement* the manner or degree. Ex. : *Je l'ai vu tant de fois chez mon frère. Elle a tant souffert après son opération. Cet acteur est tellement drôle en scène.*

1129.

Tirer, *v.t.* To pull or haul. Ex. : *Tirer sur une corde.*
To draw a cheque, line, etc.
Traîner, *v.t.* To draw or drag along. Implies a more or less sustained effort. *Voiture traînée par quatre chevaux. Traîner ses pieds.*
Entraîner, *v.t.* To draw along in the sense of carrying away. Denotes a force which rapidly overcomes. Ex. : *L'avalanche entraîna tout sur son chemin.*
Remorquer, *v.t.* To draw in the sense of towing. Ex. : *Les trains rapides sont remorqués par de puissantes locomotives.*

1130.

Laid, *adj.* Ugly, as opposed to beautiful. Especially used in a figurative sense. Ex. : *Être laid comme le péché.*
Vilain, *adj.* Ugly morally or materially. Corresponds more to "wretched" or "beastly". Ex. : *Un vilain quartier. Avoir un vilain caractère.*

LIST OF CURRENT ABBREVIATIONS USED IN THE FRENCH LANGUAGE

Abbreviation.	In Full.	Meaning.
A.	Accepté.	Accepted. (Applied to drafts, bills of exchange, etc.)
A.C.L.	Assuré contre l'incendie.	Insured against fire.
A.M.	Assurance Mutuelle.	Mutual insurance.
Amp.	Ampère.	Amp., ampere.
A P.	À protester.	To be protested. (Applied to drafts, bills of exchange, etc.)
a/s.	Aux soins de.	Care of.
A.S.P.	Accepté sans ou sous protêt.	Accepted without or under protest. (Applied to drafts, bills of exchange, etc.)
A.T.	Ancien Testament.	Old Testament.
Bd.	Boulevard.	Boulevard.
B.P.F.	Bon pour francs.	Good for Frs. (Formula preceding the amount [in figures] on a cheque, draft, money-order, etc.)
C/	Contre.	Against.
c.à.d.	C'est-à-dire.	That is to say.
C.C.	Compte courant.	Current account.
Cf.	Conférez.	Compare. Refer to.
Ch.	Chapitre.	Chapter.
Cie.	Compagnie.	Company.
cl.	Centilitre.	Centilitre.
cm.	Centimètre.	Centimetre.
C.O.	Compte ouvert.	Open account.
Ct.	Courant.	inst.
Cte.	Compte.	Account.
Cte.	Comte.	Count.
Ctesse.	Comtesse.	Countess.
dl.	Décilitre.	Decilitre.
Do.	Dito.	Ditto.
Dr.	Docteur.	Doctor. Dr.
E.	Est.	East.
E.V.	En ville.	Local. (For addresses.)
ex.	Exemple.	Example.
Fo	Folio.	Folio (No).
Fr.	Franc.	Franc.
Gal	Général.	General.
Gr.	Gramme.	Gramme.
G.V.	Grande vitesse.	Fast (goods) train.
ha.	Hectare.	Hectare.

ABBREVIATIONS

Abbreviation.	In Full.	Meaning.
hl.	Hectolitre.	Hectolitre.
ib. or ibid.	Ibidem.	In the same place.
Id.	idem.	Ditto. The same.
In-pl.	In-plano.	Broadsheet. Broadside.
Inf. or In-fol.	In-folio.	Folio.
In-4to.	In-quarto.	Quarto.
In-8to.	In-octavo.	Octavo.
In-12.	In-douze.	12 mo.
In-16.	In-seize.	16 mo.
In-18.	In-dix-huit.	18 mo.
J.-C.	Jésus-Christ.	Jesus Christ.
k., kg., kil., kilo.	Kilogramme.	Kilogramme.
Km.	Kilomètre.	Kilometre.
l.	Litre.	Litre.
LL.AA.	Leurs Altesses.	Their Highnesses.
LL.AA.II.	Leurs Altesses Impériales.	Their Imperial Highnesses.
LL.AA.RR.	Leurs Altesses Royales.	Their Royal Highnesses.
LL.EEm.	Leurs Éminences.	Their Eminences.
LL.EExc.	Leurs Excellences.	Their Excellencies.
LL.MM.	Leurs Majestés.	Their Majesties.
LL.MM.II.	Leurs Majestés Impériales.	Their Imperial Majesties.
LL.MM.RR.	Leurs Majestés Royales.	Their Royal Majesties.
m.	Mètre.	Metre.
M. or M^r.	Monsieur	M^r.
Mad. or Mme	Madame.	Mrs.
M^d.	Marchand.	Tradesman. Merchant.
M^e.	Maître.	Title given to lawyers, notaries, barristers, etc.
mg.	Milligramme.	Milligramme.
Mgr	Monseigneur.	Monsignor.
Mis	Marquis.	Marquis.
M^{ise}	Marquise.	Marchioness.
Melle	Mademoiselle.	Miss.
M^{elles}	Mesdemoiselles.	Misses.
mm.	millimètre.	Millimetre.
MM.	Messieurs.	Messrs.
MS.	Manuscrit.	Manuscript.
MSS.	Manuscrits.	Manuscripts.
N.	Nord.	North.
n/	Nous. Notre.	Us. Our.
N.B.	Notez bien.	N.B.
N.-D.	Notre-Dame.	Our Lady.
N.E.	Nord est.	North-east.
N.O.	Nord-ouest.	North-west.
N^o.	Numéro.	Number. N^o.
n/S.	Notre Sieur.	Our M^r
N.-S.	Notre-Seigneur.	Our Lord.
N.T.	Nouveau Testament.	New Testament.
N^t or Ng^t	Négociant.	Merchant.
n/v.	Notre ville.	Our town.
O.	Ouest.	West.
P.	Page.	Page.
P.	Protêt.	Protest. (Applied to drafts, bills of exchange etc.)

ABBREVIATIONS

Abbreviation.	In Full.	Meaning.
P.	Père.	Father. (In religion.)
P.A.	Pour ampliation.	True copy. (Placed at the foot of a duplicate.)
P.C.C.	Pour copie conforme.	Certified true copy.
P.D.	Port dû.	Carriage forward.
pér.	Période.	Period (electric).
P. et P.	Profits et pertes.	Profit and loss.
P. ex.	Par exemple.	For example. E.g.
P.P.	Port payé.	Carriage paid.
P.p.c.	Pour prendre congé.	To take leave. To say good-bye.
P. pon.	Par procuration.	Per procuration.
P.S.	Post scriptum.	P.S.
P.T.T.	Postes Télégraphes et Téléphones.	The French Post Office Department.
P.V.	Petite vitesse.	Slow (goods) train.
R.F.	République Française.	French Republic.
R°.	Recto.	The front of a document.
R.P.	Révérend Père.	Reverend Father.
RR.PP.	Révérends Pères.	Reverend Fathers.
R.S.V.P.	Répondez s'il vous plaît.	For reply please.
S.	Signé.	Signed.
S. or S^t.	Saint.	Saint.
S.	Sud.	South.
S.A.	Son Altesse.	His Highness.
S.A.I.	Son Altesse Impériale.	His Imperial Highness.
S.A.R.	Son Altesse Royale.	His Royal Highness.
S.E.	Sud-est.	South-east.
S.E. ou O.	Sauf erreur ou omission.	E. and O.E.
S.Em.	Son Éminence.	His Eminence.
S.Exc.	Son Excellence.	His Excellency.
S.G.	Sa Grace. Sa Grandeur.	His Grace.
S.H.	Sa Hautesse.	His Highness.
S.G.D.G.	Sans garantie du gouvernement.	Without Government guarantee. (Obligatory on all articles sold as patents.)
S.M.	Sa Majesté.	His or Her Majesty.
S.M.C.	Sa Majesté Catholique.	His Catholic Majesty. (Applied to the King of Spain.)
S.M.I.	Sa Majesté Impériale.	His Imperial Majesty.
S.M.R.	Sa Majesté Royale.	His Royal Majesty.
S.O.	Sud-ouest.	South-west.
S.P.	Saint Père (le).	Holy Father (the Pope).
S^r (le)	Le Sieur.	M^r ...
S^r	Successeur.	Successor.
S.S.	Sa Seigneurie.	His Lordship.
SS.	Saints.	Saints.
S.S.	Sa Sainteté.	His Holiness (the Pope).
S^{té}	Société.	Company.
S^{té} A^{me}.	Société Anonyme.	Joint Stock Company.
S.T.G.M.	Sa Très Gracieuse Majesté.	His most Gracious Majesty.
S.V.P.	S'il vous plaît.	If you please.
t.	Tonne.	Ton.
T.S.V.P.	Tournez s'il vous plaît.	P.T.O.

ABBREVIATIONS

Abbreviation.	In Full.	Meaning.
V.	Voir. Voyez.	See.
v/	Vous. Votre.	You. Your.
V.A.	Votre Altesse.	Your Highness.
V.C.	Votre compte.	Your account.
V.E.	Votre Éminence.	Your Eminence.
V^e or Vve	Veuve.	Widow.
V.Exc.	Votre Excellence.	Your Excellency.
V.H.	Votre Hautesse.	Your Highness.
V.M.	Votre Majesté.	Your Majesty.
V^o	Verso.	The back of a document.
Vol.	Volume.	Volume (book).
V.S.	Votre Sieur.	Your M^r ...
V.S.	Votre Sainteté.	Your Holiness.
Vte	Vicomte.	Viscount.
V^{tesse}	Vicomtesse.	Viscountess.
v/v.	Votre ville.	Your town.
W.C.	Water closet.	Lavatory.
X or N	Lettre indiquant l'anonymat.	The sign of anonymity.
7bre.	Septembre.	September.
8bre.	Octobre.	October.
9bre.	Novembre.	November.
10bre.	Décembre.	December.
Ier, Ière	Premier.	First.
2ème, 3ème, etc.	Deuxième, Troisième, etc.	Second, Third, etc.
1°	Primo.	Firstly.
2°	Secondo.	Secondly.
3°	Tertio.	Thirdly.
4°, 5°, etc.	Quatrièmement, Cinquièmement, etc.	Fourthly, Fifthly, etc.

CORRECT FORMS OF ADDRESSING AND BEGINNING LETTERS TO PERSONS OF TITLE OR HOLDING ANY OFFICE OR POSITION

BUSINESS

Monsieur le Président, Administrateur-Délégué, Directeur, etc., when writing officially to persons holding such positions, otherwise commence *Monsieur* or *Messieurs* as the case may be.

DIPLOMATIC AND CONSULAR

Ambassador	*Monsieur l'Ambassadeur.* Refer to as *Votre Excellence.*
Ambassador's wife	*Madame l'Ambassadrice.*
Consul	*Monsieur le Consul.*
Vice-Consul	*Monsieur le Vice-Consul.*

ECCLESIASTICAL

Cardinal	*Éminence.* Refer to as *Votre Éminence.*
Archbishop or bishop	*Sa Grandeur Monseigneur.* . . . Commence *Monseigneur.* Refer to as *Votre Grandeur.*
Member of a male religious community	*Mon Révérend Père* or *Monsieur et Révérend Père.*
Member of a female religious community	*Madame.* (*Madame la Supérieure* if to a Superior.)
Dean	*Monsieur le Doyen.*
Canon	*Monsieur le Chanoine.*
Archpriest	*Monsieur l'Archiprêtre.*
Priest in charge of a parish	*Monsieur le Curé.*
Priest (other than in charge of a parish)	*Monsieur l'Abbé.*
Curate	*Monsieur le Vicaire.*
Member of the Protestant clergy	*Monsieur le Pasteur.*
Rabbi	*Monsieur le Rabbin.*

(*N.B.*—In France a vicar is called a *curé* and a curate a *vicaire.*)

EDUCATIONAL

The head of a university or academy	*Monsieur le Recteur.*
The head of a college	*Monsieur le Directeur.*
The head master of a college, grammar school, etc.	{ *Monsieur le Principal.* { *Monsieur le Proviseur.*

FORMS OF ADDRESS

GOVERNMENT

The President of the French Republic	*A Son Excellence Monsieur le Président de la République* or *A Son Excellence Monsieur . . ., Président de la République.* Commence *Monsieur le Président* and refer to as *Votre Excellence.*
Prime Minister	*Monsieur le Président du Conseil.* Refer to as *Votre Excellence.*
Cabinet Minister	*Monsieur le Ministre.* Refer to as *Votre Excellence.*
Member of the Senate	*Monsieur le Sénateur.*
Member of the Chamber of Deputies	*Monsieur le Député.*

LEGAL

Judge or Magistrate	*Monsieur le Juge.*
Attorney	*Monsieur le Procureur de la République.*
Lawyer (*avocat*) Solicitor (*avoué*)	*Monsieur et cher Maître.*

MILITARY

Military officer	*Monsieur le Général, Commandant, Capitaine,* etc. When the writer also belongs to the Army it is usual to commence *Mon Colonel, Mon Capitaine,* etc.

NAVAL

Naval officer	It is customary not to use the expression *Monsieur le* before naval ranks except in the case of an *enseigne* (2nd lieutenant). Ex.: *Amiral, Commandant, Monsieur l'enseigne.* A captain commanding a vessel is addressed as *Commandant,* as is also a lieutenant holding the same position. A ship's lieutenant is styled *Capitaine,* likewise the senior *enseigne* or 2nd lieutenant.

NOBILITY

Duke	*Monsieur le Duc.* (If of royal descent address as *Altesse* or *Monseigneur* and refer to as *Votre Altesse.*)
Duchess	*Madame la Duchesse.* (If of royal descent address as *Altesse* and refer to as *Votre Altesse.*)
Marquis	*Monsieur le Marquis.*
Marchioness	*Madame la Marquise.*
Earl (or Count)	*Monsieur le Comte.*
Countess	*Madame la Comtesse.*
Viscount	*Monsieur le Vicomte.*
Viscountess	*Madame la Vicomtesse.*
Baron	*Monsieur le Baron.*
Baroness	*Madame la Baronne.*

FORMS OF ADDRESS

OFFICIAL

Notaire, Huissier, Commissaire-priseur, etc.	Monsieur et cher Maître.
Mayor	Monsieur le Maire.
Prefect of Police	Monsieur le Préfet.

ROYALTY

King	A Sa Majesté. . . . Commence Sire. Refer to as Votre Majesté.
Queen	A Sa Majesté. . . . Commence Madame. Refer to as Votre Majesté.
Prince of royal blood	Altesse or Monseigneur. Refer to as Votre Altesse.

VARIOUS

Gentleman	Monsieur.
Lady	Madame.
Unmarried lady	Mademoiselle.

NOTES

1. The above forms are used when writing to a person in his official capacity, or to someone with whom one is not personally acquainted. When on friendly or intimate terms the writer should commence, e.g., *Cher Maître, Cher Monsieur, Ma chère Baronne, Mon cher Abbé, Cher ami*, etc., etc.

2. The title, etc., employed at the commencement of a formal or official letter should be repeated when ending. Ex.: *Je vous prie d'agréer, Monsieur le Ministre, l'assurance de mon profond respect. Nous vous prions d'agréer, Monsieur le Directeur, nos salutations les plus distinguées. Veuillez agréer, Monsieur le Maire, avec nos remerciements, l'assurance de nos sentiments respectueux.*

INDEX

The figures refer to the numbers of the groups.

WHEN a word having different meanings appears in more than one group, the key-word in italics, placed afterwards within parentheses, will facilitate immediate reference to the required group number.

A

A (il y)	204	Abstraitement	27
Abaissement	33	Abuser	66
Abaisser (*to lower*)	10	Accablement	24
Abaisser (*to lower*)	142	Accabler	3
Abandon	1	Accéder	39
Abandonnement	1	Accélérer	44
Abandonner	52	Accepter	53
Abandonner (s')	22	Acclimatation	57
Abasourdir	23	Acclimatement	57
Abattement	24	Acclimater	58
Abattre (*to lower*)	10	Accolade (donner l')	224
Abattre (*to bring down*)	54	Accoler	224
Abêtir	51	Accommodement	49
Abîmer	202	Accord	56
Abjection	33	Accord (*tomber d'*)	39
Abjurer	5	Accorder	50
Abolir	2	Accoster	15
Abondamment	45	Accoter	63
Abondance (en)	45	Accoucher	16
Abonnement	1054	Accoupler	507
Abord (au premier)	47	Accourcir	19
Abord (d')	47	Accoutrer	17
Abord (de prime)	47	Accoutumance	18
Abord (dès l')	47	Accroître	48
Abord (tout d')	47	Accumulation	7
Aborder	15	Accumuler	41
Aboyer	404	Accusateur	35
Abrégé	62	Accusé	67
Abréger	19	Acerbe	34
Abroger	2	Achalandage	413
Abrutir	20	Achat	36
Absolution	112	Achever	6
Absoute	112	Acide	34
Abstraction (faire)	26	Acquiescer	39
Abstractivement	27	Acquisition	36
Abstraire	26	Acquit	37
Abstrait	4	Acquitter de (s')	9
		Âcre	34

[177]

Âcreté	38
Acrimonie	38
Acrobatie	14
Acrobatisme	14
Acte	32
Actif	13
Action	32
Actionner	11
Actuellement	30
Adhérer	39
Adjacent	64
Administration	28
Administrer	61
Adonner (s')	22
Adoucir	60
Adresse	69
Aduler	65
Advenir	998
Adversité	89
Aérage	86
Aération	86
Affaibli	76
Affaire	968
Affairé	25
Affaisser (s')	519
Affamé	713
Affecté	85
Affecter	72
Affection (avec)	88
Affectionnément	88
Affectionner	105
Affectueusement	88
Affermer	74
Affermir (*to strengthen*)	77
Affermir (*to make firm*)	189
Afféte	85
Affiche	628
Afficher	72
Affiner	983
Affinité	71
Afflictions	80
Afflouage	79
Afflouement	79
Affluence	83
Affranchir	84
Affres	75
Affreux	82
Affront	101
Affubler	17
Affûter	100
Afin de	962
Afin que	962
Agacer	102
Âgé de	103
Âge de (à l')	103
Agenouiller (s')	91
Agent de police	745
Agissant	13
Agitation	81
Agiter (*to agitate*)	92
Agiter (*to shake*)	292
Agrandir	48
Agréable	104
Agréer	53
Agréger	93
Agrès	94
Agression	97
Agreste	96
Agriculteur	95
Agronome	95
Aide	106
Aïeux	109
Aigre	34
Aigreur	38
Aiguillonner	107
Aiguiser	100
Ailleurs (d')	108
Aimer	105
Ainsi	110
Ainsi que	116
Airain	793
Aire	1061
Ais	228
Aisance (*easy circumstances*)	46
Aisance (*well off*)	117
Aise	117
Aisé	111
Aises	118
Ajourner	123
Ajouter	48
Ajustement	119
Alarme	120
Alentour	210
Alentours	121
Alerte	120
Algue	122
Aliment	115
Alimenter	871
Alinéa	124
Aliter (s')	125
Allécher	127
Allé (être)	128
Allégeance	113
Allégement	113
Alléger	126
Aller	1015
Aller à la rencontre	135
Aller au devant	135
Aller (se laisser)	22
Alliance (*ring*)	154

[178]

INDEX

Alliance (*union*)	71	Appareil	158
Allure	140	Appas	159
Alors	1118	Appât	87
Alouette	129	Appeler	865
Alphabétaire	134	Appliquer	172
Alphabétique	134	Appointements	170
Altesse	1037	Apporter	141
Altier	130	Apposer	172
Amaigrir	1119	Apprécier	166
Amaigrissement	133	Appréhender	171
Amant	131	Apprendre (*to learn*)	164
Amas	7	Apprendre (*to teach*)	168
Amasser	41	Apprêter	167
Ambiguité	132	Apprêts	160
Amélioration	137	Apprivoisé	162
Améliorer (s')	176	Approbateur	163
Amendement	137	Approbatif	163
Amener	141	Approcher	1125
Amiable (à l')	136	Approfondir	165
Amiablement	136	Approprier (s')	169
Amiante	430	Appui (*support*)	106
Amidon	431	Appui (*support*)	173
Amollir	42	Âpre	993
Amonceler	41	Après	175
Amoncellement	7	Arbrisseau	309
Amorce	87	Arbuste	309
Amoureux	131	Argent	845
Amphibologie	132	Argenterie	951
Amplement	45	Armes	174
Ampliation	1067	Armoiries	174
Ampoulé	152	Arracher	182
Amuser	145	Arranger	180
An	144	Arrêt	177
Ancêtres	109	Arriver (*to succeed*)	927
Ancien	1106	Arriver (*to happen*)	998
Anciennement	146	Arroger (s')	169
Âne	147	Arrosage	178
Anéantissement	24	Arrosement	178
Ânesse	148	Arsouille	335
Angoisses	75	Artificieux	296
Animer	107	Artistement	660
Anneau	154	Artistiquement	660
Année	144	Asbeste	430
Annoncer	150	Ascenseur	846
Annuler (*to annul*)	2	Asile	179
Annuler (*to cancel*)	1012	Assemblage	181
Anoblir	151	Assemblée	184
Anse	114	Assembler	187
Antique	1106	Asservissement	188
Antre	349	Assiette (*situation*)	183
Apercevoir	153	Assiette (*plate*)	951
Apetisser	161	Assistance	106
Aposter	959	Assister	185
Apparaître	157	Associer	93
Apparat	158	Assommoir	352

Assortiment		Balançoire
Assortiment 181	Avanie 101	
Assouvir 991	Avant (*before*) 12	
Assujettissement 188	Avant (*before*) 596	
Assurer 189	Avare 199	
Astre 697	Avaricieux 199	
Astucieux 296	Avarie 546	
Attache 191	Avarier 202	
Attachement 191	Avec 1120	
Attacher 805	Avènement 200	
Attaque 97	Avenir 201	
Attaquer 190	À venir 750	
Attaquer à (s') 190	Aventureux 254	
Atteindre 192	Aventurier 254	
Atteindre à 192	Avéré 31	
Attenant 64	Avérer 203	
Attendant (en) 143	Avers 1005	
Attendre 195	Averse 893	
Attendre à (s') 195	Avertir 205	
Attendrissement 276	Avertissement 628	
Attentat 73	Aveugle (à l') 206	
Attention 1044	Aveuglement 207	
Atterrage 197	Aveuglément 206	
Atterrissage 197	Avilir 10	
Attiédissement 193	Avilissement 33	
Attirant 59	Avis (*opinion*) 40	
Attirer 127	Avis (*notice*) 628	
Attouchement 194	Avisé 208	
Attracteur 59	Aviser 205	
Attractif 59	Avoir . . . ans 103	
Attrait 159	Avoir besoin 1113	
Attraper (*to deceive*) . . . 66	Avoir envie 113	
Attraper (*to catch*) . . . 29	Avoir été 128	
Attrayant 59	Ayant cause 661	
Attribuer (s') 169	Ayant droit 661	
Attrister 99		
Aube 156	**B**	
Aucun 874	Babiller 211	
Au demeurant 1017	Babiole 213	
Augmenter 48	Bâche 212	
Aujourd'hui 30	Bachot 214	
Aumônier 370	Badaud 215	
Auparavant 12	Badiner 217	
Auprès de (*near*) 98	Bafouer 218	
Auprès de (*attached to*) . . . 55	Bagatelle (*trifle*) 213	
Au reste 1017	Bagatelle (*no importance*) . 216	
Aurore 156	Bague 154	
Aussi (*so*) 110	Baignoire 223	
Aussi (*as well*) 658	Baille 222	
Autour 210	Bain 223	
Autres 198	Baiser 224	
Autrefois 146	Baisser 142	
Autrui 198	Balafre 221	
Avance (d') 70	Balance 1007	
Avance (en) 70	Balancer 220	
Avance (par) 70	Balançoire 694	

[180]

Balayer   *INDEX*   **Bosseler**

Balayer	986	Bénit	250
Balbutier	219	Bercail	249
Balle (*ball*)	229	Béret	247
Balle (*bale*)	234	Berge	274
Ballon	229	Berger	931
Ballot	234	Bergerie	249
Balnéable	233	Besace	251
Balnéaire	233	Bésicles	246
Bandage	232	Besoin (avoir)	1113
Bandit	335	Besogne	248
Banlieue	240	Bestiaux	257
Banqueroute	231	Bétail	257
Baptême	898	Bétise	258
Baquet	222	Beuchon	259
Baraque	321	Bévue	252
Baraquement	321	Bicoque	319
Baril	227	Bien (*well*)	8
Barillet	227	Bien (*many*)	253
Baroque	272	Bienfaisant	236
Barque	214	Bien que	981
Barre	230	Bienséance	265
Barreau	230	Bienveillant	236
Barrique	227	Biffer	266
Bas (jeter à)	54	Bigarreau	267
Bas (mettre à)	54	Bijou	255
Bassesse	33	Bille	229
Bassin	225	Binette	259
Bassine	225	Binoche	259
Basting	228	Binocle	246
Bastonnade	226	Bissac	251
Bateau	214	Bizarre	272
Bâti	341	Blafard	260
Bâtiment (*ship*)	242	Blaireau	948
Bâtiment (*building*)	235	Blâmer	261
Bâtir	245	Blé	262
Bâtisse	235	Blême	260
Bâton	244	Blessure (*wound*)	268
Battre	243	Blessure (*injury*)	1036
Battre (se)	438	Bleu	503
Baudet	147	Blottir (se)	263
Bavarder	211	Bluette	273
Beau	239	Bluter	264
Beaucoup (*much*)	8	Bocage	270
Beaucoup (*many*)	253	Bois	311
Bêcher	237	Boiter	275
Bédane	305	Bol	225
Bégayer	219	Bon	1025
Bélandre	238	Bonifier (se)	176
Belle-mère	826	Bonne	1066
Bellot	241	Bonnet de police	247
Bénéfice	241	Boqueteau	270
Bénêt	215	Bord	274
Bénévole	236	Bordure	274
Béni	250	Borne	277
Bénin	236	Bosseler	281

[181]

Bossuer INDEX Capter

Bossuer	281	Brouiller 304
Bosquet	270	Broussaille 311
Bossu	271	Broyer 312
Botte	282	Bruine 648
Bottier	491	Bruit 314
Bottine	282	Brume 648
Bouchon	804	Brun 873
Bouclier	283	Brusque 993
Boue	278	Brut 993
Bouffi	294	Bugle 313
Bouffon	421	Buisson 309
Bouffonnerie	279	Bureau 698
Bougeoir	366	Burin 305
Bouger	859	But 315
Bougie	280	Buvette 43
Bougonner	284	
Boule	229	C
Boulet	229	Cabale 301
Boulon	293	Cabane 321
Bouquin	295	Cabanon 355
Bourbe	278	Cabaret 43
Bourdon	414	Caboche 316
Bourg	285	Cache-col 317
Bourgade	285	Cache-nez 317
Bourrasque	286	Cacher 318
Bourrer	345	Cachet 1073
Bourrique	148	Cacheter 322
Bourse	287	Cachot 355
Boursouflé (*swollen*)	294	Cadeau 323
Boursouflé (*inflated*)	152	Cadet 337
Bouse	288	Cadre 324
Boussole	289	Caducité 325
Bout (*end*)	297	Café 43
Bout (*piece*)	847	Cahot 326
Boutique	290	Cahotage 326
Brancard	405	Cahotement 326
Branchage	291	Cahute 321
Branche	1058	Cailler 419
Branches	291	Calandrer 346
Branler	292	Caler 63
Brasero	300	Calme 327
Brasier	300	Calomnie 831
Brasière	300	Calot 247
Bredouiller	219	Calotte 247
Brigue	301	Campagnard 328
Brillant	303	Campagne 471
Briller	298	Canaille 335
Brimbale	114	Canari 329
Brimborion	213	Canevas 343
Briser	299	Canne 244
Broc	306	Canot 214
Brocard	307	Cantatrice 338
Broncher	308	Capitonner 345
Brosse	948	Capote 912
Brouillard	648	Capter 330

[182]

Captiver		INDEX		Chaumière
Captiver	330	Cervelet		359
Caque	227	Cervelle		359
Caquerolle	331	Cession		361
Caqueter	211	Chagrin		362
Car	340	Chahut		314
Carcasse	341	Chaland		238
Carier	353	Chaleur		385
Carillon	414	Chaloupe		214
Carnassier	354	Chambre		363
Carnivore	354	Champêtre		96
Carotteur	339	Chanceler		364
Carottier	339	Chancir		365
Carpette	1068	Chandelier		366
Carreau	336	Chandelle		280
Carrelage	924	Change		372
Carrelet	334	Change (donner le)		66
Carrer	686	Changeant		367
Carrosse	332	Changement		372
Cartel	351	Changer		368
Cas	968	Changer de		368
Cas (au)	333	Chanson		369
Cas (dans le)	333	Chansonnier		344
Cas (en)	333	Chant		369
Case	321	Chanteur		344
Casque	342	Chanteuse		338
Casquette	247	Chantre		344
Casser (*to annul*)	2	Chapelain		370
Casser (*to break*)	299	Char		371
Casserole	331	Charbon		375
Casse-tête	352	Charge (*load*)		376
Cassotte	331	Charge (*position*)		377
Catir	346	Chargement		376
Cause	968	Charger		672
Cause de (à)	340	Chariot		371
Caution	347	Charivari		314
Cave	348	Charlatanerie		378
Caverne	349	Charlatanisme		378
Cavité	360	Charme (*charm*)		159
Cécité	207	Charme (*hornbeam*)		379
Céder (*to give way*)	39	Charme (*spell*)		380
Céder (*to transfer*)	350	Charmille		379
Ceinture	356	Charmoie		379
Ceinturon	356	Charnière		381
Céler	318	Charpente		341
Cellier	348	Charretier		424
Cellule	355	Charrette		371
Cendre	692	Charrier		373
Cent	422	Châsse		374
Centaine	422	Châtaigne		382
Cependant	357	Chat-huant		398
Cerise	267	Châtier		383
Cerner	656	Chaud		385
Certainement	358	Chauffer		386
Certes	358	Chauffeur		424
Cerveau	359	Chaumière		319

[183]

| Chaussure | INDEX | Comble |

Chaussure 282	Cliché 951
Chemin 387	Clientèle 413
Chenapan 335	Cligner 403
Cheneau 754	Clignoter 403
Cher 394	Climatérique 412
Chèrement 394	Climatique 412
Chérir 105	Cloche 414
Chevelure 391	Clocher (*to limp*) 275
Cheveux 391	Clocher (*steeple*) 415
Chicane 392	Clocheton 415
Chicanerie 392	Clochette 414
Chicaneur 393	Clore 322
Chicanier 393	Clos 416
Chiffons 759	Closeau 416
Chiffre 866	Closerie 416
Chiffrer 864	Clou 316
Chiourme 384	Clouer 420
Chiper 585	Clouter 420
Chiquer 388	Clown 421
Chirurgical 389	Coaguler 419
Chirurgique 389	Cobaye 417
Choc 1030	Cocasse 418
Choir 397	Coche 332
Choisir 395	Cocher 424
Chopper 308	Cochon d'Inde 417
Choquer 396	Cœur (de bon) 536
Chouette 398	Cognée 432
Chrétienté 399	Cohue 83
Christianisme 399	Coi 327
Chuchotement 390	Coin 425
Chuchoterie 390	Col (*collar*) 436
Chutes 526	Col (*neck*) 497
Cicatrice 221	Col (*pass*) 426
Cierge 280	Colère (*anger*) 433
Cime 401	Colère (*choleric*) 434
Cinquantaine 407	Coléreux 434
Cinquante 407	Colérique 434
Cintrer 400	Colifichet 213
Circonspect 208	Colimaçon 693
Cirer 528	Colis 427
Ciseau 305	Collationner 451
Citadin 406	Collecte 428
Citoyen 406	Collection 999
Citrouille 961	Collectionner 439
Civière 405	Collègue 429
Clabaudage 408	Collerette 436
Clabauder 404	Collet 436
Clabauderie 408	Collier 436
Claie (passer à la) . . . 264	Colline 496
Clair (*clearly*) 410	Colorer 435
Clair (*light*) 423	Colorier 435
Clairement 410	Coloris 437
Clairon 313	Combattre 438
Clarté 423	Comble (*full*) 952
Clerc 402	Comble (*top*) 401

[184]

Combler		INDEX		Continuer de	
Combler	653	Conférer	457		
Comestible	440	Confiance	458		
Commande	441	Confidemment	459		
Commandement	441	Confidence	458		
Commander (*to drive*)	11	Confidence (en)	459		
Commander (*to order*)	895	Confidentiellement	459		
Comme (*as*)	116	Confier à (se)	724		
Comme (*how*)	442	Confier en (se)	724		
Commencement	443	Confins	274		
Commencer à	448	Confirmer	77		
Commencer de	448	Confondu	466		
Comment	442	Conforme	771		
Commerce	858	Confrère	429		
Commerce (fonds de)	413	Confus	466		
Commis	402	Congé	717		
Commodités	118	Congeler	419		
Communier	449	Congratulations	462		
Communiquer	449	Conjoint	463		
Compagnie	1042	Conjurateur	460		
Comparaître	157	Conjuration (*conjuration*)	380		
Comparer à	451	Conjuration (*conspiracy*)	302		
Comparer avec	451	Conjuré	460		
Compas	289	Conjurer	905		
Compétiteur	450	Connaître (*to understand*)	444		
Complainte	452	Connaître (*to know*)	461		
Complaire	446	Connexion	71		
Complet (*full*)	952	Connexité	71		
Complet (*suit*)	869	Consacrer	464		
Compléter	6	Conseil	453		
Complexion	447	Conseiller	205		
Compliments	462	Consentir	39		
Complot	302	Conserver	465		
Comploter	905	Considérable	468		
Comprendre	444	Considération	196		
Compte (en fin de)	670	Consolant	469		
Compulser	919	Consolateur	469		
Concasser	299	Consommer	470		
Concerner	445	Conspiration	302		
Concession	361	Conspirer	905		
Concile	453	Conspuer	218		
Conciliant	454	Constant	467		
Conciliateur	454	Constater	203		
Concilier	50	Constitution	447		
Concitoyen	406	Construire	245		
Concours	83	Consumer	470		
Concurrent	450	Contemplateur	481		
Condensateur	1114	Contemplatif	481		
Condenseur	1114	Contenance	480		
Condition (de)	455	Conter	478		
Conducteur	424	Contexture	479		
Conduire (*to direct*)	61	Contigu	64		
Conduire (*to lead*)	456	Continuation	474		
Conduire (*to take*)	623	Continuer	475		
Conduit	487	Continuer à	476		
Conduite	487	Continuer de	476		

[185]

Contondant	651
Contradiction	484
Contraindre à	884
Contraindre de	884
Contrarier	646
Contrat	56
Contredire	477
Contredit	484
Contrée	471
Contrefaçon	472
Contrefaction	472
Contribution	473
Contrister	99
Contusion	503
Convenance	265
Convention	56
Convier	482
Convoi	483
Convulser	485
Convulsionner	485
Copie	1067
Copieusement	45
Coque	488
Coquelicot	486
Coquillage	488
Coquille	488
Coquin	335
Corbeille	489
Corbillon	489
Cordage	490
Corde	490
Cordelière	490
Cordon	490
Cordonnier	491
Correct	492
Correctif	493
Correction	137
Correctionnel	493
Corridor	502
Corriger	383
Corsaire	494
Cortège	495
Cote	473
Côte	496
Coteau	496
Cotisation	1054
Cou	497
Couard	498
Couchant	891
Coucher	499
Coucher (se)	125
Couler	500
Couleur	437
Couleuvre	501
Couloir	502

Coupe	504
Couper	505
Couple	506
Coupler	507
Cour	508
Courbe	509
Courbé	509
Courber	400
Couronnement	1024
Courroux	433
Cours	921
Coussinet	913
Coutume	18
Couverture	510
Couvrir	511
Cracher	512
Crachoter	512
Craindre	171
Crainte	513
Crapule	335
Craqueur	764
Crasse	514
Cravache	515
Crayon	343
Créance	516
Créancier	411
Créditeur	411
Creuser (*to study*)	165
Creuser (*to dig*)	237
Creux	360
Crever	517
Cri	409
Criaillerie	409
Cribler	264
Cric	518
Crier (*to scold*)	261
Crier (*to cry out*)	629
Crierie	409
Crime	736
Crin	391
Croissance	521
Croître	48
Croix	80
Croquis	343
Crotte (*mud*)	278
Crotte (*excrement*)	288
Crouler	519
Croûte	520
Croûton	520
Croyance	516
Cru	521
Cruche	306
Cruchon	306
Crue	521
Cuisinière	953

Cuivre jaune — INDEX — **Demeurant (au)**

Cuivre jaune	793
Cultivateur	95
Cure	760
Curer	528
Cuve	222
Cuvette	225

D

Dague	522
D'ailleurs	108
Dallage	924
Dans	523
Dans l'idée	537
Dans la tête	537
Date	840
Dation	525
D'avance	70
Davantage	527
De (by)	916
De (with)	1120
Déballer	571
Debarquer	587
Débit (output)	524
Débit (shop)	290
Débit et crédit	256
Débiteur	992
De bon cœur	536
De bonne grâce	536
De bon gré	536
De bonne volonté	536
Débours	576
Déboursé	576
Débris	526
Début	443
Décamper	549
Décaper	528
Déceler	529
Décence	265
Décès	530
Décevoir	66
Déchets	526
Déchoir	397
Déclamer	531
Déclaration	704
Déclin	532
Déclinement	532
Décombres	526
Déconvenue	533
Décorer	902
Décorum	265
Découler (to flow)	500
Découler (to proceed from)	534
Découper	505
Découvrir (to perceive)	153
Découvrir (to reveal)	529
Décrasser	528
Décréditer	535
Décrépitude	325
Décrier	535
Décroissance	538
Décroissement	538
Décrotter	528
Dédain	539
Dédale	540
Dedans	553
Dedans (au)	554
Dedans (en)	554
Dédire	477
Dédommagement	541
Défaut (defect)	543
Défaut (lack)	542
Défectuosité	543
Déférer	457
Défiance	544
Défilé (pass)	426
Défilé (procession)	495
Défilement	495
Définitive (en)	558
Définitivement	558
Défoncer	545
Défunt	723
Dégât	546
Dégénération	547
Dégénérescence	547
Dégraisser	528
Degré	548
Dégringoler	397
Déguerpir	549
Déguiser	550
Déguster	551
Dehors	552
Dehors (au)	554
Dehors (en)	554
Déjoindre	604
Délaisser	52
Délateur	35
Délibérant	555
Délibératif	555
Délibératoire	555
Délié	556
Délit	736
Délivrer (to deliver)	557
Délivrer (to free)	84
Demander	833
Démarche	140
Démêloir	936
Déménager	859
Démentir	477
Démesuré	775
Demeurant (au)	1017

[187]

Demeure	559	Désespérance	705
Demeurer (*to live*)	561	Désespoir	705
Demeurer (*to remain*)	560	Déshabiller	589
Demi	562	Désignation	1041
Demoiselle	973	Désigner	564
Démolir	54	Désirer	1113
Démonstration	563	Désistement	1
Démontrer	564	Désister (se)	52
Dénégation	565	Désoccupé	590
Déni	565	Désœuvré	590
Dénier	566	Désordonné	775
Dénigrer	535	Dessein	315
Dénombrer	864	Destin	591
Dénommer	865	Destinée	591
Dénoncer	150	Détenu	67
Dénonciateur	35	Déterrer	592
Denrées	567	Détourner	618
Dentaire	568	Détraquer	584
Dental	568	Détresse	89
Dentier	569	Détroit	426
Denture	569	Détromper	586
Dénué	570	Détrousser	585
Dépaqueter	571	Détruire	54
Dépareiller	572	Deuxième	593
Déparier	572	Dévaliser	585
Départir	573	Devancer	594
Dépasser	574	Devancier	595
Dépêcher	575	Devant	596
Dépens	576	Devant (aller au)	135
Dépense	576	Devanture	696
Déperdition	577	Dévêtir	589
Dépérir	943	Dévoiler	529
Dépeuplement	579	Dévotion	597
Déplacer	859	Dévouement	597
Déplaisant	580	Dextérité	69
Dépopulation	579	Diffamable	599
Dépouillé	570	Diffamant	599
Dépourvu	570	Diffamatoire	599
Depuis (*from*)	581	Différence	600
Depuis (*since*)	974	Différent	600
Dépurer	582	Différer	123
Déraisonnable	583	Difficile	601
Déranger	859	Difficultueux	601
Derechef	876	Diligence	332
Déréglé	775	Dimensions	725
Dérégler	584	Directif	598
Dériver	534	Direction	1034
Dérober	585	Dirigeant	598
Dérober (se)	621	Diriger	61
Dès	581	Discréditer	535
Désabuser	586	Discrétion	602
Désaltérer	186	Disette	603
Description	1041	Disjoindre	604
Désembarquer	587	Disposer	167
Déserteur	588	Dissension	605

Dissentiment	. . . . .	605
Distance	. . . . . .	606
Distant	. . . .	649
Distraire	. . . . . .	145
Distrait	. . . .	4
Diurne	. . . .	607
Divertir	. . . . . .	145
Dix	. . . .	578
Dizaine	. . . .	578
Docte	. . . .	608
Docteur	. . . . . .	609
Dodu	. . . .	960
Doit et avoir	. . . . .	256
Doléance	. . . . . .	452
Domestique	. . . .	1066
Domicile	. . . . . .	559
Dominant	. . . . . .	610
Dominateur	. . . .	610
Dommage	. . . . .	546
Don	. . . .	525
Donation	. . . . . .	525
Donc	. . . .	1118
Donner (se)	. . . . .	22
Donner le change	. . . .	66
Dormir	. . . .	499
Double	. . . .	1067
Double sens	. . . .	132
Douceâtre	. . . . . .	611
Doucereux	. . . . . .	611
Douceur	. . . . . .	612
Douleur (*pain*)	. . . .	81
Douleur (*sorrow*)	. . .	362
Douter	. . . .	613
Douter (se)	. . . . . .	613
Doux	. . . .	850
Drapeau	. . . . . .	934
Drilles	. . . .	759
Droit (*duty*)	. . . . .	473
Droit (*right*)	. . . . .	984
Droite	. . . .	984
Droiture	. . . . . .	614
Drolatique	. . . . . .	418
Drôle	. . . .	418
Duper	. . . .	66
Durant	. . . .	615
Durcir	. . . .	616
Du reste	. . . . . .	1017

E

Ébahir	. . . .	23
Ébaubir	. . . . . .	23
Ébauche	. . . . . .	343
Ébouler (s')	. . . . .	519
Ébranler	. . . . . .	292
Écaille	. . . .	488

Écart (mettre à l')	. . . .	619
Écarter	. . . .	618
Écervelé	. . . . . .	701
Échanger	. . . . . .	368
Échapper à	. . . . .	620
Échapper de	. . . . .	620
Écharde	. . . . . .	907
Échauffer	. . . . . .	386
Échelon	. . . . . .	548
Échoir	. . . .	397
Éclair	. . . .	617
Éclaircir	. . . . . .	622
Éclairer	. . . .	622
Éclat (*brilliance*)	. . . .	303
Éclat (*small piece*)	. . .	907
Éclater	. . . .	517
Éclats	. . . .	847
Éconduire	. . . . . .	623
Économe	. . . . . .	624
Économique	. . . . .	624
Écorcher	. . . . . .	625
Écouler	. . . .	500
Écourter	. . . . . .	19
Écran	. . . .	918
Écraser	. . . .	312
Écrier (s')	. . . . . .	629
Écrin	. . . .	627
Écriteau	. . . . . .	628
Écrouler (s')	. . . . .	519
Écu	. . . .	283
Écumant	. . . . . .	631
Écume	. . . .	630
Écumeux	. . . . . .	631
Écurer	. . . .	528
Écurie	. . . .	664
Écusson	. . . . . .	283
Édifice	. . . .	235
Édifier	. . . .	245
Éducation	. . . . . .	632
Effacer	. . . .	266
Effaré	. . . .	633
Effarouché	. . . . . .	633
Effectivement	. . . . .	634
Effet (en)	. . . . . .	634
Effondrer (s')	. . . . .	519
Efforcer (s')	. . . . .	635
Effraie	. . . .	398
Effrayant	. . . . . .	82
Effriter (s')	. . . . . .	636
Effroi	. . . .	513
Effronté (*impudent*)	. . .	21
Effronté (*shameless*)	. .	637
Effroyable	. . . . . .	82
Effusion	. . . . . .	638
Égal	. . . .	1092

[189]

Égard	196	Enclore	656
Égarer (s')	639	Encoignure	425
Égide	283	Encolure	725
Égoïste	640	Encore (*more*)	527
Égratigner (s')	626	Encore (*as well*)	658
Éhonté	637	Encore (*again*)	876
Élaguer	641	Encourager	107
Élan	642	Endommager	202
Élancement	642	Endormir (s')	499
Élancer (s')	794	Endroit (*place*)	659
Élargir	84	Endroit (*right side*)	1005
Élever	643	Endurcir	616
Éloge	644	En effet	634
Éloigné	649	Enfanter	16
Éloignement	606	Enfermer	663
Éloigner	618	Enfin	670
Émaner	534	Enflé	294
Embêter	646	Enfoncer	545
Embranchement	1058	Enfouir	678
Embrassade	647	Enfuir (s')	621
Embrassement	647	Engendrer	16
Embrasser	224	Engloutir	671
Embrouiller	304	Engouffrer	671
Embrun	648	Enivrer (s')	758
Émietter (s')	636	Enjôler	66
Emmener	138	Enjoué	665
Émoi	650	Enlever (*to carry away*)	138
Émonder	641	Enlever (*to remove*)	1038
Émotion	650	Enluminer	666
Émoussé	651	Ennoblir	151
Émouvoir (*to affect*)	92	Ennuyant	667
Émouvoir (*to move*)	859	Ennuyer	646
Empailler	345	Ennuyeux	667
Empêchement	652	Énoncé	668
Empêcher	1115	Énonciation	668
Emphatique	152	Enquérir de (s')	669
Empire	209	Enregistrer	672
Emplacement	659	Ensanglanté	673
Emplette	36	Enseigner	168
Emplir	653	Ensemble	674
Employé aux écritures	402	Ensemencer	1033
Empois	431	Ensevelir	678
Emportement	433	Ensorcellement	380
Emporter (*to take away*)	138	Ensuite	175
Emporter (*to take*)	662	Ensuivre (s')	675
Empreindre	654	Entacher	814
Émulateur	655	Entasser	41
Émule	655	Entendre (*to understand*)	444
En	523	Entendre (*to hear*)	676
En attendant	143	Entériner	677
En avance	70	Enterrement	483
Encadrement	324	Enterrer	678
Enceindre	656	Entêté	679
Enchantement	380	Entier (en)	680
Enchérir	657	Entièrement	680

Entourer   INDEX   Faire

Entourer	656	Établo	664
Entraîner	1129	Étage	924
Entre	923	Étain	695
Entrefaites (sur ces)	143	Étalage	696
Entretemps	143	Étancher	186
Entretenir	465	État	704
Envers (*wrong side*)	1005	Été (avoir)	128
Envers (*towards*)	681	Étincelle	273
Envie (avoir)	1113	Étoile	697
Envier	1113	Étourdi	701
Environner	656	Étrange	272
Environs	121	Être	1090
Envoyer	703	Être allé	128
Épanchement	638	Étude	698
Épave	683	Étui	627
Épée	684	Évader (s')	621
Épeler	901	Évaluer	166
Épier	761	Évanouir (s')	914
Épouser	645	Éveiller	699
Épouvantable	82	Éventail	1100
Épouvante	513	Exact	492
Époux	463	Excédent	700
Épreuve	685	Excepté	702
Éprouver	1035	Excès	700
Épurer	582	Excessif	775
Équarrir	686	Exciter	107
Équipage	1082	Exemplaire	1067
Équivoque	132	Exhausser	643
Érafler	625	Exhumer	592
Errer	687	Expédier	703
Erreur	252	Exposé	704
Érudit	608	Exposition	704
Escabeau	1065	Extérieur	552
Escadre	688	Exterminer	54
Escadrille	688	Extrait	62
Escadron	688	Extrémité	297
Escarbille	692		
Escargot	693	F	
Escarpolette	694		
Esclandre	689	Fabrique	706
Escompte	690	Façade	707
Escroc	339	Face (*side*)	707
Espadon	684	Face (*face*)	708
Espérance	691	Face à main	246
Espoir	691	Facétie	279
Esquille	907	Facile	111
Esquisse	343	Façons	709
Esquiver (s')	621	Faction	1039
Essai	685	Fade	710
Essayer	635	Fagoter	17
Essor	1111	Faible	76
Est	803	Faillir	824
Est (il)	204	Faillir à	824
Estaminet	43	Faillite	231
Estimer	166	Fainéant	711
		Faire	465

Faire choix	395
Faîte	401
Fait-tout	331
Faix	376
Falot	714
Famélique	713
Famine	603
Fanal	714
Fanfaron	764
Fange	278
Farcir	345
Fardeau	376
Fatal	715
Fatigué	798
Faubourg	240
Faut (il)	712
Faute	542
Faux-col	436
Fébrile	716
Félicitations	462
Femelle	818
Féminin	818
Fer-blanc	695
Férié (jour)	717
Férir	243
Fermer	322
Fête	717
Feu	723
Feuillé	718
Feuillu	718
Fichu	317
Fidèle	467
Fiente	288
Fier	719
Fier (se)	724
Fiévreux	716
Figer	419
Figure	708
Filateur	720
Fileur	720
Filou (*cheat*)	339
Filou (*thief*)	734
Fin (*cunning*)	296
Fin (*end*)	297
Fin (à la)	670
Finalement	670
Finaud	296
Fin de compte (en) . . .	670
Finir	6
Fixage	721
Fixation	721
Flagellation	226
Flagorner	65
Flammèche	273
Flatter	65
Fleuve	732
Flot	733
Fois (à la)	674
Foison (à)	45
Folâtrer	217
Foncé	873
Fondation	735
Fondement	735
Fonds de commerce . . .	413
Fonte	722
Forban	494
Forçats	384
Forcer à	884
Forcer de	884
Forêt	310
Forfait	736
Format	725
Fort	8
Fortement	8
Fortuné	726
Fosse (*den*)	349
Fosse (*pit*)	975
Fosse (*grave*)	1075
Fou	1050
Foudre	617
Fouet	515
Fouettement	226
Fouiller	237
Foulard	317
Foule	83
Four	730
Fourbe (*rogue*)	339
Fourbe (*cheating*) . . .	737
Fourberie	737
Fourché	727
Fourchu	727
Fourmiller	728
Fournaise	730
Fourneau (*furnace*) . . .	730
Fourneau (*stove*)	953
Fourré	311
Fourreau	729
Fourrer	345
Fourvoyer (se)	639
Foyer	953
Fracas	314
Fracasser	299
Fracturer	545
Fraîcheur	731
Frais (*freshness*)	731
Frais (*expenses*)	576
Fraisil	692
Frapper	243
Frayeur	513
Frémir	740

[192]

Frimas	738	Gens	749
Fripon	339	Gérer	61
Fripouille	335	Gibbeux	271
Frissonner	740	Gibet	752
Froid	741	Giboulée	893
Froideur	741	Girandole	366
Froidure	741	Givre	738
Froment	262	Glaive	684
Fugitif	739	Glouton	753
Fuir	621	Goinfre	753
Funèbre	742	Gond	381
Funérailles	483	Gonflé	294
Funéraire	742	Gorge (*gorge*)	426
Funeste	715	Gorge (*breast*)	955
Fureur	743	Goujat	335
Furibond	744	Goulu	753
Furie	743	Gourdin	352
Furieux	744	Gourmand	753
Fuselage	341	Goûter	551
Fusiller	1074	Gouttière	754
Fusion	722	Gouvernement	28
Fustigation	226	Grâce	756
Fût	227	Grâce (de bonne)	536
Futaie	310	Gracieux	104
Futaille	227	Grand	468
Futur (*future*)	201	Grandeur	725
Futur (*future*)	750	Grandir	1121
Fuyard	739	Gratitude	1122
		Gratter (se)	626
G		Grave	757
Gâcher	202	Gravin	682
Gaffe	252	Gré (de bon)	536
Gager	751	Gredin	335
Gages	170	Gréement	94
Gai	665	Grêle	556
Gaillard	665	Grelot	414
Gaîne	729	Grelotter	740
Galant	131	Grève	755
Garant	347	Grief	762
Garde	1044	Griffer	626
Garde champêtre	745	Grimper	682
Garder	465	Gripper	29
Gardien de la paix	745	Griser (se)	758
Gare	1057	Grogner	284
Garnement	335	Grommeler	284
Gâter (*to spoil*)	202	Gronder (*to grumble*)	284
Gâter (*to decay*)	353	Gronder (*to scold*)	261
Gaucherie	746	Grosseur	725
Gazon	747	Grouiller	728
Geindre	748	Guenilles	759
Gelée	738	Guérison	760
Gémir	748	Guetter	761
Gendarme	745	Gueusard	335
Gêner	646	Guider	456
Genoux (se mettre à)	91	Guinguette	43

H

Habileté	69
Habillement	869
Habiller	78
Habit	763
Habiter	561
Habits	869
Habitude	18
Habitude (comme d')	900
Hâbleur	764
Hache	432
Haillons	759
Haleine	765
Happer	29
Harceler	102
Hardes	869
Hardi	21
Hâter (*to hasten*)	44
Hâter (*to hurry*)	575
Hâtif	766
Hausser	643
Haut (*top*)	401
Haut (*haughty*)	130
Hautesse	1037
Hautain	130
Hâve	260
Heaume	342
Hébéter	20
Herbe	747
Hésiter	220
Heure	767
Heureux	726
Heurter	396
Hibernal	320
Hibou	398
Hiémal	320
Histoire	1116
Historique	1116
Hivernal	320
Honnête	90
Honnir	218
Horloge	351
Hormis	702
Hors (*out of*)	554
Hors (*except*)	702
Houe	259
Houille	375
Huit	768
Huitaine	768
Humecter	769
Humidifier	769
Humiliation	33
Humilier	10
Hutte	321
Hymen	770
Hymenée	770

I

Idée (dans l')	537
Identique	771
Idiot	1050
Ignare	772
Ignorant	772
Il est	204
Il est nécessaire	712
Il faut	712
Illuminer	666
Ils	889
Il y a	204
Imaginer	773
Imaginer (s')	773
Imbécile	1050
Immatriculer	672
Immédiatement	777
Immeuble	774
Immobilier	774
Immodéré	775
Immondice	514
Impéritie	746
Important	468
Imposer (en)	66
Imposition	473
Impôt	473
Imprévu	776
Imprimer	654
Impudent	637
Inattendu	776
Incessamment	777
Inciter	107
Inclinaison	778
Inclination	778
Inconstant	367
Inculpé	67
Incurable	781
Indemnité	541
Indication	779
Indice	779
Indicible	782
Indiquer	564
Induire à	780
Induire en	780
Inénarrable	782
Inexprimable	782
Infirmer	2
Informer	1009
Informer de (s')	669
Infortune	89
Inguérissable	781
Inhumer	678
Inimitié	149

[194]

Injure — INDEX — Liste

Injure	1036	Lacet	792
Inoccupé	590	Lâche	498
Inopiné	776	Lâcher	791
Inscrire	672	Lacs	792
Insigne	1062	Laid	1130
Insipide	710	Laisser	52
Insouciant	701	Laiton	793
Instruction	632	Laize	269
Instruire	168	Lamanage	966
Instruire (s')	164	Lambeaux	759
Insulte	101	Lame	733
Interdit	466	Lancer	787
Intérieur	553	Lancer (se)	794
Interloqué	466	Langage	795
Intrigue	301	Langue	795
Invitation	783	Lanterne	714
Invite	783	Lardon	307
Inviter	482	Largement	8
Irraisonnable	583	Largesse	796
Ivre	784	Largeur	269
		Larmes	797
J		Larron	734
Jaboter	211	Las	798
Jacasser	211	Lavage	799
Jadis	146	Lavement	799
Jaillir	785	Léger (*fickle*)	367
Jamais (à)	786	Léger (*light*)	801
Jamais (pour)	786	Légère (à la)	802
Jaquette	763	Légèrement	802
Jaser	211	Légumier	1098
Jatte	225	Lésine	800
Jeter	787	Lésinerie	800
Jeter à bas	54	Leste	801
Joindre	15	Lettre (à la)	809
Joint	788	Lettre (au pied de la)	809
Jointure	788	Leurre	87
Jouir	1126	Leurrer	66
Jour (*light*)	423	Levant	803
Jour (*day*)	789	Lever	643
Jour férié	717	Liaison	71
Journalier	607	Libéralité	796
Journée	789	Libérer	84
Joyau	255	Liège	804
Jugement	177	Lier	805
Jurement	790	Lieu	659
Juron	790	Ligne	806
		Lignée	806
		Limace	693
K		Limaçon	693
Képi	247	Limite	277
		Limon	278
L		Liséré	274
Labeur	248	Lisière	274
Laboureur	95	Lisse	1092
Labyrinthe	540	Liste	808

[195]

Lit (se mettre au)	125	Mal (*illness*)	816
Littéralement	809	Mal (*injury*)	1036
Livre	295	Maladie	816
Livrer	557	Maladresse	746
Livrer (se)	22	Malaxer	817
Local	235	Malcontent	823
Loche	693	Mâle	818
Logement	810	Maléfice	380
Loger	561	Malencontre	533
Logis	810	Malfaisant	819
Lointain	649	Malhabileté	746
Longtemps	811	Malheur	89
Longue (à la)	670	Malin	296
Longuement	811	Mallette	821
Loques	759	Malplaisant	580
Lorgnon	246	Malpropre	1026
Lors de	976	Manche	114
Lorsque	976	Mangeable	440
Louange	644	Maniaque	1050
Louanger	65	Manières	709
Louer (*to let*)	74	Manivelle	114
Louer (*to praise*)	65	Manne	489
Loup	827	Manœuvre	822
Lourd	813	Manouvrier	822
Lueur	423	Manque	542
Luire	298	Manquer	824
Lumière	423	Manquer à	824
Luminade	423	Manquer de	824
Lunatique	1050	Mansuétude	612
Lunettes	246	Manufacture	706
Lustre	303	Maquette	825
Lustrer	346	Marâtre	826
		Marchandises	567
M		Marche	548
Mâchefer	692	Marché	56
Mâcher	388	Marchepied	548
Machine	849	Mari	463
Machiner	905	Mariage	867
Maculer	814	Marier	645
Mademoiselle	973	Marier (se)	645
Madrier	228	Marmite	331
Magasin	290	Marmonner	284
Maigre	556	Marmotter	284
Maigreur	133	Maronner	284
Maigrir	1119	Marquer	564
Mail	815	Marron	382
Maille	815	Marteau	828
Maillet	815	Masculin	818
Mailloche	815	Masque	827
Main-forte	106	Masse	828
Maint	812	Massette	828
Maintenant	30	Massue	352
Maintien	480	Matelas	829
Maisonnette	319	Matin	830
Mal (*pain*)	81	Matinal	832

Matinée	. . . . . .	830
Matineux	. . . . . .	832
Matinier	. . . . . .	832
Mauvais	. . . . . .	820
Mauviette	. . . . . .	129
Mécanicien	. . . . . .	424
Méchant	. . . . . .	820
Mécontent	. . . . . .	823
Médecin	. . . . . .	609
Médisance	. . . . . .	831
Méfiance	. . . . . .	544
Mélanger	. . . . . .	817
Mêler	. . . . . .	817
Mêler (se)	. . . . . .	817
Même que (de)	. . . . .	116
Mendier	. . . . . .	833
Mener	. . . . . .	456
Menétrier	. . . . . .	834
Mensonge	. . . . . .	835
Menterie	. . . . . .	835
Méprendre (se)	. . . .	836
Mépris	. . . . . .	539
Méprise	. . . . . .	252
Merci	. . . . . .	756
Merise	. . . . . .	267
Mésaventure	. . . . .	533
Mettre	. . . . . .	837
Mettre à bas	. . . . .	54
Mettre au lit (se)	. . . .	125
Meubles	. . . . . .	838
Meurtrissure	. . . . .	503
Mi	. . . . . .	562
Midi	. . . . . .	1059
Miettes	. . . . . .	847
Mignard	. . . . . .	839
Mignon	. . . . . .	839
Mil (*club*)	. . . . . .	352
Mil (*thousand*)	. . . . .	1124
Mille	. . . . . .	1124
Millésime	. . . . . .	840
Mince	. . . . . .	556
Mine	. . . . . .	975
Minois	. . . . . .	708
Mirer	. . . . . .	841
Misérable	. . . . . .	335
Misère	. . . . . .	89
Miséricorde	. . . . . .	756
Mixtionner	. . . . . .	817
Mobile	. . . . . .	842
Mobilier	. . . . . .	838
Mode	. . . . . .	1109
Modèle	. . . . . .	825
Modeste	. . . . . .	843
Modique	. . . . . .	843
Moineau	. . . . . .	930

Moins (au)	. . . . . .	908
Moins (du)	. . . . . .	908
Moins de	. . . . . .	909
Moins que	. . . . . .	909
Moisir	. . . . . .	365
Moisson	. . . . . .	844
Moitié	. . . . . .	562
Mollet	. . . . . .	850
Mollir	. . . . . .	42
Monceau	. . . . . .	7
Monnaie	. . . . . .	845
Monte-charge	. . . . .	846
Montrer	. . . . . .	564
Moquette	. . . . . .	1068
Morceau	. . . . . .	847
Moribond	. . . . . .	852
Mort	. . . . . .	530
Mot	. . . . . .	848
Moteur	. . . . . .	849
Motif	. . . . . .	842
Mou	. . . . . .	850
Moufle	. . . . . .	911
Mouiller	. . . . . .	769
Moulinet	. . . . . .	851
Mourant	. . . . . .	852
Mousse	. . . . . .	630
Mouvoir (*to drive*)	. . .	11
Mouvoir (*to move*)	. . .	859
Mule	. . . . . .	860
Mulet	. . . . . .	860
Multitude	. . . . . .	83
Mur	. . . . . .	853
Muraille	. . . . . .	853
Murmurer	. . . . . .	284

N

Nago	. . . . . .	854
Naguère	. . . . . .	146
Nappe	. . . . . .	855
Narine	. . . . . .	856
Narrer	. . . . . .	478
Naseau	. . . . . .	856
Natation	. . . . . .	854
Naturaliser	. . . . . .	58
Naturel	. . . . . .	447
Naufrage	. . . . . .	683
Navire	. . . . . .	242
Néanmoins	. . . . . .	357
Néant	. . . . . .	857
Nécessaire (il est)	. . . .	712
Négation	. . . . . .	565
Négoce	. . . . . .	858
Net	. . . . . .	862
Nettoyer	. . . . . .	528
Neuf	. . . . . .	879

Niais	215	Odeur		880
Nier	566	Odorant		881
Nigaud	215	Odorat		880
Nippes	869	Odoriférant		881
Niveau	1095	Œil (coup d')		890
Nobilité	870	Œillade		890
Noblesse	870	Œuvre		248
Noce	867	Office		377
Nochère	754	Oiseux		886
Noisette	868	Oisif		886
Noix	868	Ombrager		887
Nom	863	Ombrelle		888
Nombre	866	Ombrer		887
Nombrer	864	On		889
Nommer	865	Onde		733
Nourricier	875	Ondé		1088
Nourrir	871	Ondée		893
Nourrissant	875	Ondoiement		898
Nourriture	115	Ondulation		733
Nouveau	879	Ondulé		1088
Nouveau (à)	876	Opiniâtre		679
Nouveau (de)	876	Opinion		40
Noyer	868	Oppresser		3
Nuage	877	Opprimer		3
Nuancer	878	Opter		395
Nue	877	Opulence		46
Nuée	877	Ordinaire (à l')		900
Nuer	878	Ordinaire (d')		900
Nuisible	819	Ordinaire (pour l')		900
Nuit	873	Ordinairement		900
Nul	874	Ordonner		895
Numéral	872	Ordre		441
Numérique	872	Organe		896
Numéro	866	Orgue		896
Numéroter	864	Orgueilleux		719
Nutricier	875	Orient		803
Nutritif	875	Orientation		897
		Orientement		897

O

		Original		899
Obédience	882	Originel		899
Obéissance	882	Oripeaux		759
Obligeant	883	Orner		902
Obliger a	884	Orthographier		901
Obliger de	884	Os		903
Obsèques	483	Ossements		903
Observance	885	Ôter		1038
Observation	885	Où		976
Observer	1008	Ouest		891
Obstacle	652	Oui		904
Obstiné	679	Ouïr		676
Occasion (d')	1093	Ourdir		905
Occident	891	Outrage		101
Occupé	25	Outrageant		906
Occuper à (s')	892	Outrageux		906
Occuper de (s')	892	Outré		775

Outre		INDEX		Percevoir
Outre (en)	108	Parure		119
Outre cela	108	Parvenir		927
Outrepasser	574	Pas (*step*)		548
Ouvrage	248	Pas (*strait*)		426
Ouvrier (*working*)	1084	Pas (ne . . .)		861
Ouvrier (*workman*)	822	Pas de porte		413
		Passage		502
P		Passé (avoir)		929
Pacage	910	Passé (être)		929
Pacte	56	Passer		928
Paiement	935	Passer (se) (*to pass away*)		928
Paillasse	421	Passer (se) (*to happen*)		998
Paix (gardien de la)	745	Passereau		930
Palan	911	Pasteur		931
Pâle	260	Patelin		932
Paletot	912	Patelineur		932
Palier (*bearing*)	913	Pâtir		933
Palier (*level*)	1095	Pâtis		910
Palper	1035	Pâtre		931
Pâmer (se)	914	Patte		1123
Panache	915	Pâturage		910
Pancarte	628	Pâture		910
Panier	489	Paumelle		381
Papelard	932	Pavillon		934
Paquet	427	Pavoiser		902
Par (*for*)	917	Pavot		486
Par (*by*)	916	Paye		935
Parachever	6	Payer		9
Parages	659	Pays		471
Paragraphe	124	Paysan		328
Paraître	157	Pédant		937
Parasol	888	Pédantesque		937
Par avance	70	Peigne		936
Paravent	918	Peindre		938
Parce que	340	Peine (*inconvenience*)		80
Parcourir (*to scan*)	919	Peine (*mental suffering*)		81
Parcourir (*to visit*)	920	Peines		80
Parcours	921	Peinturer		938
Pardessus	912	Peinturlurer		938
Pare-brise	918	Pélisse		912
Pare-étincelles	918	Pelote		229
Pareil	771	Peloton		229
Parer	902	Pelouse		747
Paresseux	711	Pendant		615
Parfois	922	Pendant que		941
Parier	751	Pendule		351
Parmi	923	Péniche		238
Paroi	853	Pensée		942
Parole	848	Penser (*thought*)		942
Parquet	924	Penser (*to think*)		940
Part	925	Penser à		939
Partager	573	Penser de		939
Parti	926	Penture		381
Partie (*part*)	925	Percevoir (*to perceive*)		153
Partie (*party*)	926	Percevoir (*to collect*)		439

[199]

Pères	109	Pleurer	629
Périr	943	Pleurs	797
Permission	717	Pleutre	335
Permuter	368	Plie	334
Persan	944	Plier	400
Perse	944	Ployer	400
Persique	944	Plume	915
Personnel	640	Plus	527
Personnes	749	Plus (de)	108
Perte	577	Plusieurs	812
Pesage	945	Plus tôt	1080
Pesant	813	Plutôt	1080
Pesée	945	Pneumatique	232
Peuplade	965	Poêle	953
Peuple	749	Poignard	522
Peur	513	Poignée	114
Peur (avoir)	171	Poils	391
Peut (on ne)	894	Point (ne ...)	861
Picoter	946	Point du jour	954
Pièce (*barrel*)	227	Pointe	316
Pièce (*room*)	363	Pointe du jour	954
Pièce (*piece*)	847	Pointure	725
Pied	1123	Poitrail	955
Piège	792	Poitrine	955
Pieuvre	947	Poli	90
Pile	7	Police	956
Piler	312	Police (agent de)	745
Pilotage	966	Police (bonnet de)	247
Pinceau	948	Polisson	335
Piocher	237	Politique	956
Piquer	946	Poltron	498
Piquer (se)	72	Pont levant	957
Pirate	494	Pont-levis	957
Pitre	421	Port	480
Placard	628	Porte	958
Place	659	Porte-monnaie	287
Placer	837	Porter (*to move*)	859
Plage	755	Porter (*to carry*)	373
Plaie	268	Porter à	107
Plainte (*complaint*)	452	Portière (*door*)	958
Plainte (*complaint*)	762	Portière (*curtain*)	1019
Plaire	446	Portion	925
Plaisance	949	Posé	327
Plaisant	418	Poser	837
Plaisanterie	279	Position	183
Plaisir	949	Poster	959
Plan (faire un)	807	Potager	1098
Plan (lever un)	807	Potelé	960
Planche (*plank*)	228	Potence	752
Planche (*plate*)	951	Potin	314
Plancher	924	Potiron	961
Plant	950	Poulpe	947
Plante	950	Pour (*for*)	917
Plaque	951	Pour (*in order to*)	962
Plein	952	Pour (*in the opinion of*)	977

Pour que	962	Protestation 563
Pourquoi (c'est)	110	Prostration 24
Pourrir	353	Provenir 534
Poursuivre	475	Provision (par) 972
Pourtant	357	Provisionnel 972
Pousser	1121	Provisoire 972
Pousser à	107	Provoquer 102
Poussier	963	Prudent 208
Poussière	963	Pucelle 973
Pouvoir	209	Puis 175
Préalable (au)	12	Puisné 337
Préalablement	12	Puisque 974
Précéder	594	Puissance 209
Précis	62	Puits 975
Précoce	766	Pulvériser 312
Préconiser	65	Purifier 582
Prédécesseur	595	
Prélart	212	Q
Premièrement	47	Qualité (de) 455
Préparatifs	160	Quand 976
Préparer	167	Quant à 977
Près	55	Quantième 840
Près de	98	Quarantaine 978
Présent	323	Quarante 978
Présent (à)	30	Que (how) 442
Présent (être)	185	Que (when) 976
Présentement	30	Quelquefois 922
Presse	83	Quémander 833
Pressentir	1035	Quête 428
Presser (to hasten) . . .	44	Quêter 439
Presser (to hurry)	575	Queue 114
Prestance	480	Quinte 979
Prétendre	967	Quinzaine 980
Prétexter	967	Quinze 980
Prévenir (to warn) . . .	205	Quittance 37
Prévenir (to prevent) . . .	1115	Quitter 52
Prévenu	67	Quoique 981
Priser	166	Quotidien 607
Prisonnier	67	
Privé (tame)	162	R
Privé (deprived)	570	Rabaisser (to lower) . . . 10
Procéder	534	Rabaisser (to lower) . . . 142
Procès	968	Rabattre 10
Procession	495	Rabêtir 51
Prochain	964	Raboteux 993
Proche	964	Raccommodement 49
Produire (se)	998	Raccommoder (to settle) . . 50
Profit	241	Raccommoder (to mend) . 989
Promenade	970	Raccourcir 19
Promenoir	970	Raconter 478
Prône	969	Radiant 982
Prôner	65	Radieux 982
Propre	862	Radoucir 60
Propre à	971	Rafale 286
Propre pour	971	Raffermir 77

Raffiner   INDEX   Remarquer

Raffiner	983		Réclame	628
Raid	1111		Réclamer	995
Raison	984		Recoin	425
Râle	985		Récolte	844
Râlement	985		Recommander	672
Ramée	291		Réconcilier	50
Ramener	155		Reconduction	996
Ramollir	42		Reconduire	139
Ramoner	986		Reconnaissance	1122
Ramure	291		Recourbé	509
Rancart (mettre au)	619		Recourber	400
Rancidité	987		Recouvrer	997
Rancissement	987		Recouvrir (*to cover again*)	997
Rancissure	987		Recouvrir (*to cover up*)	511
Rancune	149		Récrier (se)	629
Rang	988		Rectitude	614
Rangée	988		Recto	1005
Ranger	180		Reçu	37
Rapetasser	989		Recueil	999
Rapetisser	161		Recuillir	439
Rapiécer	989		Reculer	123
Rapiéceter	989		Récurer	528
Rappeler (se)	990		Redevable	992
Rapport	71		Redouter	171
Rapporter	155		Réfléchir	1000
Rapprocher	1125		Réfléter	1000
Raser	54		Refonte	722
Rassasier	991		Réformateur	1003
Rassemblement	83		Réformation	137
Rassembler (*to assemble*)	187		Réformatoire	1003
Rassembler (*to collect*)	439		Réforme	137
Rassis	327		Refuge	179
Rater	824		Refuser	1004
Ratifier	677		Refuser à (se)	1004
Raturer	266		Regard	890
Ravaler	10		Regarder	445
Ravauder	989		Régime	28
Ravir	182		Régir	61
Ravitailler	871		Régler	9
Rayer	266		Règne	1001
Rayonnant	982		Rehausser	643
Raz de marée	733		Rein	1002
Recéler	318		Rejaillir	785
Recenser	864		Rejoindre	15
Récépissé	37		Réjouir (se)	1126
Réception	37		Relâche	1006
Recette	37		Relâchement	1006
Recevoir	53		Relâcher	791
Réchapper	620		Relater	478
Réchauffer	386		Relevé de compte	704
Rêche	993		Relever	643
Rechute	994		Reliquaire	374
Récidive	994		Reliquat	1007
Réciter	531		Reluire	298
Réclamation	762		Remarquer	1008

Rembourrer	345
Remener	139
Remettre	123
Remettre (se)	997
Remise	690
Remmener	139
Remorquer	1129
Rempli	952
Remplir	653
Remporter	662
Remuer	859
Renchérir	657
Rencontre (aller à la)	135
Rendement	524
Rendre (se)	1015
Renfermer	663
Renflouage	79
Renflouement	79
Reniement	565
Renier (*to disavow*)	566
Renier (*to deny*)	5
Renom	863
Renommée	863
Renoncement	1
Renoncer	52
Renonciation	1
Renouvellement	996
Renseigner	1009
Rente	1010
Renverser	54
Renvoyer	123
Repartir (*to rejoin*)	1011
Répartir (*to apportion*)	573
Repentance	1013
Repentir	1013
Répliquer	1011
Répondant	347
Répondre	1011
Reprendre	261
Représentation (*appearance*)	480
Représentation (*performance*)	1055
Réseau	806
Réserve	602
Résidence	559
Résilier	1012
Résolu	1014
Résoudre à	1014
Résoudre de	1014
Résous	1014
Ressemblant	771
Ressentir	1035
Ressentir de (se)	1035
Restant	1016
Reste	1016
Reste (au)	1017
Reste (du)	1017
Rester	560
Résumé	62
Rétablir (se)	997
Retard	1069
Retardataire	1018
Retenir	465
Retenue	602
Réticule	821
Retors	1078
Retoucher	383
Retourner	237
Retrancher	505
Rets	792
Réunion	184
Réunir	439
Réussir	927
Rêve	1046
Réveiller	699
Revendiquer	995
Revenir	997
Revenir à soi	997
Revenu	1010
Rêver à	940
Révérence	1027
Revers	1005
Revêtir	78
Reviser	383
Revoir	383
Révoquer	2
Richesse	46
Rideau	1019
Rien (*no importance*)	216
Rien (*nothing*)	857
Riposter	1011
Risible	418
Rivage	274
Rive	274
Rivière	732
Roc	1020
Roche	1020
Rocher	1020
Rognon	1002
Rôle	808
Romanesque	1021
Romantique	1021
Rompre	299
Rond	154
Rôt	1022
Rôti	1022
Roulement	913
Route	387
Royaume	1001
Rude	993
Ruiner	54

Ruisseau	. . . . . .	754
Rusé	. . . . . .	296
Rustaud	. . . . . .	1023
Rustique	. . . . . .	1023
Rustre	. . . . . .	1023

S

Sabre	. . . . . .	684
Sac	. . . . . .	821
Sacoche	. . . . . .	821
Sacre	. . . . . .	1024
Sacrer	. . . . . .	464
Sage	. . . . . .	1025
Saisir	. . . . . .	444
Salaire	. . . . . .	170
Sale	. . . . . .	1026
Saleté	. . . . . .	514
Salle	. . . . . .	363
Salon	. . . . . .	363
Saltimbanque	. . . . . .	421
Salut	. . . . . .	1027
Salutation	. . . . . .	1027
Sanglant	. . . . . .	673
Sanguin	. . . . . .	673
Sanguinolent	. . . . . .	673
Sarcloir	. . . . . .	259
Sardonien	. . . . . .	1028
Sardonique	. . . . . .	1028
Sasser	. . . . . .	264
Satané	. . . . . .	1029
Satanesque	. . . . . .	1029
Satanique	. . . . . .	1029
Saucisse	. . . . . .	1064
Saucisson	. . . . . .	1064
Sauf	. . . . . .	702
Saurait (on ne)	. . . . . .	894
Sauver (se)	. . . . . .	621
Savant	. . . . . .	608
Savetier	. . . . . .	491
Savoir (*to know*)	. . . . . .	461
Savoir (*to understand*)	. . . . . .	444
Savoir-faire	. . . . . .	68
Savoir-vivre	. . . . . .	68
Scandale	. . . . . .	689
Scélérat	. . . . . .	335
Séance	. . . . . .	184
Second	. . . . . .	593
Secouer	. . . . . .	292
Secours	. . . . . .	106
Secousse	. . . . . .	1030
Séculaire	. . . . . .	1040
Séculier	. . . . . .	1040
Séducteur	. . . . . .	1048
Séduisant	. . . . . .	1048
Seing	. . . . . .	1031

Selon	. . . . . .	1032
Semblable	. . . . . .	771
Semence	. . . . . .	316
Semer	. . . . . .	1033
Sens	. . . . . .	1034
Sens (double)	. . . . . .	132
Sentence	. . . . . .	177
Senteur	. . . . . .	880
Sentiment	. . . . . .	40
Sentir	. . . . . .	1035
Sergent de ville	. . . . . .	745
Sérieux	. . . . . .	757
Serin	. . . . . .	329
Serment	. . . . . .	790
Sermon	. . . . . .	969
Serpent	. . . . . .	501
Servante	. . . . . .	1066
Serviable	. . . . . .	883
Service	. . . . . .	1039
Servir de (se)	. . . . . .	1094
Serviteur	. . . . . .	1066
Souil	. . . . . .	548
Seul	. . . . . .	1127
Si (*yes*)	. . . . . .	904
Si (*so*)	. . . . . .	1128
Signalé	. . . . . .	1062
Signalement	. . . . . .	1041
Signature	. . . . . .	1031
Similaire	. . . . . .	771
Situation	. . . . . .	183
Société	. . . . . .	1042
Soin	. . . . . .	1044
Soir	. . . . . .	1045
Soirée	. . . . . .	1045
Soixantaine	. . . . . .	1043
Soixante	. . . . . .	1043
Solde (*pay*)	. . . . . .	935
Solde (*balance*)	. . . . . .	1007
Sombre	. . . . . .	873
Sommaire	. . . . . .	62
Sommet	. . . . . .	401
Sommier	. . . . . .	829
Sommité	. . . . . .	401
Songe	. . . . . .	1046
Songer	. . . . . .	940
Sonnaille	. . . . . .	414
Sonner	. . . . . .	1047
Sonnerie	. . . . . .	414
Sonnette	. . . . . .	414
Sort (*fate*)	. . . . . .	591
Sort (*spell*)	. . . . . .	380
Sorte	. . . . . .	1041
Sortilège	. . . . . .	380
Sot	. . . . . .	1050
Sottise	. . . . . .	258

Souci	1044	Tâcher à	635
Soudain	1049	Tâcher de	635
Souffle	765	Tacher	814
Souffrance	81	Tacheter	814
Souffrir	933	Tact (*tact*)	68
Souhaiter	1113	Tact (*sense of touch*)	194
Souillor	814	Tailler	505
Soûl	784	Taillis	311
Soulager	126	Tamiser	264
Soûler (se)	758	Tandis que	941
Soulever	643	Tanière	349
Soupçon	1051	Tant	1128
Soupçonner	1052	Tapage	314
Sourire	1053	Tapir (se)	263
Souris	1053	Tapis (*carpet*)	1068
Souscription	1054	Tapis (*table-cloth*)	855
Souscrire	39	Tard	1069
Soutenir	63	Tardif	1018
Soutien (*support*)	106	Targette	293
Soutien (*support*)	173	Tas	7
Souvenir (se)	990	Tasse	504
Spectacle	1055	Tâter	1035
Spiritisme	1056	Tâtonner	1035
Spiritualisme	1056	Taxe	473
Station	1057	Tellement	1128
Stupéfier	23	Témoignage	563
Subir	933	Tempérament	447
Subit	1049	Temps	767
Subsistances	567	Tendre (*soft*)	850
Succéder	927	Tendre (*new*)	879
Succursale	1058	Tendresse	276
Sud	1059	Tendreté	276
Suer	1060	Tenir	465
Suinter	1060	Tentative	73
Suite	474	Terme	277
Suivant	1032	Terminer	6
Suivre (*to attend*)	185	Terrain	1070
Suivre (*to follow*)	675	Terre	1070
Sujétion	188	Terre (tomber à)	1076
Superficie	1061	Terre (tomber par)	1076
Suppléer	1063	Terroir	1070
Suppléer à	1063	Tête (dans la)	537
Supplier	833	Têtu	679
Support	173	Texture	479
Surpasser	574	Théologal	1071
Surplus (au)	1017	Théologique	1071
Surseoir à	123	Tiédeur	193
Surtout	912	Tiers	1072
Surveiller	761	Timbre	1073
Suspecter	1052	Tintamarre	314
Suspicion	1051	Tinter	1047
Sustenter	871	Tirer (*to shoot*)	1074
		Tirer (*to draw*)	1129
T		Tissu	479
Tabouret	1065	Tissure	479

Tituber INDEX Varech

Tituber.	364
Toit.	510
Toiture.	510
Tôle	951
Tombe	1075
Tombeau	1075
Tomber.	397
Tomber à terre	1076
Tomber d'accord	39
Tomber par terre.	1076
Tome	1077
Tonneau (*tub*)	222
Tonneau (*barrel*)	227
Tordu	1078
Tors.	1078
Tortillé.	1078
Tortu	1079
Tortué	1079
Tortueux	1079
Toucher (*to concern*) . . .	445
Toucher (*touch*)	194
Tour	1081
Tourment	81
Tourner	1105
Tourner (faire)	11
Tourniquet.	851
Tournure	1081
Toutefois	357
Toux	979
Train	1082
Traîner.	1129
Trait	806
Traite	1083
Traité	56
Traitement.	170
Trajet	1083
Tramer	905
Tranche	305
Trancher	505
Transes.	75
Transférer.	350
Transfuge	588
Tranquille	327
Trappe	792
Traquenard	792
Traquet	792
Travail	248
Travaux	248
Travailleur (*worker*) . . .	822
Travailleur (*hard working*) .	1084
Travailliste.	1084
Travers (à)	1085
Travers (au)	1085
Travestir	550
Trébucher	308

Trembler	1086
Trembloter.	1086
Tremper	769
Trentaine	1087
Trente	1087
Trépas	530
Très	8
Tribu	965
Tribulations	80
Tribunal	508
Tricheur	339
Trique	352
Tristesse	362
Triturer	312
Troisième	1072
Tromper	66
Tromper (se)	836
Tromper de (se)	836
Troquer	368
Trou	1089
Troubler	92
Trouée	1089
Trouver (se)	1090
Tumulte	314

U

Unanimement	1091
Unanimité (à l')	1091
Uni	1092
Union	71
Unique	1127
Us	18
Usage	18
Usagé	1093
Usé	1093
User	1094
Usité (être)	1094
Utiliser	1094

V

Vacances	717
Vacarme	314
Vaciller	364
Vague	733
Vaguer.	687
Vain (en)	1102
Vainement	1102
Valable.	1096
Valide	1096
Valise	821
Vallée	1097
Vallon	1097
Van.	1100
Vantard	764
Varech.	122

Vareuse.	763	Violoniste	834
Vase	278	Virer	1105
Vaurien.	335	Visage	708
Végétable	1098	Viser	841
Végétal	1098	Visiter	920
Veillée	1045	Vite	1108
Veiller	761	Vitrage	336
Vénéneux	1099	Vitrail	336
Vénimeux	1099	Vitre	336
Venir (à)	750	Vitrine (*shop window*)	336
Venir à	998	Vitrine (*shop window*)	696
Ventilateur.	1100	Vivant	1107
Ventilation.	86	Vivant (bon)	1110
Venue	200	Vivement	1108
Verglas.	738	Viveur (bon)	1110
Véridique	31	Vivre	561
Vérifier.	203	Vivres	567
Vérin	518	Vogue	1109
Véritable	31	Voie (*line*)	806
Verrou	293	Voie (*road*)	387
Vers.	681	Voiler	318
Verser	9	Voisin	64
Verso	1005	Voiturier	424
Veste	763	Vol	1111
Veston	763	Volage	367
Vêtements	869	Volée	1111
Vétille	216	Voler (*to fly*)	1112
Vêtir	78	Voler (*to steal*)	585
Vétusté.	325	Voleter	1112
Veuvage	1101	Voleur	734
Vice	543	Volonté (de bonne)	536
Viduité.	1101	Voltiger	1112
Vie (en).	1107	Volume.	1077
Vieux	1106	Vouloir (*to expect*)	195
Vif	1107	Vouloir (*to wish*)	1113
Vilain (*bad*)	820	Voyage	1083
Vilain (*ugly*)	1130	Voyou	335
Vilipender	218	Vrai.	31
Ville (sergent de)	745	Vue	315
Vingt	1103		
Vingtaine	1103	**W**	
Violenter	1104	Watergang	1117
Violer	1104	Wateringue	1117
Violoneux	834	Wattman	424